Master Point Press • Toronto

ERIC KOKISH & MARK HORTON

CLOSE

ENCOUNTERS

BRIDGE'S GREATEST MATCHES

BOOK 1: 1964 TO 2001

Master Point Press
214 Merton St. Suite 205
Toronto, Ontario, Canada
M4S 1A6 (647)956-4933
info@masterpointpress.com

Websites: www.masterpointpress.com
              www.teachbridge.com
              www.bridgeblogging.com
              www.ebooksbridge.com

Library and Archives Canada Cataloguing in Publication

Kokish, Eric, author
        Close encounters : bridge's greatest matches / Eric Kokish and Mark Horton.
Contents: Book 1: 1964-2001.
Issued in print and electronic formats.
ISBN 978-1-77140-028-2 (book 1 : softcover).--ISBN 978-1-55494-630-3 (book 1 : PDF).--
ISBN 978-1-55494-675-4 (book 1 : HTML).--ISBN 978-1-77140-865-3 (book 1 : HTML)

        1. Contract bridge--Tournaments--History. 2. Contract bridge--Bidding.
3. Contract bridge--Defensive play. I. Horton, Mark, author II. Title.

GV1282.6.K65 2018   795.41'58   C2018-902754-1
                                                      C2018-902755-X

Canada███   We acknowledge the financial support of the Government of Canada.
            Nous reconnaissons l'appui financier du gouvernement du Canada.

Editor   Ray Lee
Copy editor/interior format   Sally Sparrow
Cover design   Olena S. Sullivan/New Mediatrix

1 2 3 4 5 6 7   21 20 19 18
Printed in Canada at Webcom

Publisher's Note

Close Encounters was a long time coming — indeed, as Eric notes in his Foreword, it began life as a totally different book. After initial discussions, the authors departed to their respective continents, and began to work. Both have been writing about top-level bridge for decades, and their files contain a wealth of fascinating material. Three or four years later, when the manuscript finally arrived, it was about twice the length I had envisaged — but it would have been tragic simply to discard half of it. The solution was to divide it into two books, one of which you are holding as you read this. After further lengthy discussion, we decided on a simple approach to this — we would break it into two books chronologically. That way the reader could see something of the evolution of theory and practice in bridge over the decades, and even follow the fortunes of some of the players who are recurring characters in the narrative.

Close Encounters Book 1 covers the twentieth century, beginning at the changing of the guard that ushered in the Blue Team era, and ending with the last dramatic session of the Venice Cup final in Paris in 2001. The second book covers the past twenty years, ending with the most recent World Championship in Lyon in 2017. Inevitably, the Nickell team features prominently in Book 2 — but then they have been the preeminent force in world bridge for the last thirty-odd years.

Ray Lee
Master Point Press

FOREWORD BY ERIC KOKISH

When I was more or less a callow youth, I ate up everything I could read about bridge. The day *The Bridge World* arrived in the mail was always special. So was hunting for back issues. And the annual World Championship Book: something to savor, devour, and cherish. It took me a while to start writing about bridge. I started with match reports, theory articles, and different slants I found amusing on deals I had experienced for as many different bridge magazines as I could convince of my merit, then secured a weekly column in the *Montreal Gazette*.

To give you some idea of how much I was writing in those days, I can share with you the essence of a phone call I received one rainy day from Sami Kehela, one of my idols, and eventually a cherished teammate. 'I say, Kokes,' he began, 'are you getting paid by the word?' I had to laugh because my writing style was not exactly pithy — 'pithy' being another word that often crept into our conversations. Not so much later, I noticed a comment by the much-revered Hugh Kelsey, referring to a certain earnest Canadian bridge reporter as a 'parenthetic' writer, which was also true: I often resorted to including a somewhat related idea within those curved brackets. I resolved to aim for a less-is-more approach and to limit my use of the maligned parentheses. After all, he was Hugh Kelsey; he ought to know what was good. So here I am, more than forty years later, using colons and semi-colons with great abandon, free at last to separate my thoughts.

In 1979 came my big break, when I was invited to analyze the finals of the Rio de Janeiro Bermuda Bowl for the World Championship Book, something I had wanted to do for years, trying an approach that would go far beyond reporting what happened.

It is inevitable that no one plays error-free bridge, but learning why mistakes are made, what the players are thinking, how the intangibles affect the results, which parts of the game make the difference in a match — those are things that have always interested me. I continue to hope that bringing a match to life makes reading about it an almost intimate experience. After I worked on my last World Championship Book in 2006, I thought I would miss the process terribly, but with the emergence of email (to facilitate consultation with the players) and much better record-keeping, just doing a thorough job on the final could take several months, and it had become almost an obsession for me to get everything just right.

But all that bridge writing and all those trips to major tournaments had left me with stories untold, or only partially told. The possibility of revisiting some of the most interesting matches from more than just an analytical perspective was always somewhere at the back of my mind, so when Mark expressed his interest in collaborating on just that sort of book, I was receptive.

What started out as a project called *Last Board** — a collection of single-deal chapters — has become a bird of a different feather that we call *Close Encounters*. What you will find in these two books are personal slants on some of the greatest matches ever played, including some with superb bridge, some with the other kind, but all culminating with a special ending. In most cases, at least one of us has been on site as a commentator, journalist, player or (in my case) coach, and we try to paint a picture of the tournament scene, the life and times of these important events.

We hope you enjoy the ride. Pacemaker not included.

Eric Kokish, Toronto, Canada, 2018

FOREWORD BY MARK HORTON

Bridge matches can be frustrating affairs, especially if a vast amount of your time is taken up by watching them unfold. It's tricky to entertain your audience as a VuGraph commentator or journalist if the deals are uncooperative. (One famous author of my acquaintance refuses to write up deals that end in 1NT.) However, every once in a while, one is lucky enough to be in the right place at the right time to witness the most dramatic events unfold.

We have selected contests from the last six decades that will have you metaphorically sitting on the edge of your seat. These matches are not only unbelievably exciting, but they are also instructive in so many ways. Having played and written about bridge for more than forty years, I know that there are only two ways to get better at this sometimes infuriating game — play against the best and read as much as you can. These books give you the opportunity to fulfil half of that equation.

Mark Horton, Sutton Benger, UK, 2018

---

* Available separately from Master Point Press, 2018.

Acknowledgements

Tracking down information and photographs is never easy, sometimes impossible. We could not have managed without the assistance of the ACBL, the USBF, Bridge Winners, BBO, Nikos Sarantakos and the VuGraph Project, *The Bridge World, Bridge Magazine* (RIP), *Le Bridgeur, Bridge d'Italia, International Popular Bridge Monthly* (RIP), the Internet (public domain), Tim Bourke, Francesca Canali, Wolf Klewe, Tracy Yarbro, Jeff Rubens, Simon Fellus, Richard Fleet, Gabriel Chagas, Sami Kehela, Raymond and Sally Brock, Brian Senior and so many of the players who appear in action in this book.

Contents

1. 1964 The End of an Era

The second World Bridge Team Olympiad was played in 1964 in New York at the beginning of May. The twenty-nine teams that contested the Open series included several players and captains who were to go on to great glory.

In 1964 I[†] had not yet learned how to play bridge, but six years later I picked up a copy of a book called *The Game of Bridge* written by a certain Terence Reese. As I developed an interest in the game I went on to devour almost every book he had written. Eventually I discovered that in 1965, just one year after the match described in this chapter, he had been involved in one of the greatest scandals ever to infest the game of bridge. Much later, having got to know Terence, I asked him about the Buenos Aires affair; he nodded sagely and said he had plans for something 'interesting' to be published at some point. After his death, his widow, Alwyn, invited me to their flat in Hove, but the great mass of papers we went through revealed nothing.

Some years after that (along with Raymond and Sally Brock, Brian Senior and Robert Sheehan) I was part of a group that started a bridge publishing company that we optimistically called Five Aces. We were friendly with Boris Schapiro and he agreed to write a book for us about his extraordinary career as a bridge player. Naturally we asked him what he would write about Buenos Aires 1965, to which he replied, 'I will leave nothing out'. It was not to be: he died a week later. In the end, all one can say about that extraordinary affair is that, like the mystery of the Mary Celeste, it is still the subject of speculation and controversy.

In the 1964 Olympiad, the teams played a complete round robin of 20-board matches. The matches were scored by IMPs, and the result converted to Victory Points using a scale of 6-0, 5-1, 4-2 and 3-3. The top four teams played semifinals, and the winners of those contested a final to determine the winner. It had originally been decided that those knockout matches would be over 40 boards, but this was subsequently changed to 60.

Great Britain topped the round robin, with a total of 160 VP, followed by Italy (153), USA (147) and Canada, which had won its last eight matches to qualify with 145. According to the regulations Great Britain should have faced fourth-qualifier Canada, but at the last moment it was announced that

---

† Primary author Mark Horton.

there would be a draw to decide who played whom. Four aces were put in a hat. Canada drew the ace of clubs, Great Britain the ace of hearts. When the Italian captain selected the ace of diamonds, that meant Italy would meet Great Britain.

It was generally accepted that the two most powerful bridge-playing countries in the world were Italy and Great Britain; in the previous nine years, the Italians had won the European Championships four times, just once more than the British. Italy was represented by what was already being referred to as the Blue Team: Giorgio Belladonna and Walter Avarelli, Pietro Forquet and Benito Garozzo, Massimo D'Alelio and Camillo Pabis-Ticci, with Sergio Osella, captain. They were the dominant force in world bridge, having won six Bermuda Bowls in a row, their only setback being their failure to win the first Olympiad in 1960.

The Italians were opposed by Boris Schapiro and Terence Reese, Kenneth Konstam and Maurice Harrison-Gray, Joel Tarlo and Jeremy Flint, with Dr. Sidney Lee as captain. During the championships, many thought that the player who had made the best impression was Reese, a rigid English professional with the profile of a canary, and the author of many ground-breaking bridge treatises. He was also the inventor of a complex bidding system called the Little Major, specifically designed to counter the Italians' strong club systems.

It was clear from the start that Reese and Schapiro would play all the boards in the semifinal and it was long odds that the Italians would go with their top two pairs, Belladonna-Avarelli and Forquet-Garozzo. That meant that both the Little Major as played by the British pair and the Roman Club practiced by Belladonna and Averelli would be on display throughout the match.

This is an outline of the opening bids in the Little Major:

1♣	In principle a heart suit, with 1◊ being either a negative response or the first move on a big hand
1◊	Either a spade suit or a 16-19 1NT with 1♡ being either a negative response or the first move on a big hand
1♡	Either a strong hand, usually 20 points plus, or an Acol two-bid, or a controlled psychic on balanced hands in the 3-6 range
1♠	Limited opening with length in both minors
1NT	Normal notrump, 13-15
2♣/◊	Limited opening, 12-15, no four-card major
2♡/♠	Fairly strong major-minor two-suiter
2NT	A weak three-bid in a minor or a strong minor two-suiter
3♣	A strong minor-suit hand, such as 7-3 or 6-4
3◊	A strong minor-suit hand, such as 7-3 or 6-4

Reese suggested that opponents could double the opening bids of 1♣ and 1◊ for takeout and use overcalls of the nominated suits (1♡ over 1♣ and 1♠ over 1◊ as weak takeout doubles).

The other British pairs played Acol, its cornerstones being the use of four-card majors, forcing two-bids and the weak (12-14) 1NT when not vulnerable (otherwise 15-17).

The Roman Club was based on the following opening bids:

1♣	12-16 balanced, or 21-22/25-26, or 17-20, 4/5 clubs plus 5/6 in another suit, or any shape with 3 or fewer losers, forcing for one round; club one-suiters were opened in the lowest ranking three-card suit
1◊	12-24, unbalanced with a five-card suit, usually not diamonds, forcing for one round
1♡	12-24, unbalanced, the longest suit only when minimum, forcing for one round
1♠	12-24, unbalanced, the longest suit only when minimum, forcing for one round
1NT	17-20 balanced (if 5-3-3-2 stoppers in all short suits)
2♣	12-16, 4-4-4-1 or 5-4-4-0
2◊	17-24, 4-4-4-1 or 5-4-4-0
2♡	14-16, 5/6 hearts + 4/5 clubs, 5/6 losers
2♠	14-16, 5/6 spades + 4/5 clubs, 5/6 losers
2NT	23-24 balanced, 5-3-3-2 only if long in clubs

Higher bids were sound preempts
Opener and responder both use canapé‡

Forquet and Garozzo were using the Neapolitan Club, a forerunner of Blue Club:

1♣	17+
1◊	12-16, 3+ diamonds, reverse = strong
1♡	12-16, 4+ hearts, reverse = strong
1♠	12-16, 4+ spades, reverse = strong
1NT	13-15, semi-balanced with clubs, or 16-17 balanced
2♣	12-16, 6+ clubs, or 5+ clubs and a four-card suit
2◊	7-12, six diamonds exactly
2♡	7-12, six hearts exactly

---

‡ This is a really bizarre agreement when you think about it, and can (and did) sometimes lead to chaos in competitive auctions.

| 2♠ | 7-12, six spades exactly |
| 2NT | 21-22, balanced, stoppers in all suits |

D'Alelio and Camillo Pabis-Ticci were relying on Arno, a version of the Roman Club that used a forcing opening of 1NT that promised 21+ balanced or an unbalanced game force.

Set 1 (Boards 1-20)

It sometimes happens, due to fatigue setting in, that towards the end of a major championship the standard of play is a little disappointing. Writing in the Bulletin of the Championships, editors Richard L. Frey and Albert Dormer remarked that this was not the case here; for a stretch of a great many deals the four players in the Open Room did not make the semblance of a mistake.

Board 1. Neither Vul.

```
              ♠ 9 7 6 4 3
              ♡ J 2
              ◇ Q 9 7 5
              ♣ Q 5
   ♠ J 8                        ♠ A K 10
   ♡ 9 3          N             ♡ A K Q 10 7 4
   ◇ K 8 6    W       E         ◇ A J 4 3
   ♣ A J 9 7 4 3   S            ♣ —
              ♠ Q 5 2
              ♡ 8 6 5
              ◇ 10 2
              ♣ K 10 8 6 2
```

Open Room

West	North	East	South
Forquet	Reese	Garozzo	Schapiro
	1♡[1]	dbl	pass
2♣	pass	3♡	pass
4♡	pass	4NT	pass
5◇	pass	6♡	all pass

1. Either a strong hand, usually 20+ points, or a controlled psychic on a balanced hand in the 3-6 range.

It was typical of Reese to attempt an early diversion, especially in a situation where he was protected by the partnership's system, his partner being aware that 1♡ might be based on a very weak hand. Here Reese would have passed any response other than 2NT, which would have indicated that South suspected a psych.

Terence Reese

South led the ♡5 and declarer took North's jack with the ace and played three rounds of spades, ruffing the last of these with dummy's ♡9. Then he ruffed a club, drew trumps, crossed to the ◇K, pitched a diamond on the ♣A and took the diamond finesse, taking all the tricks for +1010.

Closed Room

	West	North	East	South
	Gray	Belladonna	Konstam	Avarelli
		pass	2♣	pass
	3♣	pass	3♡	pass
	4♣	pass	4◇	pass
	4♡	pass	6♡	all pass

In this room South led the ♣6, and after pitching a diamond on the ace, declarer took a round of trumps. Then he played three rounds of spades, ruffing in dummy, ruffed a club to hand and drew the outstanding trumps before taking the diamond finesse to push the board.

Board 2. N-S Vul.

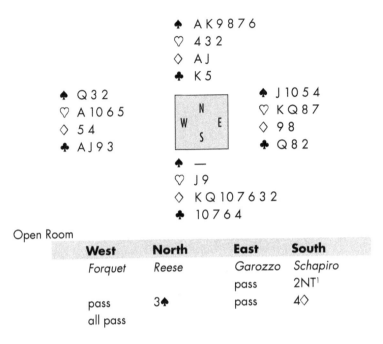

```
                        ♠ A K 9 8 7 6
                        ♡ 4 3 2
                        ◇ A J
                        ♣ K 5
     ♠ Q 3 2                              ♠ J 10 5 4
     ♡ A 10 6 5              N            ♡ K Q 8 7
     ◇ 5 4            W            E      ◇ 9 8
     ♣ A J 9 3                  S         ♣ Q 8 2
                        ♠ —
                        ♡ J 9
                        ◇ K Q 10 7 6 3 2
                        ♣ 10 7 6 4
```

Open Room

West	North	East	South
Forquet	*Reese*	*Garozzo*	*Schapiro*
		pass	2NT[1]
pass	3♠	pass	4◇
all pass			

1. A weak three-bid in a minor or a strong minor two-suiter.

Reese's minor-suit holdings made it unlikely that Schapiro held a strong hand, but hoping to find some sort of fit that made 4♠ playable he introduced his suit and then subsided. West led the ♡A and continued the suit, East winning and switching to a trump. Declarer won with dummy's ace, pitched two clubs on the top spades, drew trumps and led a club towards the king for +130.

Closed Room

West	North	East	South
Gray	*Belladonna*	*Konstam*	*Avarelli*
		pass	pass
1♣	dbl	redbl	3◇
pass	3NT	all pass	

Avarelli's initial pass was consistent with the partnership's philosophy about vulnerable preemptive bids in this position. It was standard Italian policy to double with the type of hand Belladonna held rather than overcall in spades. When South jumped to 3◇ promising a decent suit, the ever-aggressive Belladonna (he was, after all, considered the team's most dashing bidder) was willing to take a shot at game. East led the ♣2 and West won with the ace and returned the suit, the grateful declarer rapidly claiming ten tricks, +630 and 11 IMPs.

Giorgio Belladonna

Given that it was unlikely declarer would have bid 3NT without a club stopper, and surely must have a diamond fit, it looks as if the defenders will need to take their tricks on the go if they are to have a chance of defeating the contract. That points to West laying down the ♡A at Trick 2, only reverting to clubs if partner plays a discouraging card. However, West 'knows' that declarer's clubs are only ♣K5 and if East holds the ♠A, a club return will set up five tricks for the defense (East will unblock the ♣Q under the king).

Many years later, I got the opportunity to play against Belladonna and Pabis-Ticci at a Pairs tournament in Cefalu, Sicily. At the end of the round, Belladonna turned to me and said, 'You play very well, young man'. You might find that on my tombstone.

Board 5. N-S Vul.

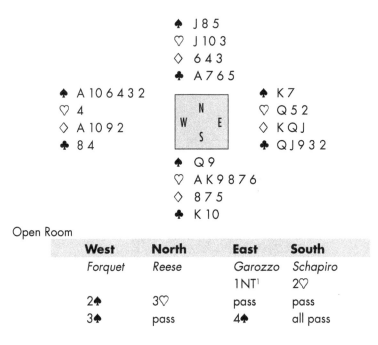

Open Room

West	North	East	South
Forquet	Reese	Garozzo	Schapiro
		1NT[1]	2♡
2♠	3♡	pass	pass
3♠	pass	4♠	all pass

1. 13-16 balanced or semi-balanced, one-suited in clubs.

When Forquet took a second bid, Garozzo (surprisingly, given his lack of aces) decided to advance to game. Reese led the ♡J and Schapiro overtook it and played king and another club. Reese won with the ace and played back a third club, ruffed by Schapiro with the queen, which did wonders for his partner's spade holding. Forquet overruffed with the ace, played a spade to the king and subsequently lost two trump tricks to finish two down, -100.

The eagle-eyed reader will have spotted that if Forquet plays the ♠10 after overruffing he will save a trick, as after North covers, the combined power of the ♠76 come into their own.

Closed Room

West	North	East	South
Gray	Belladonna	Konstam	Avarelli
	pass	1♣	1♡
1♠	pass	1NT	2♡
3♠	pass	4♠	all pass

Here Gray's jump to 3♠ more or less obliged Konstam to go on to game. This time when North led the ♡J South allowed it to hold, and when North played a second heart declarer ruffed and played three rounds of trumps. There was no way to avoid the loss of two clubs but that was only one down, -50 and 2 IMPs to Great Britain who trailed 7-11.

Board 7. Both Vul.

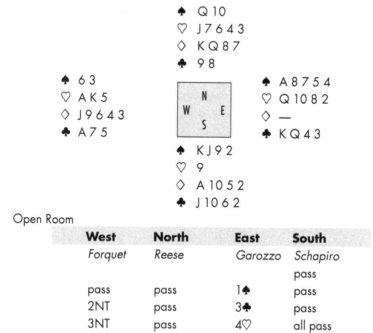

Open Room

West	North	East	South
Forquet	*Reese*	*Garozzo*	*Schapiro*
			pass
pass	pass	1♠	pass
2NT	pass	3♣	pass
3NT	pass	4♡	all pass

It's hard to imagine any modern player passing with the West hand, but both Forquet and Gray elected to do so. Knowing that West almost certainly did not have three spades, Garozzo was willing to take a third bid in the hope of finding a fit.

It's worth noting that Garozzo was happy to rebid 3♣ as opposed to bidding a direct 3♡. The huge advantage of doing that is illustrated by swapping West's minor suits around. To what extent East's strategy should be influenced by West's initial pass is unclear — it perhaps depends on how certain you are that 2NT might deliver something close to an opening bid.

South found the best lead of the ♡9. Declarer won with the ten, and ducked a spade, North winning and returning a second heart to dummy's king. Declarer played a spade to the ace, cashed the ♣K, played a club to the ace, and a third club. North ruffed and exited with a trump, and declarer could only score the master trump, finishing three down, -300. He could have saved a trick by not playing a third round of clubs, cross-ruffing diamonds and spades.

West	North	East	South
Gray	Belladonna	Konstam	Avarelli
			pass
pass	pass	1♠	pass
2NT	pass	3♣	pass
3NT	all pass		

Here too, East rebid 3♣, hoping to learn of four hearts or three spades if clubs was not the best strain. North led the ♡4 against 3NT, and declarer won in hand, cashed another top heart, took the marked finesse against North's jack and cashed a fourth heart, South discarding two diamonds and a spade. He then tested the clubs, but when they failed to divide decided to duck a spade, which meant the defenders could collect all the remaining tricks via one spade, one heart, three diamonds and a club for -200. Those 3 IMPs meant the scores were now level, 11-11.

Board 8. Neither Vul.

```
              ♠  Q
              ♡  6 3
              ◇  A 8 6 4
              ♣  A K J 8 7 6
♠ K 10 6 5                    ♠  J 9 7 4
♡ 10 9 8 7 5       N          ♡  K J 4
◇ 10 2         W     E        ◇  Q 9 5
♣ Q 4             S           ♣  10 9 2
              ♠  A 8 3 2
              ♡  A Q 2
              ◇  K J 7 3
              ♣  5 3
```

Open Room

West	North	East	South
Forquet	Reese	Garozzo	Schapiro
pass	1♠[1]	pass	1NT[2]
pass	2♡[3]	pass	3♡
pass	4♡	pass	5◇
all pass			

1. 12-15, clubs and diamonds, 5-4 or 4-5 or better.
2. Asking for the longer minor.
3. Longer clubs, presumably not minimum.

The precise meaning of 3♡ is unclear — it looks as if Schapiro wanted to make a slam try, but Reese was worried it might be natural. West led the ♡10 and declarer won with the queen, played a diamond to the ace and a diamond to the jack. When that held, he played a club to the ace, a heart to the ace and cashed the ◇K. When the ♣Q appeared on the next trick, declarer claimed the rest, +440.

Closed Room

West	North	East	South
Gray	Belladonna	Konstam	Avarelli
pass	1◇[1]	pass	1♠[2]
pass	3♣[3]	pass	3◇
pass	4◇[4]	pass	4♡[5]
pass	4♠[6]	pass	4NT
pass	5♡	pass	6◇
all pass			

1. Unbalanced with a five-card suit, usually not diamonds.
2. Natural, normally 10+ (but may be 8/9), possible canapé.
3. A four-loser hand, longer clubs, may have only three diamonds.
4. At least four diamonds.
5. Heart control.
6. Spade control.

East led the ♡4 and declarer put in dummy's queen. When that held, he cashed the ◇K and ◇A, followed by the top clubs. When the queen fell he could claim twelve tricks, +920 and 10 IMPs, restoring Italy's lead, 21-11. With North as declarer in 6◇, the heart lead meant that, had the finesse lost, he would have needed trumps to play for no losers, roughly a 39% chance. There are other issues too, so I leave to you to decide whether the Italians did well to bid the slam, or the British were unlucky to stay out of it.

Board 9. E-W Vul.

```
                    ♠ A K J 9 7 6 5
                    ♡ A Q 3
                    ◇ J
                    ♣ K J
      ♠ 10 4 3                        ♠ 8 2
      ♡ K J 10 8        N             ♡ 9 7 4 2
      ◇ K 9 8 7 2    W     E          ◇ A Q 10
      ♣ 9              S              ♣ A Q 10 6
                    ♠ Q
                    ♡ 6 5
                    ◇ 6 5 4 3
                    ♣ 8 7 5 4 3 2
```

Open Room

West	North	East	South
Forquet	Reese	Garozzo	Schapiro
	1♡¹	pass	1♠²
pass	pass	dbl	pass
2◇	2♠	3◇	pass
pass	3♠	all pass	

1. A strong hand, usually 20+ points, or an Acol two-bid, or a controlled psychic on a balanced hand in the 3-6 range.
2. Negative.

Writing in *Bridge Magazine* in 1969, Reese says that 1♠ was previously played as a step response showing controls. When he was asked how he could pass over 1♠, his explanation was that that bid showed a completely worthless hand. Writing in *The Great Bridge Scandal*, Alan Truscott suggested that Reese's pass was explicable only if North knew his partner held a singleton spade and a weak hand.

West led the ♣9 and East took two tricks in the suit and continued with the ◇A and ◇Q. Declarer ruffed in dummy, came to hand with the ♠Q, played a heart to the queen, drew trumps, and claimed nine tricks, +140.

Closed Room

West	North	East	South
Gray	Belladonna	Konstam	Avarelli
	1♣[1]	pass	1◊[2]
pass	2♠[3]	pass	3◊[4]
pass	3♡	pass	3♠
pass	4♠	all pass	

1. 12-16 balanced, or 21-22/25-26, or 17-20 with 4/5 clubs plus 5/6 in another suit or any shape with three or fewer losers.
2. 0-9.
3. Asking bid in spades.
4. Singleton or doubleton honor.

East led the ♠2, removing dummy's only entry, and declarer won with dummy's queen to play a club to the jack and queen. East continued with the ♣A, followed by the ♣10. West ruffed with the ♠10, and declarer overruffed and played five rounds of trumps. When East kept three hearts and the ◊A, he was thrown in with a diamond to lead into declarer's heart tenace, giving declarer nine tricks, for -50. That was 5 IMPs to Great Britain, edging closer: 16-21.

Once declarer has played a club at Trick 2, the defenders must discard carefully to come to five tricks. For example, if West parts with the ♡8, declarer can come to nine tricks by cashing all his trumps bar one, and then exiting with the ◊J. He can ruff the next diamond and exit with the ♡3 to endplay West.

Walter Avarelli

Board 13. Both Vul.

```
                 ♠ K J 10 9 6 4 3
                 ♡ A 5
                 ◇ 3
                 ♣ Q 7 5
  ♠ Q 5 2                        ♠ 8 7
  ♡ K Q 9 7 2        N           ♡ 10 8 6 4
  ◇ K 9          W       E       ◇ Q J 6 4
  ♣ A 9 3            S           ♣ K J 4
                 ♠ A
                 ♡ J 3
                 ◇ A 10 8 7 5 2
                 ♣ 10 8 6 2
```

Open Room

West	North	East	South
Forquet	Reese	Garozzo	Schapiro
	1◇[1]	pass	2◇[2]
pass	2♠	all pass	

1. Spades or 16-19 balanced.
2. Natural, assuming partner has opened 1♠.

Declarer lost a spade, a heart and three clubs, +110.

Closed Room

West	North	East	South
Gray	Belladonna	Konstam	Avarelli
	3♠	all pass	

Clearly the Italian pair adhered to the principle of making sound preempts when vulnerable, but here it meant they were a trick too high and -100 gave Great Britain another 5 IMPs to leave them just one behind, 21-22.

Board 14. Neither Vul.

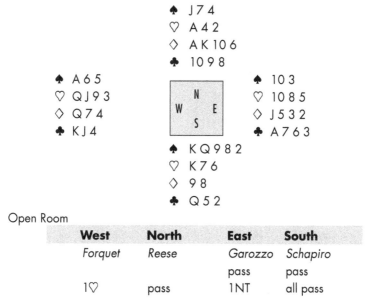

	♠ J 7 4	
	♡ A 4 2	
	◇ A K 10 6	
	♣ 10 9 8	
♠ A 6 5		♠ 10 3
♡ Q J 9 3	N	♡ 10 8 5
◇ Q 7 4	W E	◇ J 5 3 2
♣ K J 4	S	♣ A 7 6 3
	♠ K Q 9 8 2	
	♡ K 7 6	
	◇ 9 8	
	♣ Q 5 2	

Open Room

West	North	East	South
Forquet	Reese	Garozzo	Schapiro
		pass	pass
1♡	pass	1NT	all pass

South led the ♠Q (Rusinow from 'lesser' KQ holdings versus notrump) and declarer won with dummy's ace and played the ♡3. North went up with the ace, cashed the ◇A, and then went back to spades. The defenders took four tricks in that suit, and South then cashed the ♡K and reverted to diamonds. North took the king and declarer could claim the rest, two down, -100.

Closed Room

West	North	East	South
Gray	Belladonna	Konstam	Avarelli
		pass	pass
1NT	pass	pass	dbl
all pass			

Avarelli's reopening double struck gold when Belladonna had more than his share of the outstanding high cards. North led the ◇K and switched to the ♠4. Declarer won the third round of the suit and played the ♡Q, South winning with the king, cashing two spades and exiting with a diamond. North took declarer's queen with the ace and continued with the ◇10. Declarer won that with dummy's jack and played the ♡10, but North could win with the ace and cash the ◇6 for three down: -500 and 9 IMPs to Italy, making the score 31-21.

Board 15. N-S Vul.

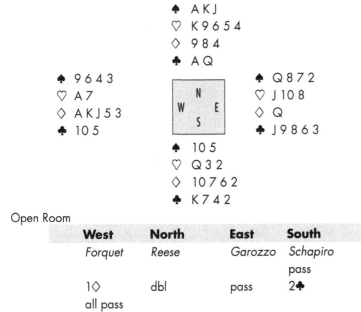

♠ A K J
♡ K 9 6 5 4
◇ 9 8 4
♣ A Q

♠ 9 6 4 3
♡ A 7
◇ A K J 5 3
♣ 10 5

♠ Q 8 7 2
♡ J 10 8
◇ Q
♣ J 9 8 6 3

♠ 10 5
♡ Q 3 2
◇ 10 7 6 2
♣ K 7 4 2

Open Room

West	North	East	South
Forquet	Reese	Garozzo	Schapiro
			pass
1◇	dbl	pass	2♣
all pass			

The disadvantages of doubling with the type of hand that North had were laid bare when Reese felt constrained to pass Schapiro's response of 2♣. (Eerily, this is just the sort of two-part bidding problem Reese would address in his classic, *Develop your Bidding Judgment*.) West started with three rounds of diamonds, and when East discarded the ♡8 and ♡10 he continued with the ◇3. Declarer pitched a heart from dummy and East ruffed and returned the ♣9 (really!). Declarer won with dummy's queen, cashed the ace and played a heart to the queen, West winning with the ace and returning the ♡7. Declarer won with dummy's king, East discarding a spade, cashed two spades, ruffed a spade, cashed the ♣K and conceded the rest for -100.

West could have ensured a two-trick defeat by switching to a spade at Trick 4, but he was no doubt anxious to eliminate the potential threat of the ◇10.

Writing about the deal, Gray opined that Schapiro might have responded 1♡ and that Reese might have bid 2♡ over 2♣. Whilst the former is a possibility I can't imagine Reese introducing such a moth-eaten suit.

Closed Room

West	North	East	South
Gray	Belladonna	Konstam	Avarelli
			pass
1◇	dbl	pass	1♠¹
pass	2♡	all pass	

1. Semi-positive, spades the shortest suit.

The Italians' system of exclusion responses simplified the process of finding a fit and enabled them to make takeout doubles on other-than-classic shapes. East led the ♠2 and declarer won with the jack, unblocked the ♣AQ, cashed the ♠A, ruffed the ♠K and played the ♣K. West ruffed with the ♡7 and declarer overruffed and ducked a heart to West's ace. When West continued with the ◇3§, East won and exited with the ♡10, but declarer could win with dummy's queen, ruff a club, draw trumps and claim nine tricks, for +140 and 6 IMPs to Italy, now ahead 37-21.

Maurice Harrison-Gray

§ No lack of imagination — EOK.

Board 17. Neither Vul.

```
                    ♠ K J 7 6 4 3
                    ♡ A 9
                    ◇ —
                    ♣ K 9 8 4 3
   ♠ Q 2                             ♠ A 10 9
   ♡ J 6 3              N            ♡ 7 5 2
   ◇ K Q 10 7 5 2   W     E          ◇ 9 8 3
   ♣ J 10               S            ♣ A Q 7 6
                    ♠ 8 5
                    ♡ K Q 10 8 4
                    ◇ A J 6 4
                    ♣ 5 2
```

Open Room

West	North	East	South
Forquet	Reese	Garozzo	Schapiro
	1◇¹	pass	2♡²
pass	3♣³	pass	3◇
pass	3♠	pass	4♠
all pass			

1. Spades or 16-19 balanced.
2. Natural, assuming partner has opened 1♠.
3. Natural, spades and clubs.

Reese's opening bid showed either spades or a strong notrump, the meaning being clear when he did not rebid 2NT. East led the ◇9 and declarer won with dummy's ace, pitching a club, and played a spade to the jack. If East wins with the ace, declarer's task will be straightforward — he can win any return in hand and play two rounds of spades, but Garozzo followed smoothly with the ten.

Benito Garozzo

As the cards lie Reese could have prevailed by playing the ♠K, but after long thought, he played three rounds of hearts pitching a club and then played a spade to the queen, king and ace. East cashed his remaining spade and exited with a diamond leaving declarer with three losing clubs, two down, -100.

Closed Room

West	North	East	South
Gray	Belladonna	Konstam	Avarelli
	2♠[1]	pass	2NT[2]
pass	3♠[3]	pass	4♠
all pass			

1. 5/6 spades + 4/5 clubs.
2. Asking.
3. Six spades.

East, hoping to protect his club holding behind declarer, led the ♠10, which ran to declarer's jack. Here too the winning line is to continue with the ♠K but when declarer cashed two hearts ending in dummy and played a spade, East won and switched to a diamond. Declarer left the ace in dummy, ruffed in hand, and exited with a spade. East won and cashed the ♣A, then a second club, and scored the ♣Q later for one down, -50 and a couple of IMPs to Italy, extending their lead to 40-21.

Board 20. Both Vul.

```
                    ♠ A Q 6
                    ♡ K 7
                    ◊ A Q J 7 4
                    ♣ 8 7 2
    ♠ J 5 4                        ♠ K 10 8 3
    ♡ J 9 8 6 2        N           ♡ A 3
    ◊ 2            W       E        ◊ K 10 8 3
    ♣ K Q J 5          S           ♣ A 10 9
                    ♠ 9 7 2
                    ♡ Q 10 5 4
                    ◊ 9 6 5
                    ♣ 6 4 3
```

Open Room

West	North	East	South
Forquet	Reese	Garozzo	Schapiro
pass	1NT	all pass	

In theory 1NT was 13-15 — why Reese refrained from opening 1◊ is unclear. East led the ♠3 and declarer took West's jack with the queen and played ◊A, ◊Q, West discarding a spade as East won with the king and returned the ♠K. Declarer won and tried the ♡K. East took the ace, cashed two spades, and continued with the ♣A and another club. West took his club winners and declarer claimed the rest, -200.

Closed Room

West	North	East	South
Gray	Belladonna	Konstam	Avarelli
pass	1♠[1]	pass	1NT[2]
pass	2◊[3]	all pass	

1. 12-24, at least one five-card suit.
2. Negative.
3. Canapé.

In the Roman Club, a single-suited hand is only opened in the long suit when the hand is of minimum strength, 12-14 points with 6/7 losers.

The British were renowned for making borderline doubles — if East had doubled 2◊ for penalties he would have picked a good moment for it. Writing about the deal in *The Blue Team in the History of Bridge*[¶], Carl'Alberto

---

¶ 2018 English translation available from Master Point Press.

Perroux, the legendary team captain who had stood down the previous year, said that he considered a double to be mandatory.

East led the ♡A, and when declarer followed with the king he switched to the ♣9, the defenders taking three tricks in the suit, after which West continued with the ♢2. East took declarer's jack with the king and continued with the ♡3, declarer winning with dummy's queen and taking the spade finesse. East won with the king and returned the three, declarer eventually losing a second spade and a diamond to finish three down, -300. Great Britain picked up 3 IMPs, but although both teams had scored on eight deals the three significant swings had gone to Italy, who led 41-24.

Set 2 (Boards 21-40)

For the second set, Italy went with the same two pairs, while for Great Britain Flint came in to partner Harrison-Gray. My inquiries suggest that they were not playing an identical system to that being used by Gray and Konstam, so that might have imposed an additional strain on their memories.

Board 22. E-W Vul.

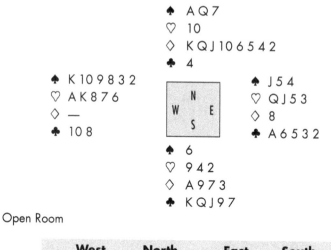

Open Room

West	North	East	South
Avarelli	Reese	Belladonna	Schapiro
		pass	1♠[1]
2♣	5♢	dbl	pass
5♡	dbl	all pass	

1. 12-15, 5+/4+ in the minors.

Facing a limited opening bid and with the potentially well-placed ♠AQ, Reese rejected the idea of taking out insurance by going on to 6♢. He led the ♣4 and declarer won with dummy's ace, drew trumps ending in dummy, and played the ♠J, overtaking it with his king. North won with the ace and switched to the ◊10. Declarer ruffed Schapiro's ace and played a spade. North won and exited with a spade, leaving declarer with a losing club, -200.

Closed Room

	West	North	East	South
	Gray	Forquet	Flint	Garozzo
			pass	1◊
	2♠	4NT[1]	dbl	5◊
	5♡	6◊	dbl	all pass

1. Roman Blackwood.

When Gray overcalled in spades, Forquet knew that finding two aces in Garozzo's hand would probably give him a play for a slam. It looks as if 5◊ promised only one ace but when Gray introduced his second suit Forquet was unwilling to risk that being a making contract and went on to what he knew must be a cheap save. West led the ♡K and switched to the ♣10. East took the ace and declarer claimed the rest, -100, giving Great Britain 7 IMPs and reducing the gap to 9, 32-41.

Board 25. E-W Vul.

```
                    ♠ K J 9 4
                    ♡ K 9 5
                    ◊ J 7 3
                    ♣ K 7 5
  ♠ A 8                            ♠ 6 5
  ♡ A Q 10 8 7 2        N          ♡ J 6 4 3
  ◊ A 9 6          W         E     ◊ 10 5 4
  ♣ A 9                 S          ♣ Q J 6 4
                    ♠ Q 10 7 3 2
                    ♡ —
                    ◊ K Q 8 2
                    ♣ 10 8 3 2
```

Open Room

West	North	East	South
Avarelli	Reese	Belladonna	Schapiro
	pass	pass	1◇[1]
1NT	2♠[2]	pass	pass
3♡	3♠	all pass	

1. Spades or 16-19 balanced.
2. Assuming partner has opened 1♠.

Facing a third-in-hand opening, Reese was content to make a non-forcing bid at his first turn and then compete on the next round. East led the ♣J (Rusinow) and West won with the ace and returned the nine, declarer winning with the king and then forcing out the ♠A. After drawing trumps, declarer gave up a diamond and could eventually pitch his losing club on the master diamond, for +170.

Closed Room

West	North	East	South
Gray	Forquet	Flint	Garozzo
	pass	pass	2♠
4♡	4♠	pass	pass
dbl	all pass		

The combination of North-South's two 'aceless wonders' was unassailable in 4♠ doubled, as East could not get in to cash a second club trick. Garozzo made his contract when the play ran along identical lines to that in the Open Room. Making +590 gave Italy 9 IMPs and advanced the score to 50-35.

Board 26. Both Vul.

```
                    ♠ A J 9 3
                    ♡ K Q
                    ◇ Q 10 8 4 3
                    ♣ K 8
   ♠ K 10 7 6 5 4                      ♠ Q 8
   ♡ 9 7 4              N              ♡ J 8 5 2
   ◇ K 7           W         E         ◇ J
   ♣ Q J              S              ♣ A 7 5 4 3 2
                    ♠ 2
                    ♡ A 10 6 3
                    ◇ A 9 6 5 2
                    ♣ 10 9 6
```

Open Room

West	North	East	South
Avarelli	Reese	Belladonna	Schapiro
		pass	pass
pass	1◇[1]	pass	1NT[2]
pass	2NT[3]	pass	3NT
all pass			

1. Spades or 16-19 balanced.
2. Assuming partner has opened 1♠.
3. 16-19.

In 1969, Reese wrote that the response of 1NT to 1◇ promised 9-10 (or a bad 11) but it's possible that in 1964 the range was 8-10. And although Schapiro was minimum, he did have a five-card suit and two aces. West led a spade and declarer put in the nine, East winning with the queen and returning a heart to dummy's queen. Declarer continued with two rounds of diamonds, and West won and switched to the ♣Q, covered by the king and ace. East returned a club, but West's jack was the fourth and last trick for the defense, +600.

Closed Room

West	North	East	South
Gray	Forquet	Flint	Garozzo
		pass	pass
pass	1◇	pass	1♡
1♠	dbl	pass	3◇
pass	3♡*	pass	5◇
all pass			

When Forquet bid 3♡, catering for good hearts with his partner, Garozzo, rightly worried about the club suit, jumped to 5♢. Declarer won the spade lead, unblocked the hearts, crossed to the ♢A, and pitched a club on the ♡A, losing only the ♣A and ♢K for +600 and a push.

Board 28. N-S Vul.

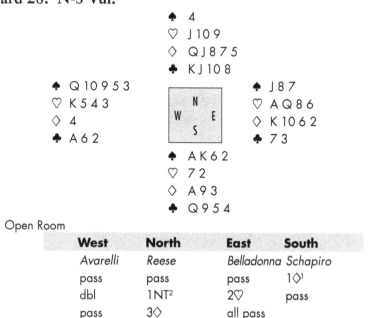

```
                    ♠ 4
                    ♡ J 10 9
                    ♢ Q J 8 7 5
                    ♣ K J 10 8
 ♠ Q 10 9 5 3                       ♠ J 8 7
 ♡ K 5 4 3         N                ♡ A Q 8 6
 ♢ 4          W         E           ♢ K 10 6 2
 ♣ A 6 2              S             ♣ 7 3
                    ♠ A K 6 2
                    ♡ 7 2
                    ♢ A 9 3
                    ♣ Q 9 5 4
```

Open Room

West	North	East	South
Avarelli	Reese	Belladonna	Schapiro
pass	pass	pass	1♢[1]
dbl	1NT[2]	2♡	pass
pass	3♢	all pass	

1. Spades or 16-19 balanced.
2. Assuming partner has opened 1♠.

With a shortage in spades West could have used a bid of 1♠ as a takeout double, so here West's double was takeout of diamonds. Even so, Reese's 3♢ looks aggressive.

West led the ♡3, and East won with the ace and switched to the ♢2. Had declarer let that run to his hand he would have been able to take nine tricks, but he went up with dummy's ace and played a second diamond, East taking the queen with the king and switching to the ♣7. Declarer could take two tricks in the suit, pitching a heart, but had to surrender a second diamond, a heart and a club for one down, -100.

Closed Room

West	North	East	South
Gray	Forquet	Flint	Garozzo
pass	pass	1♡	dbl
2NT[1]	3◇	pass	pass
3♡	all pass		

1. Good raise in hearts.

East's mildly tactical opening meant Gray was always going to compete at the three-level. South started with the ♠A, ♠K and ♠6, North ruffing and switching to the ◇7, which went to the king and ace. South returned the ♠2, ruffed by North and overruffed by declarer, who drew trumps ending in dummy and cashed the ♠Q, pitching a club. He could cash the ♣A and ruff a club, but had to lose a trick at the end to finish one down, -50.

If declarer withholds the ◇K he can always make nine tricks by ruffing out South's ace. However, if South had been sure North's ♠4 was a singleton he could have played a low spade at Trick 2, after which declarer has no real chance for nine tricks.

Italy picked up 4 IMPs, advancing the score to 55-35.

Board 29. Both Vul.

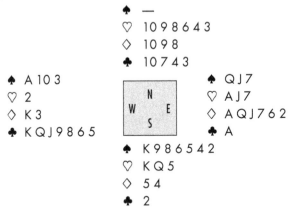

```
              ♠ —
              ♡ 10 9 8 6 4 3
              ◇ 10 9 8
              ♣ 10 7 4 3
♠ A 10 3                      ♠ Q J 7
♡ 2              N            ♡ A J 7
◇ K 3        W     E          ◇ A Q J 7 6 2
♣ K Q J 9 8 6 5    S          ♣ A
              ♠ K 9 8 6 5 4 2
              ♡ K Q 5
              ◇ 5 4
              ♣ 2
```

Open Room

West	North	East	South
Avarelli	Reese	Belladonna	Schapiro
	pass	1◇[1]	1♠
3♣[2]	pass	4◇[3]	pass
4NT	pass	5NT	pass
6◇	pass	7◇	all pass

1. Unbalanced with a five-card suit, usually not diamonds.
2. Natural.
3. Very good diamonds, 15+.

Belladonna opened 1◇ because his hand qualified for a jump rebid, which would promise 15 points or more and a very strong six-card or longer suit. Inhibited by the vulnerability and the quality of his suit, Schapiro was content to overcall at the one-level. Avarelli's 4NT looks like Roman Blackwood, but East's response (in theory 5♣ would have shown 0 or 3 aces) and the next two bids are uncharted territory. However, East knew his partner held a powerful club suit and the ♠A and he bid the grand slam confidently, selecting diamonds in case he needed to ruff out the club suit. Avarelli came under fire for not converting to 7NT, knowing that his partner must have three aces and good diamonds.

For what *The Bridge World* described as 'suspenseful minutes' the VuGraph audience held its breath. Concluding that the bidding strongly suggested that the only hope was an immediate ruff, Schapiro led the ♠5 and after declarer made the forced move of playing low Reese ruffed. One down, -100.

Closed Room

West	North	East	South
Gray	Forquet	Flint	Garozzo
	pass	2NT	pass
4♣[1]	pass	4NT[2]	pass
7NT	all pass		

1. Gerber.
2. 3 aces.

South led the ♡Q, but declarer was soon able to claim for +2220 and 20 IMPs that dramatically altered the state of the match, which was now tied at 55-55.

Board 30. Neither Vul.

```
              ♠ A 10 5 3
              ♡ 9 7 3
              ◇ A 8 5 4
              ♣ A K
  ♠ Q J 7                   ♠ 6 4 2
  ♡ Q              N        ♡ A K 10 2
  ◇ K 10 7 6    W   E      ◇ J 9
  ♣ Q 10 8 7 5     S        ♣ 9 4 3 2
              ♠ K 9 8
              ♡ J 8 6 5 4
              ◇ Q 3 2
              ♣ J 6
```

Open Room

West	North	East	South
Avarelli	Reese	Belladonna	Schapiro
		pass	pass
pass	1◇[1]	1♡	pass
1NT	pass	2♣	pass
pass	2◇	pass	pass
3♣	all pass		

1. Spades or 16-19 balanced.

Perhaps disconcerted by the previous deal, the mercurial Belladonna tried an atypical overcall and then felt compelled to remove his partner's 1NT (a contract that would make... except on a heart lead!). When Reese competed with 2◇, it was hard for Avarelli to opt to defend. His 3♣ was down in top cards, -50.

Closed Room

West	North	East	South
Gray	Forquet	Flint	Garozzo
		pass	pass
pass	1♠	pass	1NT
all pass			

West led the ♣7 and declarer won in dummy and played three rounds of spades, West winning and playing a second club. Declarer won and cashed his winners, conceding one down when the ◇K failed to appear. That gave Great Britain +50 and 3 IMPs that left them ahead by that margin, 58-55, as the match reached its halfway point.

Board 32. E-W Vul.

```
                    ♠ 10 5 3 2
                    ♡ Q J 10 4
                    ◇ 6
                    ♣ K Q 8 6
  ♠ A 7                              ♠ K 8 6
  ♡ 9 6 5 2            N             ♡ A 3
  ◇ Q 8 3         W         E        ◇ A K J 10 5 4
  ♣ J 9 5 2            S             ♣ 10 4
                    ♠ Q J 9 4
                    ♡ K 8 7
                    ◇ 9 7 2
                    ♣ A 7 3
```

Open Room

West	North	East	South
Avarelli	Reese	Belladonna	Schapiro
pass	pass	1◇[1]	pass
1♡[2]	pass	3◇[3]	pass
3NT	all pass		

1. Unbalanced with a five-card suit, usually not diamonds.
2. Negative.
3. 15+, 6+ good diamonds, 4/5 losers.

With a near maximum for his negative response, which included two golden cards, it was not difficult for Avarelli to bid game. After the lead of the ♡J, he claimed nine tricks, +600.

Closed Room

West	North	East	South
Gray	Forquet	Flint	Garozzo
pass	pass	1◇	dbl
2◇	2♡	3◇	pass
pass	3♠	all pass	

The Italians made a living by adopting thin takeout doubles with all types of hands, and here Garozzo's bold bid counted on the combination of the vulnerability and the fact that his partner was a passed hand working in his favor. Rather than introduce his weak four-card major, Gray raised diamonds. Unfortunately for Forquet, responsive doubles were not yet in use, so he had a problem now. When Forquet bid 2♡, Flint probably would have done best to bid 2NT, which reflects his playing strength (the Kaplan-

Rubens Hand Evaluator rates his hand at 18.70) and makes it relatively easy for West to go on to game. When he preferred 3◊ and Gray passed, Forquet presumably inferred spade length opposite, and decided to show his spades, knowing that Garozzo would not play him for a big hand because of his initial bid. The alternative approach for Forquet would have been to start with 2♠, perhaps competing later in hearts.

East led the ◊K and then switched to the ♠6. West won with the ace and switched to the ♣2. Declarer won with the king, played a spade to East's king, won the spade return and claimed nine tricks: +140 and 12 IMPs to Italy, reclaiming the lead at 67-58.

Jeremy Flint

Forquet's 3♠ might have been defeated. One way is for East to continue diamonds at Trick 2. Say declarer ruffs and plays a trump to the queen. If West wins that and returns a trump, East can play two more rounds and will be able to cash a diamond when he gets in with the ♡A.

Board 33. Neither Vul.

```
                    ♠ A 7 3
                    ♡ K J 5
                    ◇ 9 7 4
                    ♣ K 10 5 4
   ♠ J 10 6                          ♠ 8 5 4
   ♡ 6 4 2            N              ♡ 8 3
   ◇ K Q J       W        E          ◇ A 8 6 5 2
   ♣ A Q 7 6          S              ♣ 9 8 2
                    ♠ K Q 9 2
                    ♡ A Q 10 9 7
                    ◇ 10 3
                    ♣ J 3
```

Open Room

West	North	East	South
Avarelli	Reese	Belladonna	Schapiro
	pass	pass	1♣[1]
dbl	rdbl[2]	1◇	1♡
pass	2♡	all pass	

1. In principle a heart suit.
2. In theory no more than two hearts, at least four clubs and penalty possibilities.

West led the ◇K and continued the suit, declarer ruffing the third round and playing the ♣3. West went up with the ace and returned a heart, and declarer won and played on spades, claiming the rest when the suit divided, for +170.

Closed Room

West	North	East	South
Gray	Forquet	Flint	Garozzo
	pass	pass	1♠
pass	2♣	pass	2♡
pass	3♡	pass	4♡
all pass			

Emboldened by the result on the previous deal, Garozzo pushed on to the modest game. The play started identically, but after ruffing the third diamond declarer took two rounds of trumps and then played the ♣J. West went up with the ace and returned his remaining heart. Declarer won and tested the spades, claiming when they were 3-3. That was +420, adding 6 IMPs to Italy's total, 73-58.

Board 36. Both Vul.

```
                    ♠ J 2
                    ♡ K 6 5 3
                    ◇ A J 9 6 5 3
                    ♣ Q
    ♠ A 6 4                          ♠ K 10 8 7 3
    ♡ A 10 2         ┌─────────┐     ♡ Q 9 4
    ◇ Q 8 2          │    N    │     ◇ 10
    ♣ A J 10 6       │  W   E  │     ♣ 8 7 5 2
                     │    S    │
                     └─────────┘
                    ♠ Q 9 5
                    ♡ J 8 7
                    ◇ K 7 4
                    ♣ K 9 4 3
```

Open Room

West	North	East	South
Avarelli	Reese	Belladonna	Schapiro
1♣[1]	1◇	pass[2]	1NT
pass	2◇	2♠	3◇
3♠	all pass		

1. 12-16 balanced, or 21-22/25-26, or 17-20 with 4/5 clubs plus 5/6 in another suit or any shape with 3 or fewer losers.

2. Negative.

When Belladonna showed some modest values on the second round, Avarelli opted to bid on rather than defend. The play is not recorded, but declarer is debited with -200.

How might that happen? After a club lead to the ten and queen North returns a diamond; South wins with the king and returns a club for North to ruff. When North exits with the ♠J declarer wins with the king and plays a spade to the ace. If he now plays a low heart and guesses to put in the nine when North follows smoothly with the five, he will be two down. Notice that if declarer wins the first trick with dummy's ♣A and plays three rounds of trumps, he has every chance of recording nine tricks.

As for 3◇, it should fail if East leads a heart or a spade, but after a club lead declarer is in with a shout, needing primarily to get the trump suit right (which, depending on how West defends, may involve a first-round finesse of the ten).

Closed Room

West	North	East	South
Gray	Forquet	Flint	Garozzo
1NT	pass	2♠	all pass

Remember this was more than fifty years ago and transfers were still in their infancy, having been introduced to the English-speaking world by Oswald Jacoby in an article in *The Bridge World* in 1956.

Flint went down in 2♠, which is a little surprising. Once again, the play record is lost, but if declarer lost a club and a club ruff, then a late misguess in hearts would be one way to record only seven tricks. Great Britain recouped 3 IMPs to trail 74-61.

Board 37. N-S Vul.

```
              ♠ A J 6 5 2
              ♡ 4
              ◇ 9 7 4
              ♣ A K Q 2
♠ K Q 10 7 4              ♠ —
♡ A 10 8 6 5      N       ♡ J 9 7 3
◇ 6 3 2      W     E      ◇ K J
♣ —              S       ♣ J 9 8 6 5 4 3
              ♠ 9 8 3
              ♡ K Q 2
              ◇ A Q 10 8 5
              ♣ 10 7
```

Open Room

West	North	East	South
Avarelli	Reese	Belladonna	Schapiro
	1◇[1]	pass	2◇[2]
2♡	3♣	3♡	3♠
pass	4♠	pass	pass
dbl	all pass		

1. Spades or 16-19 balanced.
2. Assuming an opening bid of 1♠.

Belladonna attempted to lead a heart out of turn against 4♠ doubled, giving declarer the chance to prohibit a heart lead. Avarelli led the ◇3 and Schapiro took Belladonna's king with the ace and played the ♠9, ducking when Avarelli put up the queen, as Belladonna pitched a club. Avarelli cashed the ♡A and continued with a heart. Schapiro threw dummy's remaining diamonds on the

top hearts and played the ♠8 to the ten and jack. When he tried to cash the
♣A, West ruffed and exited with the ♠K. Locked in dummy, declarer could
not avoid the loss of a trump and a club, finishing two down, -500.

Schapiro's line appears to be predicated on the possibility that West's
opening lead was a singleton. However, if West's shape is 5=5=1=2 then
declarer has no winning line. Having pitched two diamonds and played the
♠8 to the ten and jack, declarer plays three rounds of clubs, but West ruffs
and his ♠K7 guarantee another trump trick.

Had he pitched a club on the second heart and played a spade to the ten
and jack he could then have returned to hand with a diamond, and played the
♠3 to the seven and ace. That leaves dummy's ♠65 as equals against West's
♠K4 and declarer can exit with a spade, leaving West helpless.

What if Schapiro had accepted the lead and put his hand down as dummy,
leaving Reese to be declarer? West wins with the ♡A and returns the suit,
declarer winning in dummy and playing the ♠9 to West's queen. He ruffs the
heart return, plays a diamond to the jack and queen and the ♠8 to the ten
and jack. He then plays a second diamond and can continue with winning
diamonds. To defeat the contract West must refrain from ruffing any of the
winning diamonds. (In *Play These Hands with Me*, Reese describes a similar
deal, entitling it 'A Long Ordeal'.)

Closed Room

	West	North	East	South
	Gray	Forquet	Flint	Garozzo
		1♠	2♣	2◇
	2♡	2♠	pass	3♠
	pass	4♠	5♡	dbl
	all pass			

East's choice of bids might not meet with universal approval; aside from his
initial overcall, if he had raised to 3♡ immediately then he could have left his
partner to make any further decisions.

North led the ♣A. Declarer ruffed and played the ♠Q, ruffing when
North covered, ruffed a club, pitched a diamond on the ♠K, and exited with
a diamond, South winning with the ace and returning the ♡K. Declarer won,
ruffed a diamond and played a club. When South pitched his remaining
spade, declarer ruffed, ruffed a diamond and played a club, scoring his last
trump *en passant* to escape for -300. The combined +800 gave Italy 13 IMPs,
extending the lead to 87-61.

Board 39. Both Vul.

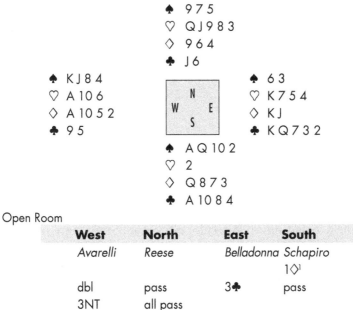

West	North	East	South
Avarelli	Reese	Belladonna	Schapiro
			1◊[1]
dbl	pass	3♣	pass
3NT	all pass		

1. Spades or 16-19 balanced.

Reese had written that a double of a Little Major 1♣ or 1◊ should presumably be for takeout (of hearts and spades respectively), but this deal suggests that the Italians were happy to maintain their policy of doubling with values, regardless of shape. With no fit for clubs, Avarelli's decision to bid game was aggressive, but perhaps he was aware of the old Russian proverb, 'If you're afraid of wolves, don't go to the woods'. Schapiro had Russian blood — maybe he mentioned that proverb to Avarelli!

North led the ♠9 and declarer won with the jack and played a club to the king and ace, South continuing with the ♠Q. Declarer won with the king and played a second club, ducking when the jack appeared. North returned his remaining spade, and South took two tricks in the suit and exited with a club. Declarer won in dummy and ran the ◊J, but there was no way to avoid losing a fifth trick at the end, -100.

For what it's worth, Belladonna would probably have made 3♣.

West	North	East	South
Gray	Forquet	Flint	Garozzo
			1♠
pass	pass	dbl	pass
pass	rdbl	pass	2♣
dbl	2◇	pass	pass
dbl	2♡	dbl	all pass

Holding three spades, Forquet's decision to redouble for rescue was unusual: perhaps he was trying to convey a near-maximum hand for his pass of 1♠. Although in theory the defenders should hold declarer to five tricks in spades, it is not always easy to defend a low-level contract. Against 2♡, East led the ♡4. West won with the ace and switched to the ♣9. Declarer took East's queen with the ace and returned a club, establishing two more tricks in the suit. East returned a spade, and declarer went up with dummy's ace and played a club, ruffed by West with the ten and overruffed by declarer, who exited with the ♡Q. East won with the king as declarer pitched a diamond from dummy, and now made the mistake of exiting with a club. That gave declarer an unexpected extra trick, and he escaped for two down. However, that was still -500 and 12 IMPs to Great Britain, who trailed 73-88 as the set came to an end.

Pietro Forquet

Set 3 (Boards 41-60)

Italy stayed with same four players, but Konstam returned to partner Harrison-Gray.

Board 41. E-W Vul.

```
                      ♠ J 10 8 7 2
                      ♡ Q 8
                      ◇ K Q 8
                      ♣ J 7 3
   ♠ Q 9 3                              ♠ A K 6 5 4
   ♡ 7 4 3              N               ♡ A K 9 6 5 2
   ◇ A 9 6 4        W       E           ◇ 7
   ♣ K Q 4              S               ♣ A
                      ♠ —
                      ♡ J 10
                      ◇ J 10 5 3 2
                      ♣ 10 9 8 6 5 2
```

Open Room

West	North	East	South
Schapiro	Belladonna	Reese	Avarelli
	pass	1◇[1]	pass
2◇[2]	pass	3♡	pass
4♡	pass	4NT	pass
5◇	pass	6♣[3]	pass
7♡	all pass		

1. Spades or 16-19 balanced.
2. Assuming an opening bid of 1♠.
3. Grand slam try.

Schapiro knew his ♠Q was important, and he gauged that Reese must have very good hearts to suggest the possibility of a grand slam. Which is how England's finest reached their 40.69% grand slam; the bridge gods were benevolent, +2210.

(Left to right) Schapiro, Belladonna, Reese, Avarelli

West	North	East	South
Forquet	Konstam	Garozzo	Gray
	pass	1♣[1]	pass
1♠[2]	pass	2♡	pass
3NT	pass	4♠	pass
5♠	pass	5NT	pass
6♣	pass	6♡	all pass

1. Strong.
2. Three controls: one ace and one king, or three kings.

When Forquet raised to 5♠, Garozzo made a grand slam try with 5NT before offering his partner a choice of trump suits. South led the ◊3 and declarer won and played a heart, taking the safety play of putting in the nine when North followed with the eight. He ruffed South's diamond return, drew trumps and claimed, +1430, but Great Britain had 13 IMPs. They had closed to within 2 IMPs at 86-88.

Board 42. Both Vul.

```
                    ♠ Q 7 5
                    ♡ A J 10 5
                    ◊ 9 8 5
                    ♣ A Q 7
    ♠ 10 4 2                      ♠ A K J 8
    ♡ 9 8 4 2          N          ♡ K 7 6
    ◊ J 4         W         E      ◊ 6 3 2
    ♣ K J 6 3          S          ♣ 10 5 4
                    ♠ 9 6 3
                    ♡ Q 3
                    ◊ A K Q 10 7
                    ♣ 9 8 2
```

Open Room

West	North	East	South
Schapiro	Belladonna	Reese	Avarelli
		pass	pass
pass	1♣[1]	dbl	pass
1♡	pass	pass	2◊
all pass			

1. 12-16 balanced, or 21-22/25-26, or 17-20 with 4/5 clubs plus 5/6 in another suit, or any shape with 3 or fewer losers.

When 1♣ is doubled, the general rule for the Roman Clubbers is that if responder is weak with three or more clubs he passes; with 8-11 he redoubles with three or more clubs, or with fewer than three clubs he bids one of a suit or 1NT; with 12 or more points, he passes and acts later, initiating a game-forcing sequence. Having passed initially, Avarelli was entitled to upgrade his hand, but when he bid 2◇, Belladonna, influenced by the initial pass didn't feel like moving forward. Certainly he was entitled to ignore any attempt by his partner to force to game! West imaginatively led the ♠10 against 2◇, and when it held, continued with the four, East winning with the king to switch to the ♣5. Declarer took West's king with dummy's ace, drew trumps and ran the ♡Q, +110.

Closed Room

West	North	East	South
Forquet	Konstam	Garozzo	Gray
		pass	1◇
pass	1♡	pass	2◇
pass	3NT	all pass	

Everyone is aware that in the 21st century light opening bids are *de rigueur*, but even in 1964, Acol, the system being employed by Konstam and Gray, had been making use of them for years. Writing in *The Acol System Today* in 1961, Reese and Albert Dormer pointed out that Acol players were always willing to open on hands that contained no more than a fair share of high cards but were likely to take more than a fair share of tricks.

Kenneth Konstam

Once South had opened it was inevitable that game would be reached. East led the ♠K and switched to the ♣4. Declarer took West's king with the ace, crossed to dummy with the ◇A and ran the ♡Q. East won and cashed the ♠A, declarer claiming the balance when the diamonds behaved, +630 and 11 IMPs. Great Britain were suddenly ahead, 97-88.

Board 43.   Neither Vul.

```
                    ♠ J 10 8 6 3
                    ♡ 2
                    ♢ K J 10 7 3 2
                    ♣ 4
  ♠ 7 2                              ♠ Q 9 4
  ♡ J 8 7            ┌─────────┐     ♡ 10 9 6 5 4 3
  ♢ 9 4             N            ♢ Q 8
  ♣ K J 10 8 7 2     W       E     ♣ A Q
                          S
                      └─────────┘
                    ♠ A K 5
                    ♡ A K Q
                    ♢ A 6 5
                    ♣ 9 6 5 3
```

Open Room

West	North	East	South
Schapiro	Belladonna	Reese	Avarelli
			1NT[1]
pass	2♠[2]	pass	3♡[3]
pass	4♠	all pass	

1. 17-20.
2. 5+ spades, 6+ HCP.
3. Maximum with a fit (which includes two of the three top spade honors).

Reese made the remarkable lead of the ♣Q. Writing in *The Great Bridge Scandal*, Alan Truscott suggested that 'this is not a lead that would be likely to occur to anyone' and implies that East must have known that West had length and strength in clubs. However, Reese was not 'anyone'. He knew that there would be around 20 points on his left, and that if anyone held the ♣K it was likely to be dummy. He also knew that South held the ♠AK, which affected the value of his ♣Q, notwithstanding the presence of the ♣9, and that his partner must hold a nearly worthless hand. Reckoning that a passive defense was unlikely to be successful, he opted for a desperate piece of deception. When the ♣Q held, Reese continued with the ace. Declarer ruffed, cashed dummy's top spades, played the two top diamonds, and then gave up a spade, claiming the rest, +450.

West	North	East	South
Forquet	Konstam	Garozzo	Gray
			2NT
pass	3♣*	pass	3NT
all pass			

North's 3♣ was Baron, asking South to bid four-card suits in ascending order, a method that has faded into obscurity. The 3NT response denied any suit other than clubs and ended the auction in a poor contract.

However, when West led the ♣J the wide-open suit was blocked. East won the first club with the ace, cashed the queen (declarer pitching a diamond from dummy) and switched to the ♠9. Declarer won with the ♠A, cashed the ◇A and played a diamond to the ten and queen. When East returned the ♠4, declarer had to play the king to secure his contract, and claimed nine tricks: +400 and 2 IMPs to Italy, which meant they trailed 90-97.

Board 44. N-S Vul.

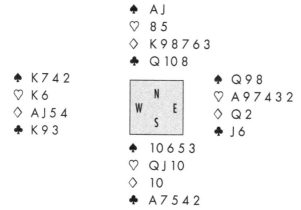

```
                    ♠ A J
                    ♡ 8 5
                    ◇ K 9 8 7 6 3
                    ♣ Q 10 8
    ♠ K 7 4 2                      ♠ Q 9 8
    ♡ K 6              N           ♡ A 9 7 4 3 2
    ◇ A J 5 4      W       E       ◇ Q 2
    ♣ K 9 3           S           ♣ J 6
                    ♠ 10 6 5 3
                    ♡ Q J 10
                    ◇ 10
                    ♣ A 7 5 4 2
```

Open Room

West	North	East	South
Schapiro	Belladonna	Reese	Avarelli
1NT¹	pass	2♣²	pass
2◇³	dbl	2♡⁴	all pass

1. 13-15.
2. Gladiator: puppet to 2◇.
3. Forced.
4. Weak.

Not vulnerable, with a weak suit, Reese decided against rebidding an invitational 3♡, which turned out to be a good move. South led the ◊10, ducked to the king, and North returned the not-quite-lowest six. South ruffed, cashed the ♣A, and switched to the ♠6. North took the ace and returned a third diamond, South ruffing when declarer pitched the ♣J. When South exited with a trump declarer claimed the rest, +110. A low club at Trick 3 would have given declarer a guess.

Closed Room

West	North	East	South
Forquet	Konstam	Garozzo	Gray
1♠	pass	2♡	pass
2NT	pass	3♡	pass
4♡	all pass		

Although the contract here was for two extra tricks, the play ran along similar lines. Here, however, North returned the ◊9 at Trick 2. So, after ruffing, South returned a spade to North's ace, ruffed the next diamond (declarer pitching a club) and cashed the ♣A. Two down, -100, and 5 IMPs to Great Britain, stretching the lead to 12, 102-90.

Board 47. N-S Vul.

```
              ♠ A 9 6
              ♡ 8 7 5 3
              ◊ A Q 5 3
              ♣ J 8
  ♠ K 3                      ♠ 10 8 7 5
  ♡ Q J 9          N         ♡ 6 2
  ◊ 9 7        W       E     ◊ 8 6 4 2
  ♣ Q 10 6 5 4 3   S         ♣ A 9 2
              ♠ Q J 4 2
              ♡ A K 10 4
              ◊ K J 10
              ♣ K 7
```

West	North	East	South
Schapiro	Belladonna	Reese	Avarelli
			1NT[1]
pass	2◇[2]	pass	3♣[3]
pass	4♡	all pass	

1. 17-20.
2. Stayman, 6+ points.
3. 17-18, both majors.

This seemingly straightforward deal was enlivened when Reese led the ♣9, no doubt reasoning as he had on Board 43 (Truscott made no mention of this deal). Without apparent pause for thought, Belladonna called for dummy's king and was soon recording +620.

The VuGraph audience (which contained many Italian supporters) was relieved, but even if declarer misguesses at Trick 1 the contract has chances. Say East switches to a trump at Trick 3. Declarer wins in dummy, draws a second round of trumps, plays the ♠Q to the king and ace and cashes a second spade, followed by three rounds of diamonds. If West refuses to ruff he is thrown in with a heart to concede a ruff and discard.

West	North	East	South
Forquet	Konstam	Garozzo	Gray
			1NT
pass	2♣	pass	2♠
pass	3NT	pass	4♡
all pass			

West led a club, and declarer played safely for ten tricks and no swing.

Board 49. Neither Vul.

```
                    ♠ A
                    ♡ 9 7 6
                    ◇ Q 10 5 2
                    ♣ J 9 7 6 4
   ♠ Q 8 7 4 3                    ♠ K 10 6 5 2
   ♡ A K 8          N             ♡ Q J 10 5 4
   ◇ K J 7      W       E         ◇ A 9 3
   ♣ K 8            S             ♣ —
                    ♠ J 9
                    ♡ 3 2
                    ◇ 8 6 4
                    ♣ A Q 10 5 3 2
```

Open Room

West	North	East	South
Schapiro	*Belladonna*	*Reese*	*Avarelli*
	pass	1◇[1]	2♣
3♣[2]	3♠	pass	4♣
6♠	all pass		

1. Spades or 16-19 balanced.
2. Game forcing.

By passing over Belladonna's 3♠ cuebid, Reese presumably denied holding the strong balanced hand type, but unless I am missing something, Schapiro's jump to 6♠ looks like a complete gamble. North led the ♣4; declarer ruffed and played a spade to the queen and ace, claiming +980.

Closed Room

West	North	East	South
Forquet	*Konstam*	*Garozzo*	*Gray*
	pass	1♠	pass
2◇[1]	pass	2♡	pass
3♠	pass	4♠	pass
5♡	pass	5♠	pass
6♠	all pass		

1. Game forcing.

In attempting to locate a definitive explanation of this sequence, I have scoured the resources of the best bridge libraries in the world, but have had no success. Having refused to cooperate over 3♠, East's retreat to 5♠ with first-round control in both minors is surprising, but not as surprising as West, a famously conservative bidder, driving to slam unilaterally. His luck was in — on another day East might have held:

♠ A K 10 6 2 ♡ Q J 10 5 4 ◇ Q 3 ♣ 2

South tried to cash the ♣A, but that did not affect the outcome, which was +980 and another push.

Board 50. N-S Vul.

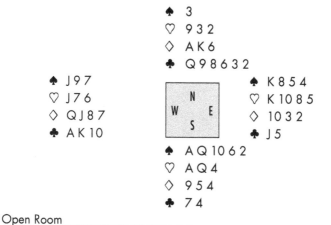

```
              ♠ 3
              ♡ 9 3 2
              ◇ A K 6
              ♣ Q 9 8 6 3 2
♠ J 9 7                        ♠ K 8 5 4
♡ J 7 6          N             ♡ K 10 8 5
◇ Q J 8 7      W   E           ◇ 10 3 2
♣ A K 10         S             ♣ J 5
              ♠ A Q 10 6 2
              ♡ A Q 4
              ◇ 9 5 4
              ♣ 7 4
```

Open Room

West	North	East	South
Schapiro	Belladonna	Reese	Avarelli
		pass	1♠
pass	2♣	pass	2♠
pass	3♣	all pass	

When Avarelli rebid a non-forcing 2♠, Belladonna judged it safer to play in clubs (and of course, it was always better to have Belladonna at the wheel rather than Avarelli). East led the ◇3 and declarer eventually took successful finesses against the major-suit kings, losing only three trumps and an odd trick for +110.

Closed Room

West	North	East	South
Forquet	Konstam	Garozzo	Gray
		pass	1♠
pass	2♣	pass	2♠
all pass			

Gray's 2♠ was non-forcing, and Konstam was reluctant to go a level higher with such a poor suit, so South was left to declare an unpleasant 5-1 fit. West led the ◊Q, won in dummy, East encouraging. Declarer led a heart to the queen, then a club, West winning with the king to continue with the ◊8. Declarer won in dummy, played a heart to the ace and a second club. West won, cashed the ◊J, and exited with the ♡J. East overtook with the king and continued with the ten. Declarer elected to ruff with the ten so West overruffed and played the ♣10. If East ruffs that with the ♠8 (or ♠K), the contract is sure to go two down, but he ruffed low, declarer overruffing with the six. Down to the ♠AQ2 declarer guessed to play ace-two rather than lead the two and so finished two down in a different way: -200. Italy recovered 7 IMPs, to trail 99-103.

Board 51. E-W Vul.

```
                  ♠  A 3 2
                  ♡  Q 10 6 4
                  ◊  J 9 2
                  ♣  A J 5
   ♠  Q J 10 5                      ♠  K 8
   ♡  J 5              N            ♡  A K 8 7 2
   ◊  10 5 3      W         E       ◊  A K 8 7
   ♣  K 7 6 2          S            ♣  10 8
                  ♠  9 7 6 4
                  ♡  9 3
                  ◊  Q 6 4
                  ♣  Q 9 4 3
```

Open Room

West	North	East	South
Schapiro	Belladonna	Reese	Avarelli
			pass
pass	1♣¹	dbl	pass²
1♠	all pass		

1. 12-16 balanced, or 21-22/25-26, or 17-20 with 4/5 clubs plus 5/6 in another suit, or any shape with 3 or fewer losers.

2. Weak, three or more clubs.

I recall having devised a defensive method against the Roman Club that required the overcaller to pass initially with all strong hands, the idea being to be able to double a rebid of 1NT for penalties. It might not be totally sound, but it did once give one of my partners the chance to double on the next round with a 23-count.

Whilst it is true that Schapiro's 1♠ might have been based on a very weak hand, Reese's pass is conservative — contrast his heart suit with the one he held on Board 15 (p. 24).

Declarer took four red winners and three trumps for +80.

Closed Room

West	North	East	South
Forquet	Konstam	Garozzo	Gray
			pass
pass	1NT	dbl	2♣
dbl	all pass		

If you play the weak notrump, being doubled for penalties is an occupational hazard. Gray's decision to run is debatable, however. Had he passed the double, East would surely have led a heart, after which declarer has every chance of escaping for one down.

Against 2♣ doubled, West led the ♠Q and East unblocked the king under dummy's ace. When declarer continued spades, West won with the ten and switched to the ♡J. East took dummy's queen with the king, cashed the ◊K and ♡A, and led the ♡8, West ruffing as declarer pitched a spade. West cashed the ♠J and played a diamond to East's ace. Back came a heart, and West overruffed declarer's ♣Q with the king, and played his remaining spade, ensuring East would score a trick with the ♣10. Four down, -700 and 12 IMPs to Italy, reclaiming the lead, 111-103.

If declarer had ruffed the fourth heart with any of his other three clubs he would have saved a trick.

Board 52. Both Vul.

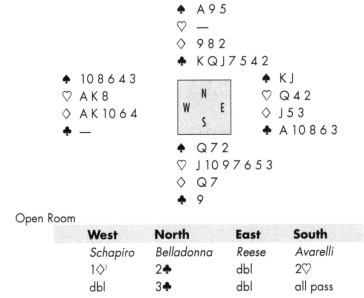

```
                    ♠ A 9 5
                    ♡ —
                    ◇ 9 8 2
                    ♣ K Q J 7 5 4 2
    ♠ 10 8 6 4 3              ♠ K J
    ♡ A K 8          N        ♡ Q 4 2
    ◇ A K 10 6 4   W   E      ◇ J 5 3
    ♣ —              S        ♣ A 10 8 6 3
                    ♠ Q 7 2
                    ♡ J 10 9 7 6 5 3
                    ◇ Q 7
                    ♣ 9
```

Open Room

West	North	East	South
Schapiro	Belladonna	Reese	Avarelli
1◇¹	2♣	dbl	2♡
dbl	3♣	dbl	all pass

1. Spades or 16-19 balanced.

Reese and Schapiro made a living by doubling low-level contracts and, had Belladonna not retreated to 3♣, perfect defense would have allowed East-West to collect +1100 against 2♡ doubled.

Reese made the unfortunate lead of the ♠K (remember the opening bid promised spades or a strong notrump), won by Belladonna, who played a diamond to the queen. Schapiro won and played back a spade to dummy's queen. When Belladonna called for the ◇7 it was virtually impossible for Schapiro to play low, which would allow Reese to win and switch to the ♣10, restricting declarer to six tricks. (Declarer can eliminate this remote possibility by playing dummy's ◇7 on the first round of the suit.) After winning with the ◇A, Schapiro continued with the ♣10. Reese could have ruffed this and exited with the ♣10, ensuring a two-trick penalty, but instead he threw a heart. On the next spade, Belladonna discarded a diamond and Reese... ruffed with the ♣10! That meant declarer could concede a trick to the ♣A and escape with eight tricks, -200. Discarding instead of ruffing, a theme that Reese knew all too well, ensures three trump tricks for East and +500. Evidently, fatigue had started to set in.

West	North	East	South
Forquet	Konstam	Garozzo	Gray
1♠	2♣	dbl	2♡
3◊	pass	3NT	all pass

When Forquet decided against doubling 2♡, Garozzo naturally bid game. South led the ♡J against 3NT and declarer won in dummy and played a spade to the jack and queen. He won the heart return in dummy, played a spade to the king, a diamond to the ace and then a spade, taking all the remaining tricks for +660. That was 10 IMPs to Italy, 121-103.

No doubt Konstam would have bid 3♣ if 2♡ had been doubled, but it's worth analyzing the defense against a heart contract. West cashes a top diamond and switches to a spade, East winning with the king and returning the jack. Declarer wins with the queen and plays the ♡9, but West wins and plays a third spade for East to ruff. East cashes the ♣A and plays a diamond, West winning and playing a fourth spade, allowing East to score a trick with the ♡Q. Then a club from East ensures two more trump tricks for West — if declarer ruffs with the jack West will simply discard. Declarer is held to four tricks.

Board 53. N-S Vul.

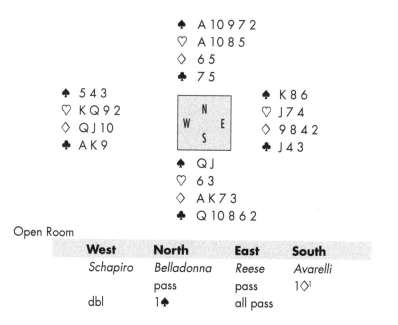

Open Room

West	North	East	South
Schapiro	Belladonna	Reese	Avarelli
	pass	pass	1◊[1]
dbl	1♠	all pass	

1. Unbalanced with a five-card suit, usually not diamonds.

When Schapiro made an Italian-style double, Belladonna had the option of redoubling to promise 8-11 but, with a minimum, preferred 1♠. Despite heroic efforts I have been unable to determine how the play went, but the result was +80.

Closed Room

	West	North	East	South
	Forquet	Konstam	Garozzo	Gray
		pass	pass	pass
	1♡	1♠	pass	2♠
	all pass			

Having decided to pass his 12-count, Gray felt compelled to do something opposite Konstam's overcall, but game was surely unlikely facing a passed hand. Even so, the defense had to be very good to defeat 2♠ and we must assume it was, as the contract failed by a trick, -100. Another 5 IMPs to Italy, who had run off 34 IMPs over the last four deals to lead 126-103

One can speculate how the defenders held declarer to seven tricks. If East leads a trump, declarer wins in dummy and plays a heart, which forces West to put up an honor, returning a spade when it is ducked. (If West plays low, declarer ducks the heart to East who cannot profitably play a spade, while playing a club allows declarer to establish the suit eventually.) Declarer lets that run to East's king and now a club switch is essential — and if declarer plays low from dummy West must put in the nine and then switch to diamonds. (Yes, East can switch to the ♣J instead of a low one but West can play him for the ♣Jx anyway.) Declarer wins in dummy and plays a heart to the eight; East wins with the jack and plays a second club, West winning and playing another diamond. If East fails to switch to clubs, perhaps preferring a diamond, declarer wins in dummy and plays a heart to the eight and jack. The next diamond is taken in dummy and declarer ruffs a diamond, draws the outstanding trumps and plays a club to the ten, endplaying West.

Board 55. Both Vul.

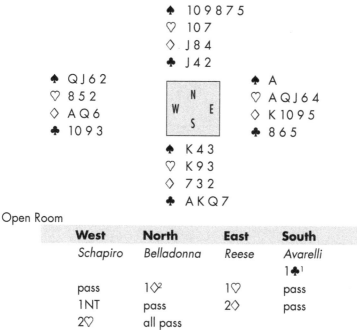

```
                ♠ 10 9 8 7 5
                ♡ 10 7
                ◇ J 8 4
                ♣ J 4 2
  ♠ Q J 6 2                        ♠ A
  ♡ 8 5 2          N              ♡ A Q J 6 4
  ◇ A Q 6      W       E          ◇ K 10 9 5
  ♣ 10 9 3          S             ♣ 8 6 5
                ♠ K 4 3
                ♡ K 9 3
                ◇ 7 3 2
                ♣ A K Q 7
```

Open Room

West	North	East	South
Schapiro	*Belladonna*	*Reese*	*Avarelli*
			1♣¹
pass	1◇²	1♡	pass
1NT	pass	2◇	pass
2♡	all pass		

1. 12-16 balanced, or 21-22/25-26, or 17-20 with 4/5 clubs plus 5/6 in another suit, or any shape with 3 or fewer losers.
2. 0-9.

There is no play record, but declarer took nine tricks for +140.

We can imagine that South cashed three clubs and switched to a diamond, declarer winning in hand and playing the ♡A followed by the queen. Were South to play a fourth club rather than a diamond, North could ruff with the ten, promoting a second trump trick for South if declarer overruffs and plays trumps. It's still possible to arrive at nine tricks by discarding a diamond from dummy on the fourth club, overruffing, and then abandoning trumps, playing South for the ♡K9x, eventually executing an endplay.

Closed Room

West	North	East	South
Forquet	Konstam	Garozzo	Gray
			1♣
pass	pass	2♡	pass
pass	2♠	3◇	pass
4♡	all pass		

When Konstam refused to go quietly over 2♡, Garozzo took a second bid, and that was enough to persuade Forquet that his side might have a play for game. Declarer finished two down, so having lost three club tricks, he must have taken a heart finesse, after which South played a fourth club, North's ruff promoting South's ♡9 for -200. That meant 8 IMPs to Great Britain, and a lifeline, with the deficit only 111-126.

Board 57. E-W Vul.

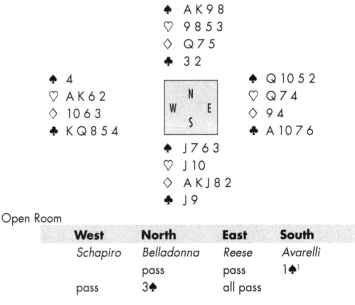

```
              ♠ A K 9 8
              ♡ 9 8 5 3
              ◇ Q 7 5
              ♣ 3 2
  ♠ 4                        ♠ Q 10 5 2
  ♡ A K 6 2         N        ♡ Q 7 4
  ◇ 10 6 3       W     E     ◇ 9 4
  ♣ K Q 8 5 4       S        ♣ A 10 7 6
              ♠ J 7 6 3
              ♡ J 10
              ◇ A K J 8 2
              ♣ J 9
```

Open Room

West	North	East	South
Schapiro	Belladonna	Reese	Avarelli
	pass	pass	1♠[1]
pass	3♠	all pass	

1. In general, two-suited hands are opened in the shorter suit (or the lower-ranking if equal in length).

Facing a passed partner and perhaps with an eye to the vulnerability, Schapiro apparently declined to get involved. On another day, he might well have doubled 1♠.

Yet another deal where I can only speculate about the play. Declarer managed eight tricks, -50. The way for the defense to be certain of a two-trick set is to cash a top heart and then play two rounds of clubs, East winning and continuing with the ♡Q and a heart. Declarer ruffs and can try playing a spade to the ace followed by a low spade, but East goes in with the queen and plays a club, ensuring a second trump trick.

If West cashes two top hearts and then switches to clubs, East winning the second round and returning a diamond, declarer can win, cross to a top spade and continue with a low one, restricting East to one trump trick, but is more likely to cash dummy's top spades, hoping the queen will fall. Unless Schapiro did double 1♠, when declarer would be likely to play for the spades to be 4-1. Solve that one, Hercule!

Closed Room

West	North	East	South
Forquet	Konstam	Garozzo	Gray
	pass	pass	1◇
1♡	1♠	2♡	2♠
3♣	3◇	pass	pass
3♡	all pass		

Having overcalled on a four-card suit and caught a raise, Forquet introduces his clubs on the next round. When Konstam shows his diamond support, Gray decides he has had enough and then declines to compete in spades, perhaps worried that he might drive East-West into a making game. Give East a fourth heart and you would like to be in game, but on this layout, when North cashed a spade and switched to a trump, declarer could take only eight tricks, -100. So another 4 IMPs to Great Britain, now within striking distance at 115-126.

There was no swing on either Board 58 or Board 59, so the next board was the last of this classic encounter.

Board 60. N-S Vul.

```
              ♠ Q
              ♡ 10 7 3 2
              ◇ K J 2
              ♣ Q 10 9 8 6
♠ 3                          ♠ J 10 9 7 2
♡ A J 9 6 5 4      N         ♡ K Q
◇ 10 8 7 6     W     E       ◇ 9
♣ J 4              S         ♣ K 7 5 3 2
              ♠ A K 8 6 5 4
              ♡ 8
              ◇ A Q 5 4 3
              ♣ A
```

Open Room

West	North	East	South
Schapiro	*Belladonna*	*Reese*	*Avarelli*
pass	pass	pass	1♣[1]
1♡	pass[2]	2♡	3◇[3]
pass	4♣[4]	pass	4♠[5]
pass	5◇[6]	pass	6◇
all pass			

1. 12-16 balanced, or 21-22/25-26, or 17-20 with 4/5 clubs plus 5/6 in another suit, or any shape with 3 or fewer losers.
2. 0-9.
3. Asking in diamonds.
4. ◇Kxx or ◇KJx.
5. Asking in spades.
6. Singleton or doubleton spade honor.

Looking at the North-South hands, 6◇ is clearly where you would like to be assuming reasonable breaks — if trumps are 3-2 then only a 5-1 spade break will be too tough to handle.

West led the ♡A and continued the suit. Declarer ruffed, played a spade to the queen, cashed the ◇K, and, playing a diamond to the queen, received the bad news. He played the ♠A, ruffed by West and overruffed with dummy's jack. Declarer ruffed a heart, drew the outstanding trump, and cashed the ♠K. The ♣A was declarer's ninth and last trick, -300. The escape hatch was open — could Konstam and Gray find their way through it?

Closed Room

West	North	East	South
Forquet	Konstam	Garozzo	Gray
2♡	pass	pass	3♡
pass	5♣	pass	5♠
all pass			

After West's weak two-bid, Gray had to decide how best to describe his hand. A Leaping Michaels 4◇ would probably be the majority choice in 2018, but in 1964 his options were more limited and he eventually fell back on cuebidding to show a powerful two-suited hand. Had Konstam contented himself with 4♣, Gray would have continued with a non-forcing 4♠, but the jump to 5♣ meant he had to introduce his spades (or perhaps more sensibly, diamonds, the lower of the marked spade-diamond two-suiter) one level higher.

Afterwards, Gray maintained that their agreement was that advancer was not allowed to jump because of the danger (as here) of partner being short in that suit. At that time, few partnerships had agreements about what a jump in a suit not promised should mean in a forcing auction, and what 4◇ over 4♣ would imply about expected length in the pointed suits.

West led the ♡A and there was no way for declarer to avoid the loss of a heart and two spades. One down, -100 and 5 IMPs to Great Britain, leaving Italy ahead by a nose at the wire, 126-120.

Had Gray and Konstam found a way to stop at 4♠, their +620 would have combined with Reese and Schapiro's +300 for a gain of 14 IMPs and Great Britain would have pulled out the match at the eleventh hour by 3 IMPs, 129-126. If they had come to rest in 5◇, Forquet would have needed to start with two rounds of hearts to be 100% sure of defeating the contract.

There was talk that Reese could have doubled 6◇. He knew his spade holding might be a nuisance and there was at least a possibility that the trumps might be breaking badly. Against that, there seems to be no reason that South could not have started with six diamonds and five spades, when 6◇ would be more or less cold. I suspect no one would have mentioned it had it not been necessary to achieve +800 to make up for the poor result in the Closed Room. Let's see... +800 and -100 = 700 net to Great Britain = 12 IMPs = Great Britain 127, Italy 126. (And in any case, declarer can get out for two down with card-perfect play, which would have kept the bridge scribes busy for weeks.)

Epilogue

The Italians went on to defeat the United States (Jordan, Robinson, Stayman, Mitchell, Krauss, Hamman) by 46 IMPs, 158-112, in the 60-board final.

At the Victory Banquet, they named Great Britain as the 'first power in European bridge'. However, it was to be twenty-seven years before the British won another European Championship, by which time Italy had recorded another seven victories. It was, in fact, the end of an era.

Cover of the ACBL Bulletin, June 1964

(Back l-r) D'Alelio, Pabis-Ticci, Forquet, Belladonna, Garozzo, Avarelli
(Front l-r) Perroux, Gruenther (WBF honorary president), Osella

2. 1979 Flying Down to Rio

Flying Down to Rio was significant for being the first screen pairing of Fred Astaire and Ginger Rogers, who became iconic dance partners, making ten movies between 1933 and 1949. Beautiful Rio de Janeiro, with its glorious beaches, panoramic views and lively vibe, was the host city for the 1979 Bermuda Bowl, the first in which the defending champions were not automatically entitled to compete. It was also the first time all the (then six) World Bridge Federation zones were represented.

The Rio World Championship, however, was *not* the first pairing of screens with bridge tables; that security idea had made its debut at the 1975 Bermuda Bowl. Ironically, while those first screens kept partners from seeing each other's facial expressions and gestures, they did not prevent partners from 'dancing' on each other's feet — gingerly or otherwise — to convey illicit information. That technical flaw might not have become an actionable issue had not two of Italy's players, Gianfranco Facchini and Sergio Zuchelli been detected brazenly 'doing the dirty' at the table early and often. Their impropriety soon came to be known as The Foot Soldiers' Affair and scandalized that World Championship. Those events led to a change in the screen design: they were extended under the table to the floor, forming a barrier running diagonally between two table legs.

I[**] had been in Rio and São Paulo and Buenos Aires as a player the previous year for a circuit of wonderful invitational tournaments, and would visit Brazil in different bridge roles in the next three decades, but I was not there in 1979, which would be my first assignment as principal analyst for the World Championship book. Bidding and play was recorded manually, usually by volunteers, so I would have to rely on those records and in some cases the players' recollections to do my job properly.

[**]   Primary author Eric Kokish

The favorites in Rio were USA (Ed Theus, NPC: Malcolm Brachman and Mike Passell, Billy Eisenberg and Eddie Kantar, Bobby Goldman and Paul Soloway), and Italy (Guido Barbone and Sandro Salvetti, NPCs: Giorgio Belladonna and Vito Pittalà, Dano De Falco and Arturo Franco, Benito Garozzo and Lorenzo Lauria), and those two teams did indeed emerge from the Round Robin. Thanks to a dominating performance in their three round robin matches, Italy started the 96-board final with a particularly significant carryover of 37 IMPs. The teams would play 64 boards on the first day with 32 more on the morrow.

BRACHMAN team, 1979
(Top to bottom, left to right) Kantar, Eisenberg, Goldman, Soloway, Brachman, Passell

(Left to right) Garozzo, Lauria, De Falco, Belladonna

The Italians got off to a fast start, but the Americans kept the set close. Italy won the session 41-35, and led 78-35, but the second set was all USA:

Board 19. E-W Vul.

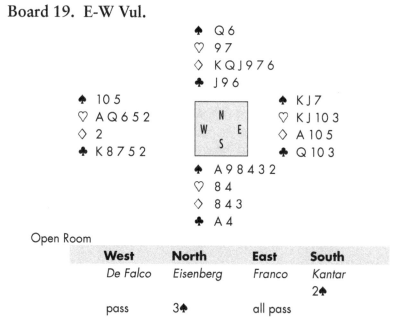

```
               ♠ Q 6
               ♡ 9 7
               ◇ K Q J 9 7 6
               ♣ J 9 6
♠ 10 5                          ♠ K J 7
♡ A Q 6 5 2        N            ♡ K J 10 3
◇ 2            W       E        ◇ A 10 5
♣ K 8 7 5 2        S            ♣ Q 10 3
               ♠ A 9 8 4 3 2
               ♡ 8 4
               ◇ 8 4 3
               ♣ A 4
```

Open Room

West	North	East	South
De Falco	Eisenberg	Franco	Kantar
			2♠
pass	3♠	all pass	

Kantar would have liked a stronger internal suit for a weak two-bid, but traded on the vulnerability and rank of his long suit to act while the price was right. That handcuffed De Falco, who might have risked a direct move with short spades. Eisenberg did what he could with a blocking raise to 3♠. While an objective panel of expert bridge analysts would surely fault De Falco for passing out 3♠, with Franco marked with some high cards that might well combine to offer a play for a vulnerable game, there can be no doubt that De Falco knew passing was more dangerous than bidding and so was heroic in its own way! He led his singleton diamond and the defenders took all their tricks: ◇A, two diamond ruffs, two hearts, a club and two late trump winners. Declarer finished with five tricks, four down, -200.

Closed Room

West	North	East	South
Passell	Lauria	Brachman	Garozzo
			pass
pass	1◇[1]	1♡	1♠
4♡	all pass		

1. 11-15, no four-card major.

In first and second seat, Garozzo-Lauria's weak two-bids were constructive, nominally 9-13, with some texture, so when Garozzo and Passell passed (today an opening 1♡ by West would have plenty of expert support), Lauria, prevented by system from opening 2◇ or 3◇, tried 1◇. Brachman's decision to overcall on his four-card suit gave his side an easy ride to their money contract. Brachman might have had to guess both black suits to get home in 4♡, but Garozzo led the ♠A and switched to the ♣4, so declarer coasted home with eleven tricks: +650 and 10 IMPs for the USA.

Lorenzo Lauria

Board 20. Both Vul.

```
              ♠ 8 4
              ♡ Q 8 7 4
              ◇ 10 4
              ♣ A 7 6 4 2
  ♠ A                        ♠ Q J 7 3 2
  ♡ K 9 6 3      N           ♡ J 10 2
  ◇ K J 7 3 2  W   E         ◇ A Q 8
  ♣ Q 10 9       S           ♣ K J
              ♠ K 10 9 6 5
              ♡ A 5
              ◇ 9 6 5
              ♣ 8 5 3
```

Open Room

West	North	East	South
De Falco	Eisenberg	Franco	Kantar
1♡	pass	1♠	pass
2◇	pass	3♣[1]	pass
3NT	all pass		

1. Fourth-suit forcing.

Eisenberg led the ♣4, fourth best, and declarer won with dummy's king (♣3, count, from South) and played a heart to the nine. North won with the queen and continued with the ♣2, so when South gained the lead with the ♡A he could return a club giving the defenders five tricks, +100.

Closed Room

West	North	East	South
Passell	Lauria	Brachman	Garozzo
1◇	pass	1♠	pass
1NT	pass	2♣[1]	pass
2♡	pass	3NT	all pass

1. New minor forcing.

Lauria also led the ♣4 but his lead was attitude: the lower the card the greater the interest in the suit. Declarer won with dummy's king (eight from South, reverse count), played a spade to the ace, a diamond to the queen, and the ♣Q, South winning with the king. Garozzo was certain of the club position — if declarer held the ace he would have played dummy's jack at Trick 1 and his partner's attitude lead (the deuce was missing) made it clear he could not have a suit headed by the ♣AQ. If he returned a club, declarer would win and have two spades, five diamonds and two clubs.

Garozzo, at single dummy, found one of the most interesting plays ever made at this level — a diamond, aiming to tangle declarer's communications. Declarer won in dummy and could not play a club as North would win and exit with a club, eventually endplaying declarer. Passell, not without hope, cashed the ♠J, but now the writing was on the wall: when he continued with the ♣J, North could win and play a heart allowing South to win and cash two spades for one down, a flat board.

Benito Garozzo

Might declarer have overcome this brilliant defensive move? After the diamond return, he could strand his spade winner in dummy and cash his remaining diamond tricks. If North has blanked the ♡Q to retain four clubs, declarer can exit with a club, win the club return and sagely play the ♡K. If North has come down to two hearts and three clubs, declarer can exit with a low heart instead of a club and must come to two more tricks.

Had declarer crossed to the ◇A rather than the queen at Trick 3, he could have succeeded in a less dramatic way by playing for diamonds 3-2: win the diamond return with the jack and lead a club. If North ducks, declarer has four black-suit tricks and overtakes the ◇Q; if North takes the ♣A (best) to exit in clubs, declarer must use dummy's ◇Q to enter dummy to play a heart to his king — frightening but effective.

Board 25. E-W Vul.

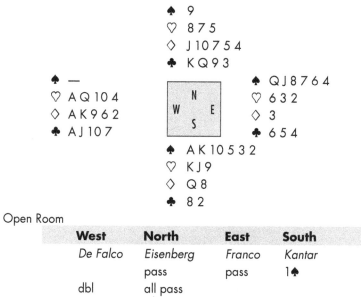

```
                    ♠ 9
                    ♡ 8 7 5
                    ◇ J 10 7 5 4
                    ♣ K Q 9 3
   ♠ —                              ♠ Q J 8 7 6 4
   ♡ A Q 10 4          N            ♡ 6 3 2
   ◇ A K 9 6 2      W     E         ◇ 3
   ♣ A J 10 7          S            ♣ 6 5 4
                    ♠ A K 10 5 3 2
                    ♡ K J 9
                    ◇ Q 8
                    ♣ 8 2
```

Open Room

West	North	East	South
De Falco	Eisenberg	Franco	Kantar
	pass	pass	1♠
dbl	all pass		

West led the ◇A and continued with the ◇9, East ruffing to return the ♡6. West won with the ten and played the ◇K, East pitching a club. Declarer ruffed, and played a club, West taking the ace and playing a diamond to dummy's ten. East discarded his remaining club as declarer discarded the ♡K. When declarer played dummy's ◇J, East ruffed in with the ♠J and declarer got rid of his last heart. He ruffed the heart return, exited with the ♠5 to the nine and jack, ruffed the next heart with the ♠10 and claimed one down, -100.

Closed Room

West	North	East	South
Passell	Lauria	Brachman	Garozzo
	pass	pass	2♠[1]
dbl	all pass		

1. 9-13.

West led the ◇A and continued with the ◇6, East ruffing and returning the ♡6 to West's ten. Passell made a fine play by switching to the ♣7 to attack dummy's late entry to potential impending diamond winners. Declarer won with dummy's ♣K and played the ◇J, ruffing when East pitched a heart. He continued with a club and West took the ace, cashed the ♡A and gave Brachman a heart ruff. Garozzo took East's exit of the ♠J with the ♠K and played the ♠5 but East won cheaply and exited with his remaining club, forcing declarer, who was trump-tight, to ruff and surrender a trick to the ♠Q for three down, -500 and a well-earned 9 IMPs for USA.

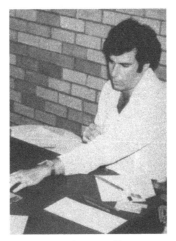

Mike Passell

Spearheaded by a huge card turned in by Brachman-Passell, USA won the second 16-board stanza 71-3 to take the lead by 25 IMPs, 106-81. With Brachman, the team's sponsor, having fulfilled his board requirements to qualify for a medal, American spirits were understandably high: since the team could field its front four the rest of the way, the position was far brighter than it had been to start the day.

In an interview with Dorthy Francis for the Daily Bulletin, Brachman confided that his main goal in playing with professionals was to become a better bridge player. 'I know there are many who do not like the idea of having a sponsor represent USA, particularly in the final, and I confess I'm hoping we've given them something to think about. I was hoping to wipe out much of our deficit and knew we had some good results, but really, I was more concerned about mistakes I had made. After comparing scores, I'm euphoric.'

In Set Three, the Italians outscored USA 47-3 over the first eight boards to take a 17-IMP lead, with momentum at their backs, prompting some opportunistic spectators to ask, 'Where is Brachman?' However, in the second half of the set, the Americans convincingly outplayed their rivals, outscoring them 37-8 to reclaim the momentum. Italy won the set, 55-40, but at the half-way mark, USA was still ahead by 10 IMPs, 146-136.

Although Italy made no headway in Set Four, the final deal was a morale booster:

Board 64. E-W Vul.

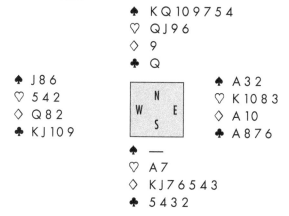

```
                        ♠ K Q 10 9 7 5 4
                        ♡ Q J 9 6
                        ◇ 9
                        ♣ Q
   ♠ J 8 6                                   ♠ A 3 2
   ♡ 5 4 2                                   ♡ K 10 8 3
   ◇ Q 8 2          N                        ◇ A 10
   ♣ K J 10 9    W     E                     ♣ A 8 7 6
                     S
                        ♠ —
                        ♡ A 7
                        ◇ K J 7 6 5 4 3
                        ♣ 5 4 3 2
```

Open Room and Closed Room

West	North	East	South
Goldman	Belladonna	Soloway	Pittalà
De Falco	Eisenberg	Franco	Kantar
pass	4♠	dbl	all pass

With no attractive lead, both Easts made the unfortunate choice of the ♠2.
Both declarers discarded a club from dummy, took the jack with the king,
and led the ◇9. East went in with the ace, West following low. With the
diamonds as they are, declarer has only one discard for a heart coming, so a
black-suit continuation suffices for the defense.

Franco switched to the ♣A and continued the suit, took the ♠Q with the
ace and, after considerable thought, switched to the ♡10. Eisenberg ran that
to his queen, drew trumps, and eventually lost the last trick to the ♡K for one
down, -100.

Soloway switched to hearts immediately, but did not cater to the actual
position, as Franco had done. When he led the three and Belladonna played
dummy's seven, Goldman could not play a card to cover it. Declarer discarded
the ♣Q on the ◇K, ruffed a club, knocked out the ace of trumps, won the
heart continuation with the ace, ruffed a club, drew trumps and conceded a
trick to the ♡K for +590 and a 12-IMP Italian gain.

The remarkable heart-spot layout aside, Belladonna was faced with a
possible losing option at Trick 3: if West had the ♡K, and the ♡10 was coming
down tripleton, the winning play would be the ♡A to discard the club loser
on the ◇K, hoping to lose only to the ♠A and ♡K.

Arturo Franco

USA won the final set of the day 43-34, and led by 19, 189-170 overall at the close of play.

The fifth segment the next morning was excellent for USA, 46-10, so the Italians started the last 16-board set trailing by 55 IMPs, 180-235. No one's idea of a close encounter.

Session Six (Boards 81-96)

Board 81. Neither Vul.

```
              ♠ 8 4 2
              ♡ J 9 5 3
              ◇ 8 7 4 3
              ♣ 7 2
♠ A K Q J 3              ♠ 6
♡ K 8 4        N        ♡ A 10 7 2
◇ J         W     E     ◇ K Q 10 9 6
♣ Q 9 8 3      S        ♣ 6 5 4
              ♠ 10 9 7 5
              ♡ Q 6
              ◇ A 5 2
              ♣ A K J 10
```

Closed Room

West	North	East	South
Goldman	*Belladonna*	*Soloway*	*Pittalà*
	pass	pass	1♠
1NT	pass	2♠	pass
3♠	pass	3NT	all pass

Italy started the last set badly. Pittalà's typical suit-quality-insensitive four-card 1♠ opening gave Goldman a tough problem, which he solved by overcalling 1NT with a hand you might not find in any textbook. That worked well for him, although his natural 3♣ dissuaded North from leading his partner's suit against 3NT. Belladonna chose the ♣7 because a short-suit lead was more likely than either four-card red suit to hit a five-card canapé in Pittalà's hand. Pittalà cleared clubs; Goldman overtook the ◊J, and lost only to the ◊A and ♣10 for +400.

Bobby Goldman

Open Room

West	North	East	South
De Falco	Eisenberg	Franco	Kantar
	pass	pass	1♣
dbl	pass	2♣	pass
3♠	pass	4◊	pass
4♠	all pass		

De Falco's takeout double of 1♣, coupled with his bulky jump in spades over Franco's cuebid, worked badly, as Franco could not bid 3NT. Today, virtually no serious player would do anything other than overcall 1♠, but the Italian style had been and would continue to be for many years, 'double when too strong for a rather limited overcall'. Against 4♠, Eisenberg led the ♣7, ruffed away De Falco's queen, and then switched to the ♡3 when he read Kantar's third-round ♣J as suit-preference. Although that gave declarer the chance for four heart tricks, that would get him to only nine winners, so De Falco drew trumps and played a diamond and went two down, -100. That was 11 IMPs to USA, ahead by 66, 246-180.

The situation was dire for the Italians, but as always, they mounted a charge, starting with:

Board 82. N-S Vul.

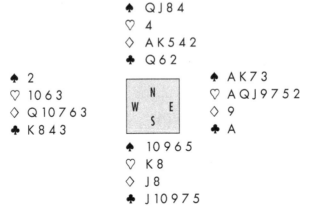

```
                    ♠ Q J 8 4
                    ♡ 4
                    ◇ A K 5 4 2
                    ♣ Q 6 2
    ♠ 2                           ♠ A K 7 3
    ♡ 10 6 3          N          ♡ A Q J 9 7 5 2
    ◇ Q 10 7 6 3   W     E       ◇ 9
    ♣ K 8 4 3         S          ♣ A
                    ♠ 10 9 6 5
                    ♡ K 8
                    ◇ J 8
                    ♣ J 10 9 7 5
```

Closed Room

West	North	East	South
Goldman	Belladonna	Soloway	Pittalà
		2♣[1]	pass
2◇[2]	dbl	2♡	pass
3♠[3]	pass	4NT[4]	pass
5♣[5]	pass	6♡	all pass

1. Strong.
2. Artificial, neutral.
3. Splinter for hearts.
4. RKCB for hearts.
5. 0 keycards.

When his partner admitted to holding no keycards, Soloway had the chance to sign off in 5♡; however, there were several reasons why he elected to continue on to 6♡. The first was predicated on the possibility that partner might just hold the five outstanding low hearts, in which case it would not be possible to 'misguess' trumps. The second was that if partner held only four hearts the slam would depend on no more than the trump position in an eleven-card fit. The third was that even opposite a three-card holding in trumps the slam would have play. The final, and perhaps most compelling reason, was that it had to be odds-on that the Italians, looking for opportunities, would bid a slam in the other room.

The case for bidding six would have been even stronger had Belladonna not been able to double 2◇ for the lead, and Pittalà duly led the ◇J, so declarer had to lose a diamond and the ♡K, one down, -50.

Paul Soloway

Open Room

	West	North	East	South
	De Falco	Eisenberg	Franco	Kantar
			1♣[1]	pass
	1◇[2]	pass	2♡	pass
	3♡	pass	5♡	all pass

1. Strong.
2. 0 or 1 controls (A=2, K=1).

Once West supports hearts, there are many ways to advance with the East hand. The objection to going down a scientific route is that you may tip South off to the best lead. For example, after 4♣-4♡; 4♠-5♣; 6♡, South is virtually certain to lead a diamond. When Franco bid 5♡ as a general try, De Falco judged that a singleton spade, three trumps headed by the ten and the ♣K were not what his partner was looking for.

With a blind lead, Kantar looked no further than his sequence in clubs. Declarer could ruff his losing spades in dummy and dispose of his diamond on the ♣K for +480.

Ironically, Soloway's wager that his counterparts would be in six did not pay off, and Italy recovered the 11 IMPs lost on the previous deal, 191-246.

These were the cards on the next deal:

Board 83. E-W Vul.

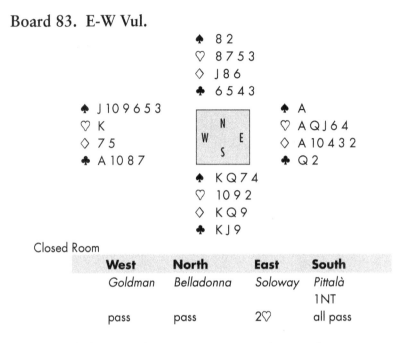

                82
                8 7 5 3
                J 8 6
                6 5 4 3

    J 10 9 6 5 3   A
    K   A Q J 6 4
    7 5   A 10 4 3 2
    A 10 8 7   Q 2

                K Q 7 4
                10 9 2
                K Q 9
                K J 9

Closed Room

West	North	East	South
Goldman	Belladonna	Soloway	Pittalà
			1NT
pass	pass	2♡	all pass

Pittalà picked a good moment to treat his weak notrump as strong, representing 15-17. This tactical effort gave Goldman-Soloway a tough time. Soloway came to eleven tricks in 2♡ for +200.

Vito Pittalà

West	North	East	South
De Falco	Eisenberg	Franco	Kantar
			1♣
1♠	pass	2♣	pass
2♠	pass	3♡	pass
3NT	all pass		

Against 3NT, Eisenberg led the ♣6: deuce, jack, ace. De Falco continued clubs to build a ninth trick if hearts were coming in, while he still had an entry. Kantar took the ♣Q with the king and switched to a spade, but with the ♣9 falling, De Falco had ten tricks: a spade, five hearts, a diamond and three clubs, +630. So 10 more IMPs to Italy, 201-246.

Two flat boards ate away two more chances for Italy to tighten up the match, but then:

Board 86. E-W Vul.

```
                    ♠ K Q 9 5
                    ♡ J 6 4 2
                    ◇ 10 7
                    ♣ J 6 4
      ♠ 10 7                        ♠ A 8 4 2
      ♡ A 9 5 3          N          ♡ Q 7
      ◇ K J 9 5 3    W       E      ◇ A 6 4
      ♣ A 9              S          ♣ Q 8 7 2
                    ♠ J 6 3
                    ♡ K 10 8
                    ◇ Q 8 2
                    ♣ K 10 5 3
```

West	North	East	South
De Falco	Eisenberg	Franco	Kantar
		1♠	pass
2◇	pass	2NT	pass
3NT	all pass		

Franco's four-card 1♠ opening led to a virtually forced auction ending at 3NT, and Kantar's entirely normal low-club lead gave declarer his ninth trick, +600.

West	North	East	South
Goldman	*Belladonna*	*Soloway*	*Pittalà*
		1♣	pass
1♡	1♠	pass	2♠
3◇	pass	3♡	pass
3♠	pass	4♡	all pass

Although Goldman was strong enough to respond in his longer suit, he tried 1♡, concerned that with his two weak spades, competition by the opponents might make it tricky to get hearts into play. That modest distortion might not have mattered, but Belladonna, looking for any opportunity, stuck out his neck at favorable vulnerability to overcall 1♠ on something short of a wing and a prayer. When Pittalà raised to 2♠ Goldman forced with 3◇, but was unable to convince Soloway that he did not hold at least five hearts. Although Soloway had a spade guard and could have bid 3NT after his preference to 3♡ caught a last-chance 3♠ from Goldman, his hand seemed better oriented to suit play opposite West's expected short spades, so he bid 4♡, which went down four on a spade lead, -400. That was a further 14 IMPs, 215-246. The lead was down to 31 IMPs, with ten boards to play. Much more interesting now.

Board 87. Both Vul.

```
              ♠ Q
              ♡ K J 10 7
              ◇ J 7 4
              ♣ A J 4 3 2
  ♠ A 9 2                    ♠ K 10 8 5
  ♡ 9 8 6 2        N         ♡ Q 4
  ◇ 8 2        W     E       ◇ Q 10 9 6 5
  ♣ 9 8 7 6        S         ♣ K Q
              ♠ J 7 6 4 3
              ♡ A 5 3
              ◇ A K 3
              ♣ 10 5
```

Closed Room

West	North	East	South
Goldman	Belladonna	Soloway	Pittalà
			1♠
pass	2♣	pass	2♠
pass	2NT[1]	pass	3NT
all pass			

1. Forcing.

With such weak spot cards in the black suits, 3NT was not a good contract. Soloway led the ◊9, promising no higher card or the ten and a non-touching honor, and declarer was apparently off to a good start. However, to the dismay of the many Italian supporters in the audience, Belladonna did not let the lead run to his hand: he played dummy's ace (◊8 from Goldman, who would have played the jack had he held it) and ran the ♣10 to the king.

Soloway had every reason to switch to spades and chose the ♠10, which would be best if declarer had the ace, the nine, or no significant card. When declarer played low from dummy Goldman would have done best to take the ♠A to play a diamond, but he followed low, perhaps convinced that Belladonna held ◊QJ10x to explain his play at Trick 1. Declarer gratefully won with the queen and cashed the ♣A. When the queen fell one option was to continue with two more clubs, establishing a long card in the suit. However, that might expose him to three spade losers if East started with honor-ten-third, and Belladonna suspected that East's failure to switch to a heart rather than a spade suggested that he held the ♡Q. Backing his judgment, he led the ♡J and ran it when it was not covered. He had nine tricks now by cashing hearts, but chose not to put his faith in hearts providing four tricks, and so changed tack and cleared clubs, discarding a diamond and a spade from dummy. When West won, he returned his remaining diamond and declarer finished with a surprise overtrick, +630.

Open Room

West	North	East	South
De Falco	Eisenberg	Franco	Kantar
			1♠
pass	2♣	pass	2◊[1]
pass	2NT	all pass	

1. Ostensibly natural.

Eisenberg, who ran the lead of the ◊10 (which suggested an honor) to his jack, was pleased to take nine tricks in 2NT after scoring his ♠Q in the fashion of

Belladonna, but +150 was not good enough to save the board for USA and Italy gained 10 more IMPs, 225-246.

A couple of deals later, East-West had to deal with a difficult combination:

Board 89. E-W Vul.

```
              ♠ K 7
              ♡ Q J 10 9
              ◇ 10 8 5
              ♣ A K 8 2
♠ A Q J 8 6 4              ♠ —
♡ 8 7 5 3        N        ♡ A K 6
◇ Q 6 2      W     E      ◇ A K J 7
♣ —              S        ♣ Q 7 6 5 4 3
              ♠ 10 9 5 3 2
              ♡ 4 2
              ◇ 9 4 3
              ♣ J 10 9
```

Closed Room

West	North	East	South
Goldman	Belladonna	Soloway	Pittalà
	1♡	2♣	pass
2♠	pass	3◇	pass
3♠	all pass		

Belladonna's four-card 1♡ opening allowed Soloway a natural overcall in his longest suit. As 3◇ showed extra values over the constructive but non-forcing 2♠, Goldman may have considered his 3♠ forcing. However, as Goldman could have forced with 3♡, Soloway, after giving serious thought to both 3NT and a raise to 4♠, eventually decided to try for a plus in 3♠. Belladonna led the ♡Q, but the 3-3 diamond break was sufficient compensation for the 5-2 trump split and declarer collected ten tricks with three club ruffs in hand, two other trump tricks, two hearts and three diamonds, +170.

Open Room

West	North	East	South
De Falco	Eisenberg	Franco	Kantar
	1♣	1◇	pass
2♣[1]	pass	3♣	pass
3♠	pass	3NT	pass
4♠	all pass		

1. Both 1♠ and 2♠ would have been non-forcing.

As Franco did not have a natural 2♣ overcall available over Eisenberg's 1♣, he settled for 1◊ on his strong four-card suit, which improved De Falco's hand significantly; he started with a cuebid before introducing his long suit. As he had not yet shown his sixth spade and thought his club void dreadful for notrump, he made the winning decision to convert 3NT to 4♠. Eisenberg led the ♣A and declarer ruffed, cashed the ♠A and continued with the ♠Q, North winning to switch to the ♡J. Declarer won with dummy's ace, ruffed a club and cashed the ♠J. When North discarded, declarer needed some luck and he got it: he cashed three diamonds and the ♡K and then ruffed a club for +420 and another 10 IMPs for Italy.

The margin was now only 11 IMPs, 235-246, and Italy still had seven deals to wipe out what was left of the American lead. The way things had gone so far in this set, who would have bet against Italy at this point?

The next three deals passed by without significant incident, although on Board 90, neither North-South pair got past 4♡ on these cards:

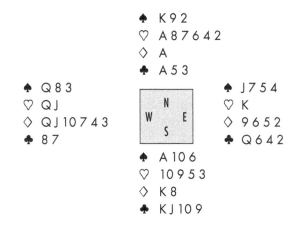

With the South hand, Pittalà raised Belladonna's limited fourth-seat 1♡ to 4♡. At the other table, Eisenberg as North had to deal with a third-seat 1◊ from De Falco, West. He doubled, again not the action an expert would choose today. Kantar cuebid 2◊ and raised Eisenberg's jump to 3♡ to game. The indicated line of play in 6♡ on a neutral diamond lead would be: ♡A, ♣A, ♣K, ◊K to throw a club, club ruff, trump. West would have to play a spade and declarer would play for split honors and make his slam. The chance for the ♣Q to come down in two or three rounds would preclude the need to guess spades. Not an easy combination.

The American lead was just 10 IMPs with four to play, but Board 93 seemed to have some life in it.

Board 93. Both Vul.

```
                    ♠ 6
                    ♡ 6 5 4 3
                    ◇ A K Q 2
                    ♣ J 6 4 3
  ♠ 10 9 8 5                      ♠ A Q 3 2
  ♡ J 10 8 2          N           ♡ A Q
  ◇ 10 7 3      W         E       ◇ J 8 6
  ♣ 7 5              S            ♣ K Q 8 2
                    ♠ K J 7 4
                    ♡ K 9 7
                    ◇ 9 5 4
                    ♣ A 10 9
```

Closed Room

West	North	East	South
Goldman	Belladonna	Soloway	Pittalà
	pass	1♣	pass
pass	pass		

This looked very good for Italy when Soloway was left to rot in 1♣ in his 4-2 fit, down four for -400 — the second time in the space of a few deals that his side had gone four down, vulnerable (Pittalà found the best lead of a diamond).

Open Room

West	North	East	South
De Falco	Eisenberg	Franco	Kantar
	pass	1♣¹	pass
1◇²	pass	1NT	pass
2♣³	pass	2♠	pass
pass	dbl	all pass	

1. Strong, artificial.
2. 0 or 1 controls.
3. Stayman.

Franco and De Falco found a much better contract after a strong club opening when they located their 4-4 spade fit and stopped at 2♠, but Eisenberg saved the day for USA by reopening with a shape-perfect takeout double at his fourth turn to bid. Kantar passed for penalty, and then found the winning diamond lead to set the contract two tricks, -500. The American gain was only 3 IMPs, increasing the lead to 13, 249-236, but any sort of gain had been a long time coming and must have felt like a breath of fresh air to the U.S. supporters watching at the tables and in the VuGraph theater.

Billy Eisenberg

Board 94. Neither Vul.

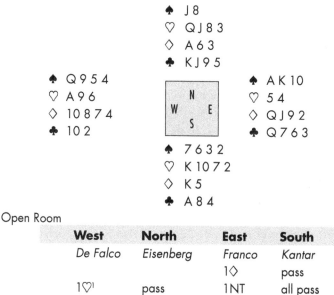

```
                    ♠  J 8
                    ♡  Q J 8 3
                    ◊  A 6 3
                    ♣  K J 9 5
   ♠ Q 9 5 4                        ♠  A K 10
   ♡ A 9 6           N              ♡  5 4
   ◊ 10 8 7 4      W     E          ◊  Q J 9 2
   ♣ 10 2            S              ♣  Q 7 6 3
                    ♠  7 6 3 2
                    ♡  K 10 7 2
                    ◊  K 5
                    ♣  A 8 4
```

Open Room

West	North	East	South
De Falco	Eisenberg	Franco	Kantar
		1◊	pass
1♡[1]	pass	1NT	all pass

1. A diamond raise would be 'positive' so this would be the start of a canapé or an artificial negative.

Once Kantar did not come in over 1◊, there was no safe way into the auction. Against 1NT, the American defense was pretty: ♠7 ducked to the ten; two high spades (diamond discard); ◊J to the ace; heart to the ten, ducked; ♡2 ducked to the jack; ♣J to surround dummy's ten, ducked; club to the ace; revert to hearts. Declarer took five tricks for two down, -100.

Closed Room

West	North	East	South
Goldman	Belladonna	Soloway	Pittalà
		1◇	dbl
2◇	3◇	pass	3♡
pass	4♡	all pass	

Pittalà, who had reason to believe the match was within reach, pressed his luck with a light takeout double, and Belladonna's cuebid handily located the heart fit and propelled his side to a worthwhile 4♡. Goldman led the ◇4 (ace, nine, five). Soloway took the ♠J continuation with the king (deuce, five) and switched accurately to a trump to the nine and jack. A second spade was taken by the ace (three, four), and Soloway tried to cash the ◇Q in case declarer had the ♠Q9 to discard dummy's diamonds. Whether Goldman would have played five-four in spades with ♠7654 is worth considering after the fact, but it would have been better this time for the defense to clear hearts. Declarer took the ◇K, ruffed a spade, and came off dummy with a trump, hoping to score four club tricks for the contract.

When Goldman won with the ♡A and returned a trump (diamond from East) it was clear to declarer that East held the ♣Q, so he led the ♣J from dummy and passed it when it was not covered. Club to the ace and the last trump; West could keep the ◇10 and the high spade and East could keep his clubs after dummy's diamond discard, so declarer lost the last trick to the ♣Q for one down, -50. That was 4 IMPs to USA, extending the lead to a more substantial 17 IMPs, 253-236, with only two deals to play.

Pittalà was playing East for the ♡A and West for the ♣Q when he led the second trump from dummy, but he could have made his pushy 4♡ and swung 12 IMPs had he placed those honors in their actual positions: ♣J, ♣A, spade ruff, trump. West could win and force declarer with a diamond, but the last two tricks would be taken by the ♡K and dummy's ♣K.

The Closed Room was more than a board ahead and the score on Board 95 was posted by the time the Open Room players picked up their cards. The VuGraph audience could see that Italy had logged a good result.

Board 95. N-S Vul.

```
                      ♠ 3
                      ♡ A 9 8 7 2
                      ◇ 6 5
                      ♣ Q 10 9 5 3
    ♠ J 9                              ♠ A K 10 8 6 2
    ♡ K 4 3          ┌─────────┐       ♡ Q J 10
    ◇ A J 9 8        │    N    │       ◇ Q 7 2
    ♣ J 8 7 6        │  W   E  │       ♣ K
                     │    S    │
                     └─────────┘
                      ♠ Q 7 5 4
                      ♡ 6 5
                      ◇ K 10 4 3
                      ♣ A 4 2
```

Closed Room

West	North	East	South
Goldman	Belladonna	Soloway	Pittalà
			pass
pass	pass	1♠	pass
1NT	pass	2♠	pass
2NT	pass	3NT	all pass

Belladonna led the ♣3, low from interest. The defenders played four rounds of the suit, Goldman discarding deuce-seven of diamonds and then a spade from dummy, not enjoying it much. Declarer won the ♣J and ran the ♠J, which was allowed to hold. When North showed out (♡9), declarer took dummy's top spades (♡3, ♡2) and played the now-bare ◇Q, covered by Pittalà. Goldman took the ◇A and ◇J and played the ♡4. North took his ace, cashed the ♣10 and exited with a heart, tucking declarer in hand to surrender a diamond trick at the end for two down, -100.

As Italy, except for a miracle grand-slam swing, needed to gain on *both* the last two deals, this one held some promise because the Italian East-West might be permitted to make 4♠ and perhaps even 3NT, and if they stopped short of game, 6 IMPs (+140) or 7 IMPs (+170) would come in.

While the Open Room players were bidding Board 95 the Closed Room had moved on to 96, which appeared to be a routine no-play game for North-South — good news for USA.

Board 96. E-W Vul.

```
                    ♠ Q 6 2
                    ♡ 9 7 6 4
                    ◇ A K J 10
                    ♣ J 7
   ♠ 10 9 7 5              N          ♠ 4
   ♡ A 5 3            W         E     ♡ Q J
   ◇ 9 7 2                S          ◇ 8 6 4 3
   ♣ Q 10 6                          ♣ A K 9 8 4 2
                    ♠ A K J 8 3
                    ♡ K 10 8 2
                    ◇ Q 5
                    ♣ 5 3
```

Closed Room

West	North	East	South
Goldman	*Belladonna*	*Soloway*	*Pittalà*
pass	1◇[1]	pass	1♠
pass	1NT	pass	2♣[2]
pass	2♠	pass	4♠
all pass			

1. 2+ diamonds, possible canapé.
2. Checkback.

But the American supporters' sense of relief was short-lived.

Belladonna, with a strong suit to mention, could hardly resist opening in second seat at the prevailing vulnerability and state of the match. Soloway decided not to risk a thin vulnerable 2♣ overall once his partner had passed as dealer, so Goldman had little to go on when choosing his opening lead against 4♠ (the fact that a minimum 1♡ overcall would require less than a minimum 2♣ overcall was not a strong clue). He elected, not unreasonably, to lead a low heart, which presented Pittalà with his tenth trick. With trumps 4-1 declarer did not have time to build a second heart winner after discarding clubs on high diamonds, so settled for an excellent +420.

Excellent indeed, as we would learn later that in the Open Room Franco and De Falco would have no difficulty defeating 4♠ after giving their opponents a rough ride in the auction:

West	North	East	South
De Falco	Eisenberg	Franco	Kantar
pass	pass	2♣*	dbl
3♣	dbl*	pass	3♠
pass	4♠	all pass	

When Eisenberg did not open, Franco had a light but normal natural limited 2♣ opening in third position. North could not comfortably commit to hearts, so competed with a responsive double, and when he raised 3♠ to 4♠ he could not be sure he was facing a five-card suit. De Falco had an easy club lead and East cashed two clubs before switching to the ♡Q; Kantar saved a trick by covering, but he was one down, -50.

The spectators knew that Board 96 was overwhelmingly likely to earn Italy 10 IMPs, which would make the match score USA 253, Italy 246. The fate of the match would hang on Board 95; Italy needed 7 IMPs to tie, 8 IMPs or more to win the Bermuda Bowl.

Board 95. N-S Vul. *(repeated for convenience)*

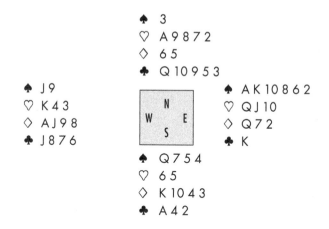

```
              ♠ 3
              ♡ A 9 8 7 2
              ◇ 6 5
              ♣ Q 10 9 5 3
♠ J 9                          ♠ A K 10 8 6 2
♡ K 4 3           N            ♡ Q J 10
◇ A J 9 8      W     E         ◇ Q 7 2
♣ J 8 7 6         S            ♣ K
              ♠ Q 7 5 4
              ♡ 6 5
              ◇ K 10 4 3
              ♣ A 4 2
```

With +100 in the Bank of Italy for defeating East-West's 3NT in the Closed Room, achieving +140 in a spade partial in the Open Room would leave Italy exactly 1 IMP short, but +170 would mean overtime! However, if Franco and De Falco reached game they would have to make it for Italy to prevail.

	West	North	East	South
	De Falco	Eisenberg	Franco	Kantar
				pass
	pass	pass	1♠	pass
	2♣	pass	2♠	pass
	2NT	pass	3NT	all pass

As De Falco's passed-hand 2♣ response was non-forcing, it was highly unusual with such a short and weak suit, but it had the effect of buying him a heart lead in 3NT. He won with the king (six from South) to ensure a later heart entry to dummy, and ran the ♠J. The American supporters in the audience, who could see all the cards, were willing Kantar to win (had he done so the defenders would have needed to cash out accurately), but after a great deal of thought, he followed low, as Pittalà had done in the Closed Room. Declarer played a second spade; when Eisenberg discarded the ◊5, he took the ♠A and called for the ◊Q (king, ace, six) then led a heart.

Now it was Eisenberg's turn to take some time. By now he knew that his partner had the ♣A; if he held ace-eight-low, Eisenberg could take the ♡A and arrange to cash out the clubs, which would be essential if declarer was poised to take four diamond tricks. The club shift would be wrong, however, if it destroyed the defensive timing and squeezed Kantar out of an exit card (imagine declarer with ◊AJ93 rather than ◊AJ98 and we'll soon see what could happen). On this layout it would be safe to duck the heart, or win and clear the suit. Eisenberg decided to go in with the ♡A to switch to the ♣3 — his lowest — to express his interest in having that suit returned. South took the king with the ace and returned the ♣4 to the eight and nine. Although Eisenberg could not be sure of the exact diamond position, he knew that cashing the ♣Q would establish a club trick for declarer, almost certainly his ninth winner, so Eisenberg exited with a heart to dummy's queen, hoping his partner had a safe discard. Kantar, who had to keep his spades and diamonds, released his remaining club.

With the lead in dummy we can see why the location of the ◊3 was so important: trade the ◊3 for the ◊8 and declarer *could* make the contract — diamond to the nine, ◊J, exit with the ◊3. South, unable to unblock, would be forced to win the fourth diamond and would have to lead into dummy's ♠K10. With his actual diamond holding, De Falco realized that Kantar would not allow himself to be endplayed to concede the last two spade tricks to dummy and would play the ◊10 under the jack. That would give De Falco an extra diamond trick, but he would have to surrender the last two tricks in clubs to North. There remained but one obscure chance — De Falco cashed dummy's ♠K and played a diamond to the jack hoping North had started with 1=5=3=4 shape and had bared the ◊10. When that slim chance did not materialize, all declarer could do was exit with a diamond, scoring the eight at the end for one down, -50, 2 IMPs to Italy, 238-253. The 10-IMP Italian gain on Board 96 would make the final score USA 253; Italy 248.

Suppose East-West had found a route to 4♠?

If South leads a heart and North ducks, declarer will almost certainly go down, but he would be disappointed after the fact to discover that he could have made it: ♡Q, ◊Q covered, ♠A, diamond to the eight, ♠K, diamond to the nine (North unable to ruff that or the ◊J, as declarer discards the ♣K). The defenders are restricted to three tricks. That would be a remarkable sequence of plays to find, but some way short of impossible.

Giorgio Belladonna

When the players emerged, Belladonna (who had almost single-handedly turned the match around) and Pittalà had every reason to think they had done enough to pull out the match. After the score comparisons revealed that Italy had fallen 5 IMPs short, Belladonna could not conceal his emotions. He announced his official retirement from World Championship play, concluding an era of personal excellence that began in 1957.

The final Daily Bulletin included this summary: 'Belladonna, the top-ranked player in the world, who is now retiring, had won thirteen previous Bermuda Bowl contests, more than any other player. But today he lost his *greatest* battle. Today's contest was more important to Belladonna than any previous Bermuda Bowl because he wanted to prove that Italy could win just as well under the new security measures with table screens as they did when they dominated world bridge before screens were introduced. Belladonna today walked off the world bridge scene in tears.'

His disenchantment was painfully apparent; he remarked that he was prepared to leave the game to the younger players who contended that they were the strongest. He no longer wished to be associated with several of the Italian players, serving notice to the rest of the world that the legendary Italian *esprit de corps* was sadly missing.

Epilogue

However, the bridge muse is a powerful one, and Belladonna returned once more in 1983 — and to no one's surprise became involved in another final with a dramatic conclusion. In the Bermuda Bowl final in Stockholm, the Aces (playing under that name for the last time) edged Italy by 5 IMPs in a match decided in the last three boards. That story is included in the second edition of Alan Sontag's classic book, *The Bridge Bum.*

Belladonna and Kantar compare scores

3. 1979 The History Boys

Cincinnati, also known as the Queen City, the Queen of the West, the Blue Chip City and the City of the Seven Hills, whose beloved Reds lost the National League baseball pennant to the Pittsburgh Pirates in September, 1979, played host to the ACBL's Fall North American Bridge Championships (a.k.a. the Fall Nationals) in November of the same year. In unrelated, but not fake U.S. news, Jack Haley (the Tin Man in *The Wizard of Oz*), Zeppo Marx, and Mr. Ed (the talking horse) all passed away.

When the scores after the sixth and final session in the main event, the Reisinger Board-a-Match Teams, were totaled, REINHOLD (Bud Reinhold, Bobby Levin, Russ Arnold, Jeff Meckstroth, Eric Rodwell) had amassed 37.13, while the defending champions, the ACES (Bob Hamman, Bobby Wolff, Fred Hamilton, Ira Rubin) had finished with 37.05 (fractions due to carryover formula). As the Conditions of Contest specified that the margin of victory had to be 0.25 or more, the teams went into the record books as co-titleholders.

REINHOLD *team*
(l-r) Arnold, Rodwell, Meckstroth, Levin, Reinhold

The ACES
(l-r) Hamman, Wolff, Hamilton, Rubin

However, that was not the end of the matter. The Reisinger was one of four qualifying events for the U.S. Team Trials (for the 1980 Olympiad) due to take place only a few days later, but only one team could emerge. Thus, after two long tension-filled sessions that day, there would be a playoff between the Reisinger co-winners for a place in the Team Trials. It was history in the making — the first-ever Reisinger playoff — and not just sudden-death or a handful of boards; the Directors dusted off the Conditions of Contest to reveal an obscure regulation stating that the two teams would have to contest another 12 deals (still scored at Board-a-Match) to break the tie.

There was a complication: REINHOLD would normally have fielded Levin and Arnold, leaving the triumvirate's third member — team sponsor Reinhold — on the sidelines, but Arnold, who had not played in the final session, was already on his way back to Florida. REINHOLD's request for a postponement was politely refused.

Despite the playoff start time of 1 a.m., there were huge crowds of spectators in both rooms.

Board 1. Neither Vul.

```
              ♠ 5
              ♡ Q J 10 6 5
              ◇ 5 4 2
              ♣ J 9 7 6
♠ 7                          ♠ J 10 6 4 3 2
♡ 9 8 7 3         N          ♡ —
◇ A Q 9       W     E        ◇ K 10 6 3
♣ K 8 5 3 2       S          ♣ A Q 4
              ♠ A K Q 9 8
              ♡ A K 4 2
              ◇ J 8 7
              ♣ 10
```

Open Room

West	North	East	South
Reinhold	Wolff	Levin	Hamman
	pass	pass	1♣[1]
pass	1♡[2]	2♠	dbl
all pass			

1. Strong, artificial, forcing one round.

2. Artificial negative.

South took five trump tricks, but there was no way the defenders could generate a sixth trick, so REINHOLD scored up +470. It's interesting to note that in 1979 Hamman had a penalty double of 2♠ available; even then, it was more common to treat this double as takeout, and today it's almost universal to double for takeout when a pass by a strong hand would not be forcing on a weak one.

Closed Room

West	North	East	South
Hamilton	*Meckstroth*	*Rubin*	*Rodwell*
	pass	pass	1♣[1]
pass	1◇[2]	1♠	dbl
rdbl[3]	pass	2◇	pass
pass	2♡	pass	pass
3♣	pass	3◇	3♡
all pass			

1. Strong, artificial, forcing one round.
2. Artificial negative.
3. Rescue.

Here too, the strong-club opener could double for penalty, but the context was different, as apparently at the one-level opener's pass would be forcing. Given the Open Room result, the number of tricks Meckstroth took in 3♡ was irrelevant, but the play was of some interest.

East led the ◇3 and the defenders cashed three tricks in the suit and then switched to spades. Declarer took the ace and played a trump to the queen, which eventually led to West scoring a trump trick by ruffing spades with his remaining equal intermediates for one down, -50. Had declarer started with one of dummy's top trumps he would have managed safe club ruffs and been able to neutralize West's trumps. REINHOLD 1, ACES 0.

Board 2. N-S Vul.

```
                    ♠ K J 5 3
                    ♡ 8 6 5
                    ◇ K J 7 2
                    ♣ 7 2
     ♠ A 9 8                          ♠ 10 6
     ♡ K 7 4 3          N             ♡ A Q 9
     ◇ A Q 10 9    W         E        ◇ 6 5 4
     ♣ Q 8             S             ♣ K J 6 5 4
                    ♠ Q 7 4 2
                    ♡ J 10 2
                    ◇ 8 3
                    ♣ A 10 9 3
```

	West	North	East	South
Open Room	Reinhold	Wolff	Levin	Hamman
Closed Room	Hamilton	Meckstroth	Rubin	Rodwell
			pass	pass
	1NT	pass	3NT	all pass

After identical auctions, North led the ♠3 at both tables, declarer winning the
third round as North ensured that his partner would win the fourth. In the
Open Room, Reinhold led the ♣8 to the jack and ace, and after cashing the
♠7, on which declarer threw a diamond from both hands, Hamman switched
to the ◇8. Declarer went up with the ace, unblocked the ♣Q, crossed to
dummy with a heart and cashed the ♣K. When declarer, perhaps showing his
fatigue, inexplicably discarded a heart and exited with a club, North could
dispose of his remaining heart. A second diamond through the queen-ten
allowed North to take the rest, which added up to down four, -200. That
would be a tough result to duplicate.

Indeed. Hamilton, after the same start to the play in the Closed Room,
discarded a diamond on the ♣K and then cashed his three remaining heart
winners when the suit broke 3-3 for the normal one down, -50. The score
was even. REINHOLD 1, ACES 1.

Board 3. E-W Vul.

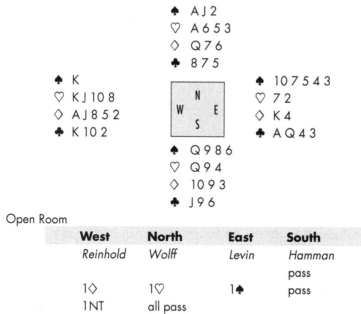

```
            ♠ A J 2
            ♡ A 6 5 3
            ◇ Q 7 6
            ♣ 8 7 5
♠ K                        ♠ 10 7 5 4 3
♡ K J 10 8        N        ♡ 7 2
◇ A J 8 5 2    W     E     ◇ K 4
♣ K 10 2          S        ♣ A Q 4 3
            ♠ Q 9 8 6
            ♡ Q 9 4
            ◇ 10 9 3
            ♣ J 9 6
```

Open Room

West	North	East	South
Reinhold	*Wolff*	*Levin*	*Hamman*
			pass
1◇	1♡	1♠	pass
1NT	all pass		

Appreciating Reinhold's discomfort on the previous deal, Wolff risked a truly vile 1♡ overcall to stir the pot before calm was restored. Against 1NT, he led the ♣8, and the trick continued with the four, jack and king. Declarer continued with a diamond to the king, and another diamond to the jack and queen. At first blush, it may have seemed that it was asking a lot for Wolff to find the switch to the ♠A, but if South would have raised with four-card heart support, it was likely that declarer's shape was 1=4=5=3. However, Wolff continued with a second club. Declarer won and cashed all his minor-suit winners ending in dummy. This was the position:

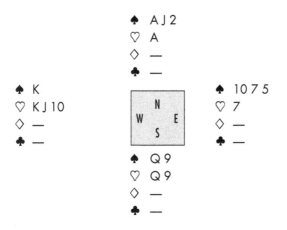

With the spade suit blocked (South would have done better to keep a third spade and release a heart — probably the queen, given that overcall!), declarer can secure a ninth trick by leading a heart to the ten. When, instead, he exited with a spade, North won, returned a spade to South's queen and claimed the last two tricks, holding 1NT to two, +120.

```
                    ♠ A J 2          (repeated for convenience)
                    ♡ A 6 5 3
                    ◇ Q 7 6
                    ♣ 8 7 5
      ♠ K                        ♠ 10 7 5 4 3
      ♡ K J 10 8      N          ♡ 7 2
      ◇ A J 8 5 2   W   E        ◇ K 5
      ♣ K 10 2        S          ♣ A Q 4 3
                    ♠ Q 9 8 6
                    ♡ Q 9 4
                    ◇ 10 9 3
                    ♣ J 9 6
```

Closed Room

	West	North	East	South
	Hamilton	Meckstroth	Rubin	Rodwell
				pass
	1◇	pass	1♠	pass
	1NT	pass	2♣	all pass

Rubin's 2♣ was not an encouraging move and could easily have delivered four spades and at least five clubs, so might not have led to a superior 5-3 spade fit had West held three of those. Meanwhile, 2♣ took the partnership out of a higher-scoring strain with insufficient evidence to support the decision. South led the ♡4 to the ten and ace, Rubin concealing the two. North returned the ♡6 to the queen and king, and declarer tried the ♠K. North won and switched to a trump, won in dummy. Declarer threw a spade on the ♡J, came to the ◊K, ruffed a spade, cashed the ◊A, ruffed a diamond and ruffed a spade, which added up to ten tricks for a lovely +130 and a win for ACES, ahead now 2-1. Rubin's unusual action had paid off in a way that could not easily have been foreseen.

Ira Rubin

In fact, as it went, had Rubin played to set up the diamonds without giving up a spade he would have taken eleven tricks, which would have been necessary to push the board had Reinhold guessed accurately in the endgame to land +150. North can deny declarer an eleventh trick in clubs by withholding the ♡A on the first round.

Could the defense have held 2♣ to nine tricks to win the board for REINHOLD? The short answer is yes; the long answer is that only one card gets the job done. It's somewhat intuitive to think that South must lead a trump, but something else to divine that it must be the jack!

If South starts with the ♣6 or the ♣9, declarer wins with dummy's ten, comes to hand with a diamond, and plays a heart to the ten. When North ducks, declarer can cash dummy's ◊A, ruff a diamond and play a second heart. North wins, but now playing two rounds of spades can be countered by ruffing, cashing the ♡K and then taking three more trump tricks via a high crossruff.

Leading the ♣J stops this line of play. If declarer wins in hand and plays a heart to the ten, North must duck and declarer cannot untangle his tricks if the rest of the defense is equally efficient. Say he continues with a diamond to the king and a second heart. North wins, and must cash the ♠A and continue with the jack. Declarer ruffs in dummy, but lacks the necessary communications to score more than nine tricks. Winning Trick 1 with dummy's king removes a vital high trump entry to dummy.

Board 4. Both Vul.

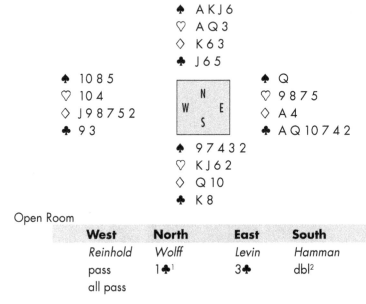

```
              ♠ A K J 6
              ♡ A Q 3
              ◇ K 6 3
              ♣ J 6 5
♠ 10 8 5                        ♠ Q
♡ 10 4          N              ♡ 9 8 7 5
◇ J 9 8 7 5 2  W   E           ◇ A 4
♣ 9 3             S            ♣ A Q 10 7 4 2
              ♠ 9 7 4 3 2
              ♡ K J 6 2
              ◇ Q 10
              ♣ K 8
```

Open Room

West	North	East	South
Reinhold	Wolff	Levin	Hamman
pass	1♣[1]	3♣	dbl[2]
all pass			

1. Artificial, 17+, forcing one round.
2. Negative double.

Hamman's double of Levin's enterprising jump to 3♣ was value-showing, and with his balanced hand, Wolff elected to pass for penalty. South led a heart and North won with the ace and switched to a trump, ducked to the king. A second trump left declarer looking at only six tricks and almost surely a lost board, but after cashing three more clubs declarer played the ♡8. South went in with the jack and exited with a spade. Declarer ruffed the second round of spades with his last trump and played the ♡9. When Hamman misjudged by playing the ♡K, crashing the queen, Wolff's earlier spade discard meant that the defense could cash only one spade as Levin discarded his diamond loser. Now Wolff had to play a diamond and Levin took the last two tricks with the ◇A and the ♡7 to escape with seven tricks, -500, an excellent result for REINHOLD as North-South were entitled to the vulnerable game bonus.

Closed Room

West	North	East	South
Hamilton	Meckstroth	Rubin	Rodwell
pass	1♣[1]	2♣	2♠[2]
pass	3♠	pass	4♠
all pass			

1. Artificial 16+, forcing one round.
2. Game force.

Rubin's less-adventurous 2♣ gave North-South plenty of room to bid their vulnerable game with no realistic temptation to propose defending 2♣ doubled. Rodwell lost tricks to the two missing aces, +650 and a win for REINHOLD, tying the score at 2-2.

BAM scoring has traditionally stressed the wisdom of taking actions that will most often ensure at least a half-point (a tie) while expecting better judgment, greater skill in the play and opponents' errors to create a significant number of wins. Levin's atypical 3♣ (indifferent intermediates in clubs, good defense, potentially fine dummy for hearts or diamonds) offers us a glimpse of what might reasonably happen after stepping out just a bit. First, 3♣ made it much more difficult for North-South to reach their best contract; second, it created a 'win or lose' scenario rather than the expected tie at North-South +650; third, it may well have played a role in steering the defenders wrong as they were not focused on declarer having both a fourth heart and a second ace. One conclusion we can take from this deal is that sometimes you must give to get, i.e., put yourself at some risk if your objective is to win rather than tie a board against a very strong team.

On Board 5, the East players were dealt:

♠8 ♡Q 9 6 2 ♢Q 5 3 2 ♣Q 10 6 3

There were two different auctions that led to 3NT, to be declared by North:

West	North	East	South
Reinhold	Wolff	Levin	Hamman
	1NT	pass	2♢[1]
pass	2NT[2]	pass	3NT
all pass			

1. Game-forcing Stayman.
2. No four-card major.

Closed Room

West	North	East	South
Hamilton	Meckstroth	Rubin	Rodwell
	1NT	pass	2♡[1]
pass	2♠	pass	3NT
all pass			

1. Transfer, at least five spades.

Provided with different major-suit length information at the two tables, which of your four-card suits would you choose to lead?

The full deal will show you how your choice(s) would have fared:

Board 5. N-S Vul.

```
                      ♠ K Q
                      ♡ J 3
                      ◇ A 10 9 8 7
                      ♣ A J 5 2
      ♠ J 9 7 6 3         N          ♠ 8
      ♡ K 10 8 4      W       E      ♡ Q 9 6 2
      ◇ K J               S          ◇ Q 5 3 2
      ♣ 8 7                          ♣ Q 10 6 3
                      ♠ A 10 5 4 2
                      ♡ A 7 5
                      ◇ 6 4
                      ♣ K 9 4
```

In the Closed Room Rubin did not lead from his strongest suit — he chose the ♡2, knowing dummy would have at most three of those. That proved a big success. Meckstroth won the third round of the suit with dummy's ace, discarding a diamond from his hand. When East discarded a diamond on the second round of spades declarer was at the crossroads. Should he play on clubs, which would give him a chance of making the contract (to be precise, the prospect of taking four club tricks is 19.37%) but might lead to a second undertrick, or should he play on diamonds, which would most often give him two tricks in the suit, but give up on making the contract and leading to one down?

In a seemingly normal contract, against what would usually be the normal lead, making the contract at BAM scoring is often not as important as taking the maximum number of available tricks. Meckstroth went after diamonds and finished one down, -100.

In the Open Room, although declarer could have significant length in one or both minors, dummy did not investigate further, so would not have an obvious weakness in a major. That was enough to convince Levin to lead his best suit, in which he needed only to find partner with the jack to be off to a good start. While the reasoning was sound enough, the low-club lead cost a fast trick and gave declarer hope. Wolff played low from dummy (this time the nine would have put more pressure on the defense, as we will see) and won with the ♣J. When declarer cashed the second high spade, Levin had a second tough decision. A diamond discard would have been best but he parted with a heart. Now Wolff continued with the ◊8 from hand, which ran to the jack. Reinhold did not switch to hearts, instead returning partner's suit, so Wolff could clear diamonds and claim ten tricks: one heart and three of each of the other suits for +630 and an easy win on the board. If Reinhold switches to hearts, Wolff ducks twice, wins the third round and can build two more diamond tricks by conceding the third round to East, who is out of hearts, for +600; that heart discard by Levin was fatal.

Declarer can make 3NT on a club lead even if East keeps his fourth heart, but must judge to play dummy's nine at Trick 1 — not such a good idea if the ten or queen were going to appear from West (that would give up his chance for four club tricks). When the ♣9 holds he starts spades, East doing best to discard a diamond on the second round. Declarer ducks a diamond to West, who switches to hearts. Declarer wins the third heart, parting with a diamond. He cashes the ♣K, then the ♠A, reducing to the ◊A10 and ♣AJ. East, down to:

$$♡9 \quad ◊Q5 \quad ♣Q10$$

cannot spare a minor-suit card, so must release the ♡9. Now declarer can play two rounds of diamonds, forcing East to lead into the club tenace. Declarer takes three spades, a heart, a diamond and four clubs. REINHOLD 2, ACES 3.

Board 6. E-W Vul.

```
              ♠ 8 7 5
              ♡ J 9 7 4
              ◇ Q 10 9 6 2
              ♣ Q
♠ 6 2                         ♠ A J 10 4
♡ A 6 2          N           ♡ K 3
◇ K 5        W       E       ◇ A J 8
♣ A K 10 7 6 2    S          ♣ 8 5 4 3
              ♠ K Q 9 3
              ♡ Q 10 8 5
              ◇ 7 4 3
              ♣ J 9
```

West	North	East	South
Reinhold	Wolff	Levin	Hamman
		1♣	pass
3♣[1]	pass	3NT	pass
4NT[2]	pass	5♡[3]	pass
5NT[4]	pass	6◇[5]	pass
6NT	all pass		

1. Game-forcing raise.
2. Blackwood.
3. Two aces.
4. Blackwood.
5. One king.

Against 6NT, Hamman led the ♠K. Levin won and established his twelfth trick in spades, for +1440. With only 27 combined HCP and no short suit in either hand, that was a very good-looking result for REINHOLD, especially as it was possible that 6NT could fail on an admittedly unlikely rounded-suit lead, declarer relying on one of two spade finesses. He would take one spade finesse, but would then be able to cash the ♡K and run clubs, discarding a spade and the ♡3 (if the defense had not killed that possibility) before committing himself. He would always have the option of cashing the ♠A with the diamond finesse in reserve, the winning line, or cashing the ace-king of diamonds and falling back on the second spade finesse if needed, going down.

Closed Room

West	North	East	South
Hamilton	Meckstroth	Rubin	Rodwell
		1♣	pass
3♣[1]	pass	3NT	pass
4♣	pass	4◇[2]	pass
4♡[3]	pass	4♠[4]	dbl
pass	pass	4NT	pass
5◇[5]	dbl	5♡[6]	pass
6♣	all pass		

1. Game-forcing raise.
2-6. Control bids.

When Rodwell doubled 4♠, Hamilton passed to give his partner a chance to redouble to show first-round spade control, but Rubin preferred a 'nothing more to say' 4NT. Although Hamilton tried to offer a choice between 6♣ and 6NT, the partnership subsided in 6♣, the right slam at IMP scoring (cold with trumps 2-1). Indeed, reaching any slam was not routine, and in such cases, it is good strategy at BAM to play in the safest contract. Accordingly, after the ♠K lead, Rubin was not going to risk going down by taking the diamond finesse to try for an overtrick once he judged that reaching slam might be enough to win the board. As is often the case on such many-outcome slam-zone deals, once Levin and Reinhold had achieved their maximum result at the other table, +1370, +1390, or -100 would all have lost the board. That was another win for REINHOLD, tying the match at 3.

Fred Hamilton

Board 7 was the first push, both teams recording +680 in a routine 4♡. REINHOLD 3.5, ACES 3.5.

Board 8. Neither Vul.

```
              ♠ J 9
              ♡ A 3
              ◇ J 9 7 6
              ♣ K Q 10 8 7
♠ 7 2                           ♠ K 10 6 5 4 3
♡ K J 8 7 6 2      N            ♡ Q 9 5
◇ Q 8 2         W     E         ◇ A 3
♣ 9 4              S            ♣ J 5
              ♠ A Q 8
              ♡ 10 4
              ◇ K 10 5 4
              ♣ A 6 3 2
```

Open Room

West	North	East	South
Reinhold	*Wolff*	*Levin*	*Hamman*
2♡	pass	2NT¹	pass
3♡²	all pass		

1. Forcing inquiry.
2. Minimum.

Levin was not really looking for game, but as he was going to raise as a blocking move he decided to make a show of strength with little risk, and was pleased to buy the contract quietly in 3♡. North led the ♣K, cashed the ♣Q, and switched to the ◇6, declarer ducking to South's king. Hamman returned the ♡4 to the ace and three rounds of spades followed, but Reinhold could ruff high and claim, two down, -100. As North-South could make 4♣ or 4◇ as well as a very lucky 3NT with the double finesse against the ♠K10, that was a fine result for REINHOLD.

Bud Reinhold

Closed Room

West	North	East	South
Hamilton	Meckstroth	Rubin	Rodwell
pass	1◇[1]	1♠	2◇[2]
2♡	pass	3♡	3♠[3]
pass	3NT	all pass	

1. 2+ diamonds, 10-15.
2. Inverted raise, more like a natural two-over-one.
3. Values in spades.

Even though Hamilton did not open 2◇ (which would show either a weak 2♡ or a strong 2◇) his side was still able to compete to 3♡, but North had been given the opportunity to open and South was going to drive to game. The 3NT contract was terribly fragile on the lead of the ♡5, but declarer won the first heart, cashed the ♣K, and led the ♠J to the king and ace. He returned to hand with the ♣Q and ran the ♠9 successfully, crossed to the ♣A to cash the ♠Q and claim nine tricks. Plus 400 was a win for REINHOLD.

Jeff Meckstroth

Note that Meckstroth did not believe he was in the normal contract and could not know whether his teammates would get their hearts into the picture. Had he known the result at the other table, he would have settled for a gentle partial in a minor. However, once he had landed in 3NT, he had every reason to try to make it, even though the chance of success was only 25%; his counterparts were likely to be plus and any minus figured to be a loss. A different approach would be to assume the contract at the other table was five of a minor and that either of those games would fail; if that were so, cashing out for one down at 3NT (with the small chance that the ♠10 would drop doubleton for his ninth trick) would tie the board. The complexity of estimating what is likely to happen at the other table in time to influence your strategy is one of the elements that make BAM such a fascinating and challenging form of scoring. REINHOLD 4.5, ACES 3.5.

Board 9. E-W Vul.

```
                        ♠ 6 4 3
                        ♡ J 10
                        ◇ J 5 4 3
                        ♣ K Q 7 5
        ♠ 5                               ♠ K 8 7
        ♡ Q 9 4 3 2          N            ♡ A 8 6 5
        ◇ 9 2           W         E       ◇ A K Q 7 6
        ♣ J 10 9 3 2         S            ♣ 4
                        ♠ A Q J 10 9 2
                        ♡ K 7
                        ◇ 10 8
                        ♣ A 8 6
```

Open Room

West	North	East	South
Reinhold	*Wolff*	*Levin*	*Hamman*
	pass	1◇	1♠
pass	2♠	pass	3◇[1]
pass	3♠	all pass	

1. Initially a try for 3NT.

Although Levin knew his partner would be relatively short in spades, he was reluctant to double 2♠ for takeout with a singleton club. Reinhold led the ◇9 against 3♠; Levin won with the ◇Q, cashed the ◇K and continued with the ◇7. Declarer ruffed with the ♠J, crossed to dummy with a club, and played a spade to the queen. When he tried to return to dummy with a club, East ruffed and played the ◇A. Declarer ruffed high, drew the outstanding trump, crossed to dummy with a spade, and played the ♡J. East spared declarer a modest guess (Reinhold, known to be at least 5-5, had not doubled 1♠) by going up with the ace, and North-South had +140.

Had Wolff tried 3NT he would have either made four or gone down four if subjected to an early guess in hearts!

Closed Room

West	North	East	South
Hamilton	*Meckstroth*	*Rubin*	*Rodwell*
	pass	1◇	1♠
pass	pass	2◇	2♠
all pass			

While it might seem mildly surprising that the normally-aggressive Meckstroth did not raise to 2♠ at favorable vulnerability, at BAM it's so often important to avoid blowing a trick on the opening lead, and that seems to have been the key issue for North in this case. Although Rubin could reopen over 1♠ with a takeout double and convert clubs to diamonds, he was not keen to do that any higher than the two-level, and was not strong enough for 1NT (18-19). Rather than pass, he opted for an imperfect rebid of his top-heavy suit, but no one disturbed Rodwell's 2♠.

The early play was the same as in the Open Room, but after the first spade finesse, Rodwell cashed the ♠A and exited with a spade. East won and exited in diamonds, and when clubs did not behave declarer had to guess hearts. Rubin was marked with the ace for several reasons, so he took it immediately. That was +140 for Rodwell and a tied board, leaving REINHOLD ahead, 5-4.

It's not always easy to outbid the spade suit, but had East-West found a way to get together in hearts there were ten tricks available to them. Do you think a negative double of 1♠ would receive significant support on a modern expert bidding panel? Or perhaps a takeout 2NT over 2♠?

Board 10. Both Vul.

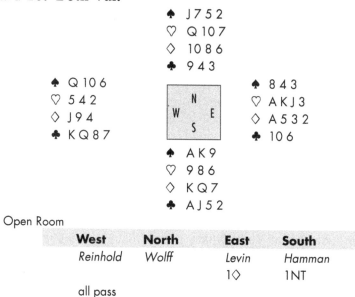

```
              ♠ J 7 5 2
              ♡ Q 10 7
              ◇ 10 8 6
              ♣ 9 4 3
  ♠ Q 10 6                      ♠ 8 4 3
  ♡ 5 4 2          N            ♡ A K J 3
  ◇ J 9 4       W     E         ◇ A 5 3 2
  ♣ K Q 8 7        S            ♣ 10 6
              ♠ A K 9
              ♡ 9 8 6
              ◇ K Q 7
              ♣ A J 5 2
```

Open Room

	West	North	East	South
	Reinhold	Wolff	Levin	Hamman
			1◇	1NT
all pass				

After an opening bid by East, it makes some sense for West to double 1NT to try for +200, which might be required to save the board if East-West could score +110 or more on their cards at the other table. Reinhold passed, however, and, somewhat surprisingly, rejected an attractive lead in partner's suit to gamble on finding him with a supporting honor in clubs. The ♣7 went to the ten and jack, and Hamman passed the ♡9, hopefully. Levin won the jack and continued clubs; West cleared the suit when declarer ducked, East parting with a spade. Declarer played a second heart and East won to return the ♠8. Declarer won with the ♠A, cashed the ♠K, and exited in hearts. East won and was careful not to cash the long heart, exiting with a diamond, trying to look like a man who had started with ace-jack-fifth with 3=3=5=2 shape.

Hamman could have ensured five tricks by playing an honor, but his best chance for six tricks was to play low from hand, even though that carried the risk of holding himself to only four. It's human nature to do what it takes to avoid -200 on a partscore hand, so it's not surprising that Hamman played low, although that amounted to playing East to have erred by not cashing the third heart before exiting in spades. West won with the ◊J and cashed his black-suit winners before putting East in with the ◊A to cash the long heart for three down, -300, a plus position for REINHOLD despite the apparently unpromising opening lead.

Closed Room

West	North	East	South
Hamilton	Meckstroth	Rubin	Rodwell
		pass	1NT
all pass			

It must seem odd to see East pass as dealer, more so when you learn that his partnership opens virtually *any* four-card major, but Ira 'The Beast' Rubin, widely recognized by his peers as a great theoretician, relied on one of his more arcane principles when he declined to open: 'If you can't comfortably rebid in a not-unlikely situation, it's better to pass than open with minimum values'. The dreaded case for Rubin would be an auction that started 1♡-2♣. Now 2◊ would not be appropriate with only four cards in each suit, while 2NT with an unstopped tripleton would risk misplacing the declaration, something important for him.

Hamilton, unwilling to guess which modest honor-holding to lead from with no evidence from the auction, selected the ♡5, top of nothing and ultra-passive. Rubin took two tricks in the suit and switched to the ◊2. Rodwell put up the king and when it held, led a low club: seven, nine, ten. East switched to the ♠8, and declarer won to continue with the ♣A and ♣J. West won, cashed the other club, and exited with a heart, East winning and playing another spade, legitimately holding declarer to four tricks, -300, for a flat board. REINHOLD 5.5, ACES 4.5.

When declarer wins the first spade, he does best to exit with a third heart, East winning to play a second spade. Declarer wins and exits with a spade to West's queen; now the best he can do is play a top club, but declarer ducks, and must score a second diamond or club for five tricks. So both South players could have won the board by arranging to go -200, normally a terrible result when the points are evenly divided. How ironic!

Board 11. Neither Vul.

```
              ♠ 10 5 4
              ♡ A Q 4 2
              ◇ K 10 5 2
              ♣ A 10
♠ A 7                          ♠ Q J 9 6
♡ K 10 9 3        N            ♡ 8 7 6
◇ 4 3         W       E        ◇ 7
♣ K 9 6 3 2       S            ♣ Q J 8 7 5
              ♠ K 8 3 2
              ♡ J 5
              ◇ A Q J 9 8 6
              ♣ 4
```

Open Room

West	North	East	South
Reinhold	Wolff	Levin	Hamman
			1♠[1]
pass	2◇	pass	3◇
pass	3NT	all pass	

1. At least four spades, possible canapé.

East led the ♣Q, which held, and continued with the ♣5 to the king and ace. Declarer cashed six rounds of diamonds: West pitched a spade, a club and two hearts, while East parted with two spades, two hearts and a club. When the ♡J was covered by the king and ace declarer had four heart tricks, and +460. If West is going to discard two hearts, East must not part with *any* of his, which is probably too difficult in real life, though possible if East knows early enough that West has the ♠A. Today, just following four-three in diamonds to send a suit-preference message might be sufficient, but if West is going to part with one club he might as well discard two, along with a spade and a heart, and East could keep all his clubs.

Bob Hamman and Bobby Wolff

Closed Room

West	North	East	South
Hamilton	Meckstroth	Rubin	Rodwell
			1◇[1]
pass	1♡	pass	1♠
pass	2♣[2]	pass	2◇
pass	3NT	all pass	

1. 2+ diamonds, 10-15.
2. Fourth-suit forcing.

East led the ♣7 to the king and ace and declarer cashed the diamonds. Here too, East relinquished two hearts, two spades and a club, but West threw three clubs and only *one* heart (as North had bid the suit), restricting declarer to nine tricks (with the successful heart finesse).

That was a win for the ACES, so with just one deal remaining the score was tied once again.

REINHOLD 5.5, ACES 5.5.

Board 12. N-S Vul.

```
                 ♠ J 8 7 2
                 ♡ A
                 ◇ A 5 4 2
                 ♣ A Q 9 7
  ♠ A Q                          ♠ 10 6 3
  ♡ J 6 4 2          N           ♡ 9 8 7 5
  ◇ K J 8 7 6     W     E        ◇ Q 9 3
  ♣ J 6              S            ♣ K 8 4
                 ♠ K 9 5 4
                 ♡ K Q 10 3
                 ◇ 10
                 ♣ 10 5 3 2
```

Open Room

West	North	East	South
Reinhold	*Wolff*	*Levin*	*Hamman*
pass	1◇	pass	1♡
pass	1♠	pass	2♠
all pass			

When Reinhold passed as dealer, North-South settled in 2♠ on a combination that offered some acceptable play for game. Levin led the unbid suit, the ♣4 going to the jack and queen. Wolff led a spade to the king and ace, and West cashed the ♠Q before reverting to clubs. Declarer took the ace, drew the outstanding trump, cashed the ♡A and gave up a club, claiming ten tricks, +170.

This room had finished well ahead of the other, and the spectators, knowing that the match was tied, considered it unlikely that Meckstroth and Rodwell (they had not yet obtained the sobriquet of Meckwell) would reach 4♠. They were prepared to fill up on coffee to watch a second overtime, this one a sudden-death finale — the first team to win a board would get the spoils of victory.

Closed Room

West	North	East	South
Hamilton	Meckstroth	Rubin	Rodwell
1◊	pass	1♡	pass
2♡	dbl	pass	2♠
all pass			

Hamilton, with an easy rebid (1NT over a 1♠ response, or 2NT over 2♣), had a normal opening bid in the partnership style (in contrast to the East hand on Board 10). Meckstroth had to pass, but was not hard-pressed to double 2♡ for takeout. That sort of 'live' double implies a different minimum for different partnerships, but with so much strength in hearts, North's short suit, Rodwell settled for a simple 2♠.

West led a heart to dummy's ace, and declarer cashed the ◊A, ruffed a diamond, and cashed the top hearts. Had he pitched dummy's diamonds, all would probably have been well, but he threw two clubs. A club to the queen lost to the king, and the defense played two rounds of trumps, then a diamond, forcing declarer to use his remaining entry to hand while the clubs were blocked. That meant dummy had a losing diamond at the end and Rodwell's +140 left REINHOLD a trick short of tying the match at sixes!

By winning the final board (with an overtrick), the Aces prevailed in the playoff 6.5-5.5, earning them a place in the upcoming Team Trials for the 1980 Olympiad. They added Paul Soloway to play with Rubin and Mike Passell to play with Hamilton and won those Trials, but they would lose the Olympiad final to France, 131-111, in Valkenburg, Netherlands, in one of the hardest-fought and best-played matches in World Championship history.

Two years later, the REINHOLD team, the loser of this historic Reisinger playoff, with the addition of John Solodar, won the Bermuda Bowl in Port Chester, New York. Meckstroth and Rodwell, both of whom, like Levin, were in their early twenties in Cincinnati, have been winning World titles ever since.

4. 1985 Breathless

You leave me... aaah... breathless
Jerry Lee Lewis, 1958 (Sun Records)

In 1985 the U.S. Open Trials were staged in Memphis, Tennessee. The playoff would normally have involved four teams, but Peter Pender, Hugh Ross, Chip Martel and Lew Stansby had won two of the qualifying events, the 1983 Grand National Teams and the 1984 Vanderbilt, which earned them an automatic place in the final. They added a third pair, Bob Hamman and Bobby Wolff, and appointed a captain, Alfred SHEINWOLD.

(l-r) Stansby, Martel, Ross, Pender

In the final SHEINWOLD faced the 1983 Spingold winners: George ROSENKRANZ (NPC), Jeff Meckstroth, Eric Rodwell, Larry Cohen, Marty Bergen, Eddie Wold and Mark Lair. Lair had replaced Dr. Rosenkranz, who, as a Mexican national, was ineligible to represent USA in world competition. This team had beaten the Reisinger winners — Cliff RUSSELL (NPC), Richard Pavlicek, Bill Root, Edgar Kaplan, Norman Kay, Mike Lawrence, Peter Weichsel — convincingly, 294-167, in the semifinal.

ROSENKRANZ team
(l-r) Meckstroth, Rodwell, Cohen, Bergen, Wold, Rosenkranz

The 128-deal final proved to be one of the most dramatic matches in the history of bridge. Space restricts me[††] from doing more than point out the highlights — but there were plenty of those.

Set One (Boards 1-16)

Board 4. Both Vul.

```
              ♠ A Q J
              ♡ 10 6 5 2
              ◇ Q
              ♣ A J 10 6 3
 ♠ K 4 3                        ♠ 9 8 6 5 2
 ♡ 9 4           N             ♡ A K 8 3
 ◇ A K 8 4   W       E         ◇ 2
 ♣ K Q 5 4       S             ♣ 9 8 2
              ♠ 10 7
              ♡ Q J 7
              ◇ J 10 9 7 6 5 3
              ♣ 7
```

Open Room

West	North	East	South
Meckstroth	Martel	Rodwell	Stansby
1NT	pass	2♣[1]	pass
2◇[2]	pass	3♣[3]	pass
3◇[4]	pass	3♠[5]	pass
4♠	all pass		

1. Asking for a five-card major.
2. None.
3. Inquiry.
4. No four-card major.
5. Five spades and four hearts, limited hand.

The high-tech (for the times) auction led to a 22-point game that needed much more luck than it got; Rodwell lost a club, a club ruff, three spades and a late heart (after a first-round spade to the king, North could draw trumps) for three down, -300.

††   Primary author Eric Kokish

Closed Room

West	North	East	South
Ross	Bergen	Pender	Cohen
1◇	pass	1♠	pass
2♣	pass	pass	3◇
dbl	all pass		

Ignoring the opening bid and the vulnerability, South, true to his principles about disturbing apparently comfortable contracts, boldly reopened in his LHO's suit (1◇ promised 4+ diamonds unless West was 4=4=3=2 and had 15+ HCP). West led the ♣K and declarer won with dummy's ace.

There is a route to nine tricks: club ruff, spade finesse, club ruff, spade finesse, heart discard on the ♠A, club ruff; with those seven tricks in, declarer still has the ◇Q opposite ◇J1097. However, Cohen played the ◇Q at Trick 2. That gave Ross the chance to win and switch to hearts, which would give the defenders five tricks — four top cards in the red suits plus a heart ruff — but Ross ducked, and now the road to nine tricks was reopened. However, declarer played not an essential club but a heart, and Pender won; the defenders were again poised to collect five tricks. No, East returned a club, so declarer was on track for a third time, but when he ruffed and played the ◇9, West won and put an end to the dizzying table tennis exchanges by playing a heart, the subsequent ruff securing that elusive setting trick, -200, and 11 IMPs for SHEINWOLD where it might well have been 9 IMPs to the other guys.

Hugh Ross

Board 7. Both Vul.

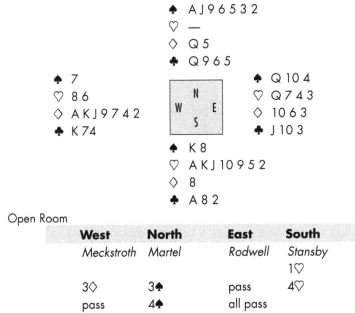

West	North	East	South
Meckstroth	Martel	Rodwell	Stansby
			1♡
3◇	3♠	pass	4♡
pass	4♠	all pass	

In 4♠, declarer ruffed the second diamond in dummy, ruffed a heart, crossed to the ♠K, ruffed a heart, and played the ♣A and another spade, with the ♣A the entry to the good hearts to discard clubs: +650.

Closed Room

West	North	East	South
Ross	Bergen	Pender	Cohen
			1♡
2◇	3♠[1]	pass	4◇
pass	4♠	pass	4NT[2]
pass	5◇[3]	pass	5♡[4]
pass	6♠	all pass	

1. Less than a high-card invitation.
2. RKCB for spades.
3. One keycard.
4. Asking for the ♠Q.

Bergen felt his seventh spade might be as good as the queen. The resulting 6♠ was certainly odds-against, but hardly outrageous; it had no chance on this layout when the defenders took their diamond trick and waited for their trump trick. That was -100, so SHEINWOLD gained 13 IMPs.

Board 9. E-W Vul.

```
                    ♠ K 8 4
                    ♡ 7
                    ◇ A 8 7 4 3
                    ♣ K 6 4 3
  ♠ A J 10 6                          ♠ 3
  ♡ A 10 8 6 5          N             ♡ Q 9 3
  ◇ 2            W            E       ◇ Q J 9 6 5
  ♣ J 8 2               S             ♣ A 10 9 7
                    ♠ Q 9 7 5 2
                    ♡ K J 4 2
                    ◇ K 10
                    ♣ Q 5
```

Open Room

West	North	East	South
Meckstroth	Martel	Rodwell	Stansby
	pass	pass	1♠
pass	1NT[1]	pass	pass[2]
2♡	2♠[3]	4♡	dbl
all pass			

1. Forcing opposite a sound opening bid or any distributional hand.
2. Relatively balanced minimum, normally a 2♡ rebid with this shape.
3. Inferentially a three-card limit raise as North-South do not play Drury.

Martel did not have a Drury 2♣ available, so had to choose between a heavy 2♠ and a hopeful not-quite-forcing 1NT, intending to jump to 3♠ over a 2♣ or 2◇ rebid. Once Stansby's pass confirmed that game would be out of reach, Martel was pleased to describe his three-card limit raise with a free bid of 2♠. That did not seem to mean much to Rodwell, who completed a typical Meckwell effort, squeezing every drop out of two average hands to bid a thin vulnerable game.

North led the ♠4 to the queen and ace and declarer continued with a diamond to the nine and ten. Stansby switched to the ♣Q; when Meckstroth let it hold, South continued clubs, the jack winning. Declarer ruffed the ♠6, ruffed a diamond, and played the ♠10, ruffing away North's king to lead dummy's now-blank queen of trumps. When South covered, declarer could win, drive out the ♡J, win the spade return, draw trumps, and claim, +790. Declarer would have failed had South not covered the ♡Q with the ♡K: declarer would either have to shorten his trumps in order to return to hand, or allow South to score a club ruff.

On this layout declarer can improve his chances by leading the ♠10 at Trick 5; it doesn't matter whether North covers, although it is best to do so. The difference is that there is another trump left in dummy when declarer leads the ♡Q, so it does not help South to refuse to cover; declarer can drive out the ♡J and eventually discard a losing spade on a club winner.

There is one more intriguing aspect to this deal; if South were to switch to the ♡K at Trick 3, declarer would have no legitimate way to come to more than nine tricks.

Closed Room

West	North	East	South
Ross	Bergen	Pender	Cohen
	1◇	pass	1♠
pass	2♠	pass	3♠
all pass			

On this layout declarer was always struggling, and Cohen did well to take eight tricks, down one, -50. ROSENKRANZ gained 12 IMPs.

Board 13. Both Vul.

```
              ♠ A 9 8 6
              ♡ 10 8 7 6 5 2
              ◇ 6
              ♣ K 8
♠ Q 10 7 2              ♠ K 4
♡ 9 3          N         ♡ A Q J
◇ A J 10 5 3  W   E      ◇ K Q 8 4
♣ 10 2          S        ♣ J 9 6 5
              ♠ J 5 3
              ♡ K 4
              ◇ 9 7 2
              ♣ A Q 7 4 3
```

Open Room

West	North	East	South
Meckstroth	Martel	Rodwell	Stansby
	pass	1NT	pass
2♣[1]	pass	2◇[2]	pass
2♠[3]	pass	2NT	pass
3NT	all pass		

1. Asking for a five-card major.
2. None.
3. Four spades, at best invitational.

South led the ♣4 and North won with the king. As declarer was marked with four or five clubs from the spots on display, Martel switched accurately to a heart, which ensured that the defenders would be able to take three clubs, a heart and a spade; one down, -100.

Had North returned a club at Trick 2, South would have needed to switch to a spade or a diamond, which is far from obvious.

Closed Room

West	North	East	South
Ross	Bergen	Pender	Cohen
	2♡	2NT	pass
3♣[1]	pass	3◇[2]	pass
3NT	all pass		

1. Stayman.
2. No four- or five-card major.

Although Cohen was well aware of Bergen's penchant for opening all sorts of hands with a weak two-bid, he hoped for a decent suit at the prevailing vulnerability and so led the ♡K against 3NT. Declarer won and could set up his ninth trick in spades. That was +600, and another 12 IMPs for SHEINWOLD.

After a busy first segment, SHEINWOLD led by 26 IMPs, 51-25.

Larry Cohen

Set Two (Boards 17-32)

Lest we forget how beautiful bridge can be, consider this deal:

Board 23. Both Vul.

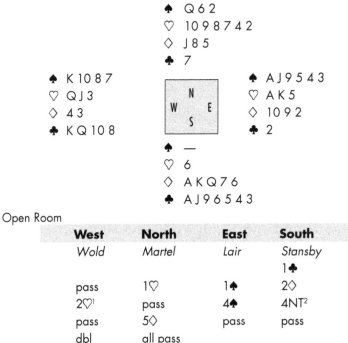

```
                    ♠ Q 6 2
                    ♡ 10 9 8 7 4 2
                    ◊ J 8 5
                    ♣ 7
  ♠ K 10 8 7                        ♠ A J 9 5 4 3
  ♡ Q J 3            N              ♡ A K 5
  ◊ 4 3          W       E          ◊ 10 9 2
  ♣ K Q 10 8         S              ♣ 2
                    ♠ —
                    ♡ 6
                    ◊ A K Q 7 6
                    ♣ A J 9 6 5 4 3
```

Open Room

West	North	East	South
Wold	Martel	Lair	Stansby
			1♣
pass	1♡	1♠	2◊
2♡[1]	pass	4♠	4NT[2]
pass	5◊	pass	pass
dbl	all pass		

1. Good raise in spades.
2. Confirming the fifth diamond.

On deals of this type (on which declarer, with a big two-suiter, eventually plays in his shorter suit), traditional wisdom advocates a forcing defense, threatening declarer with the loss of control before he can enjoy the long suit. With an imposing holding in declarer's long suit it is perhaps more intuitive to lead trumps to prevent declarer from establishing that important suit with ruffs in the shorter-trump hand, and that is the strategy Wold adopted. Stansby won with dummy's ◊J, played the ♣A and ruffed a club with the ◊8. Lair overruffed and continued with the ♡A and ♡K. Declarer ruffed and then ruffed a club, East overruffing a second time and playing a spade. Declarer ruffed, drew West's lone outstanding trump, and conceded a club (in effect losing *three* club tricks) with a long trump remaining to use the long clubs: two down, -500.

Had Stansby divined the minor-suit layout, he could have saved a 300-point trick by winning the first trump in hand, playing the ♣A, ruffing a club with the jack, and cashing two high trumps. Then, retaining trump control, he could concede two clubs and, eventually, a heart.

Closed Room

	West	North	East	South
	Wolff	Cohen	Hamman	Bergen
				1♣
	pass	1♡	2♠[1]	3♢
	4♠	pass	pass	4NT[2]
	pass	5♢	dbl	all pass

1. Intermediate.
2. Confirming the fifth diamond.

Hamman and Wolff probably led trumps against games and slams far less often than most expert partnerships, and here Wolff relied on his picture of the hand to try to shorten declarer's trumps by leading spades. Bergen ruffed East's jack, and played the ♣A, followed by a club ruff with the eight. If East makes the reflex play of overruffing to continue the force, declarer counters by ruffing a club with the jack, drawing the remaining trumps in two rounds, and conceding a club while retaining a controlling trump to cash the established clubs, going just one down.

But Hamman, appreciating that it is rarely right for the defender with the long trumps to overruff when declarer is struggling to establish a long side suit, backed his judgment by allowing the ♢8 to win the trick. Declarer called for a heart, but Hamman won and played a second spade. Declarer ruffed and ruffed a club with the ♢J. He ruffed a heart and ruffed another club, but now East could overruff and play a third spade. Declarer could take only eight tricks (five trumps in hand, the ♣A and two club ruffs in dummy) for three down, -800 and 7 IMPs for SHEINWOLD.

Perhaps you will not be surprised to learn that this remains one of my all-time favorite deals!

Bob Hamman

Board 26. Both Vul.

```
                    ♠ Q 9 6 4
                    ♡ Q J 10 5 3
                    ◊ 5
                    ♣ K 10 8
    ♠ 3 2                          ♠ A K J 5
    ♡ 9 8 7 6          N           ♡ A 4
    ◊ 10 9 6        W   E          ◊ K 2
    ♣ J 5 4 2          S           ♣ Q 9 7 6 3
                    ♠ 10 8 7
                    ♡ K 2
                    ◊ A Q J 8 7 4 3
                    ♣ A
```

Open Room

West	North	East	South
Wold	Martel	Lair	Stansby
		1♣	1◊
pass	1♡	1♠	3◊
pass	3NT	all pass	

There was no defeating this pushy vulnerable game, with the East-West layout meeting any possible North-South requirement; bidding 3NT was the main task. The final result was +630, when Lair eventually led a third round of spades.

Closed Room

West	North	East	South
Wolff	Cohen	Hamman	Bergen
		1NT[1]	dbl
2♣	pass	2♠	3◊
pass	3♡	all pass	

1. Normally 15-17 but possibly 13-14 with 3=3=3=4 or 3=3=2=5 pattern

Hamman's 1NT has much to recommend it, especially in his Blue Club methods: he got his strength across and avoided any complications arising from a heavy 1♠ or a sub-minimum strong club or ugly 2♣ opening. There is no indication that Wolff's 2♣ was other than natural, but Hamman took the opportunity to show his lead-worthy spades on the way to 3♣. Whether North-South were on firm ground after Cohen passed 2♣ is far from clear, but 3♡ was a better contract than 3NT, albeit with a much lower upside.

Again, Hamman conducted a first-class defense: he led the ♠K, but did not continue to give Wolff a ruff. He switched to a club, ducked dummy's ♡K, took the heart continuation and switched to the ◊K, stranding declarer in dummy while cutting his communications. Had Cohen guessed the trump position, he could have played both the ◊Q and ◊J, discarding a club and a spade. Instead, he discarded a club and then tried a spade, playing West for the jack. East took two spade winners and gave West a fourth-round spade ruff for the setting trick. One down, -100, 12 more IMPs to SHEINWOLD.

Board 27. Neither Vul

```
                    ♠ K 7 5 3 2
                    ♡ 8
                    ◊ A 2
                    ♣ Q 10 4 3 2
  ♠ Q J 10                          ♠ 8 4
  ♡ Q J 10 7          N             ♡ A K 2
  ◊ K J 3         W       E         ◊ Q 10 8 7 5
  ♣ J 9 8             S             ♣ 7 6 5
                    ♠ A 9 6
                    ♡ 9 6 5 4 3
                    ◊ 9 6 4
                    ♣ A K
```

Open Room

West	North	East	South
Wold	Martel	Lair	Stansby
			pass
pass	2♠[1]	pass	2NT[2]
pass	3♡[3]	pass	4♠
all pass			

1. Weak two-bid.
2. Artificial game try.
3. Shortness in hearts.

Martel's short and spotless third-seat weak two-bid would not be found in the trade literature, not even in Marty Bergen's advice to the lovelorn column in the ACBL *Bulletin*, but it worked a treat here: 4♠ was cold for +420. Curiously, it may have been easier for North-South to reach game after Stansby's initial pass than if he had opened everyone's three-honor-tricks 1♡ or a weak notrump.

Closed Room

	West	North	East	South
	Wolff	Cohen	Hamman	Bergen
				1♡
	pass	1♠	pass	1NT
	pass	3♣[1]	all pass	

1. The end, often four spades and at least six clubs.

That bridge can be a strange game was highlighted by the events in this room. Bergen and Cohen had made a living out of their unusual (to say the least) preempts, but here Cohen was himself preempted out of the opportunity to use one *à la* Martel by Bergen's opening bid. Cohen might well still have bid game had Bergen raised to 2♠, as many systems would advocate. But over the 11-13 1NT rebid here he chose to give up on game; his 3♣ did not invite correction, which explains Bergen's pass. That was +130, 8 IMPs to SHEINWOLD.

Board 32. E-W Vul.

```
    ♠ A K J 6 4              ♠ 3
    ♡ Q 5          N         ♡ A J 9 8 4 3
    ◇ A J 10 8 7  W   E      ◇ Q 9
    ♣ 6               S      ♣ A J 9 8
```

West	East
Wold	Lair
1♠	2♡
3◇	3♡
4NT*	5♡*
6♡	pass

Playing 2/1 GF, Wold knew he was facing at least an opening bid and chose Blackwood as the easiest way to reach a possibly cold seven; he was not going to stop short of six.

Eddie Wold

West	East
Wolff	Hamman
1◊	1♡
2♠	3♣*
3◊	3♡
4♡	pass

Playing four-card majors and canapé in a strong club system, Wolff's first three bids described 5-5 in a good hand not quite strong enough to open 1♣, but whether his raise to 4♡ suggested his actual shape and such strong heart support is not as clear. (Forty years later West would probably bid 4♣ over 3♡, unambiguously a slam try in hearts.) Hamman knew slam could not be excellent and did the right thing on the actual lie of the cards by passing, as there was no winning line available for twelve tricks. Eleven tricks in 4♡ was worth +650 while 6♡ scored -100, so SHEINWOLD gained 13 IMPs and won the set 56-26 to lead in the match by 56, 107-51.

Set Three (Boards 33-48)

Spoiler alert: in case you have begun to wonder why this match is being included in a book about 'close encounters', you may soon be unable to resist the urge to exclaim 'Seriously?' to anyone who will listen.

Board 34. N-S Vul.

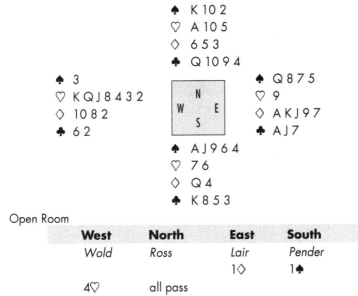

```
                    ♠ K 10 2
                    ♡ A 10 5
                    ◇ 6 5 3
                    ♣ Q 10 9 4
   ♠ 3                          ♠ Q 8 7 5
   ♡ K Q J 8 4 3 2        N     ♡ 9
   ◇ 10 8 2           W       E ◇ A K J 9 7
   ♣ 6 2                   S     ♣ A J 7
                    ♠ A J 9 6 4
                    ♡ 7 6
                    ◇ Q 4
                    ♣ K 8 5 3
```

Open Room

West	North	East	South
Wold	Ross	Lair	Pender
		1◇	1♠
4♡	all pass		

Ross, who had resisted the temptation to gamble 4♠, led the ♠K, hoping to hold the lead should a switch seem opportune. When Pender discouraged with the ♠6 (reverse attitude), Ross continued his very thoughtful defense by switching to the ♣Q. Declarer won with dummy's ace and played a heart to the king and ace. North continued with the ♣10, ducked, and played a third club. Declarer in due course took a losing diamond finesse for -50. Although South would have a thin overcall at unfavorable vulnerability without the ◇Q, he was much more likely to appreciate diamond shortness than a doubleton queen in RHO's suit, and Ross's carding pointed to Pender's hand being 6=2=1=4 or 5=2=1=5.

Closed Room

West	North	East	South
Wolff	Rodwell	Hamman	Meckstroth
		1♠[1]	pass
2♡[2]	pass	3◇[3]	pass
3♡	pass	3NT	pass
4♡	all pass		

1. Possible canapé.
2. Forcing for one round.
3. Longer diamonds than spades.

Hamman's 1♠ opening kept North-South out of the auction. Rodwell led the ♣10 and when declarer played low from dummy, Meckstroth, with a nasty decision (the ten was from either a Q109 or a ten-high holding) misguessed by winning with the king. He now played the ♠A and another spade. Declarer ruffed and forced out the ♡A. When North continued with a club, Wolff permitted himself a small chuckle, and rejected the finesse. When he later ruffed another spade the king fell, so he had a discard for his third diamond after all: +420 and 10 IMPs to SHEINWOLD.

As long as South was not dealt the well-guarded ♢Q, Wolff was not going to have to guess diamonds even if the ♠K were not coming down: North, with the ♣Q (when finessing the jack would have worked) and three low diamonds, would be exposed to a show-up squeeze to reveal the diamond position on the run of the trumps.

Bobby Wolff

Then SHEINWOLD gained another 12 IMPs thanks to some remarkable luck: Hamman-Wolff reached and made an unlikely vulnerable 5♢ that required no more than two combined losers from KJ1073 opposite 62 in trumps and QJ opposite A10963 in clubs, while Wold-Lair had to fail in a superior 4♠ on a 5-2 fit when trumps broke 5-1. Then came Board 37, which could have gone the other way:

Board 37. North-South Vul.

```
                        ♠ K 10 9 5
                        ♡ K 5
                        ◇ 10 5
                        ♣ A J 8 5 4
    ♠ 8 7 4 2                              ♠ A 3
    ♡ Q J 10 6 2          N               ♡ 9 8 7 4 3
    ◇ 3               W       E           ◇ K J 7 2
    ♣ K Q 3               S               ♣ 10 2
                        ♠ Q J 6
                        ♡ A
                        ◇ A Q 9 8 6 4
                        ♣ 9 7 6
```

Open Room

West	North	East	South
Wold	Ross	Lair	Pender
	pass	pass	1◇
2♡	dbl*	5♡	dbl
all pass			

I can understand Wold's atypical weak jump overcall at favorable colors, but as it was the catalyst for Lair to bounce to 5♡, down three doubled, -500, saving against who knew what — and probably nothing — Wold must take responsibility for this one.

Closed Room

West	North	East	South
Wolff	Rodwell	Hamman	Meckstroth
	1◇[1]	1♡	2◇[2]
4♡	pass	pass	5◇
pass	pass	dbl	all pass

1. 2+ diamonds, 10-15.
2. Like a standard 2/1 response.

The Closed Room auction was not of the same species, but East-West were also up to a high level in hearts in a hurry, nudging South into 5◇ when North did not double 4♡. Hamman thought he might have a trump trick or two when he doubled even though 1◇ didn't mean much; he was surely disappointed to see all those trumps come down in dummy. Rodwell won the heart lead (deuce from Wolff) and led the ♣6 to the eight, ten and ace. A club would have been best now, but Hamman returned his remaining spade, declarer overtaking in hand to lead the ◊10. Because of the blocked spade position, declarer had no safe way back to hand without playing clubs, so on the existing lie, Hamman could cover with profit. When he did not, Rodwell could have made his contract by running the ten (second diamond finesse, ◊A, spade). One club would go on the ♡K, another on the fourth spade. Unfortunately for ROSENKRANZ, Rodwell called for dummy's ◊Q and cashed the ace, and so lost two trumps and the ♠A for one down, -200. That was 12 IMPs more to SHEINWOLD, part of the run that extended the lead to 100 IMPs, 155-55.

Board 41. E-W Vul.

```
              ♠ A K Q 9 4 3
              ♡ A 9 6 4 3
              ◊ —
              ♣ A 10
♠ J 7 2                        ♠ 10
♡ Q 5            N             ♡ J 10 8 7 2
◊ K Q J 8 7 5 2  W   E         ◊ 4 3
♣ 7              S             ♣ Q J 6 4 3
              ♠ 8 6 5
              ♡ K
              ◊ A 10 9 6
              ♣ K 9 8 5 2
```

Open Room

West	North	East	South
Wold	Ross	Lair	Pender
	2♣[1]	pass	2NT[2]
pass	3♠	pass	4NT[3]
pass	5◊[4]	pass	5♡[5]
pass	5NT[6]	pass	6◊[7]
pass	7♠	all pass	

1. Strong.
2. Four controls (A=2; K=1).
3. RKCB for spades.
4. Four keycards.
5. Asking for the ♠Q.
6. The ♠Q, no side king.
7. Grand slam try.

The final 7♠ was an excellent contract, and with East-West silent in the auction, Ross took a straightforward line after East led the ♡J. He won with dummy's king, came to hand with a trump, ruffed a heart (West following with the queen) ruffed a diamond, and ruffed another heart with dummy's ♠8. He needed hearts 4-3 or an opponent with only two hearts unable to overruff the eight after one round of trumps. Wold's overruff was a cruel blow; one down, -50.

Closed Room

	West	North	East	South
	Wolff	Rodwell	Hamman	Meckstroth
		1♣[1]	pass	2♣
	2◇	2♠[2]	pass	3♣[3]
	pass	3♡	pass	3♠
	pass	4♣[4]	pass	4◇[5]
	pass	4NT[6]	pass	5♡
	pass	5NT[8]	pass	6♡[9]
	pass	6♠	all pass	

1. Strong.
2. Natural, 'support ask'.
3. Three spades, no top honor.
4-5. Control bids.
6. RKCB for spades.
7. One keycard.
8. King ask.
9. Two kings.

As 5NT invited a grand slam, Meckstroth might well have bid seven on the strength of his holding in Rodwell's second suit. Stopping at six on hands of this type (twelve 'sure' winners with good play for thirteen) was not in keeping with their slam strategy at that time, but it's possible that they were influenced by the recent run of deals in which optimism had not worked well for them.

In 6♠, Rodwell played as safely as possible for twelve tricks. He ruffed only one heart and ran his trumps, squeezing East in hearts and clubs for a thirteenth trick that would have been worth considerably more to Ross at the other table. That was +1010 for Rodwell and 14 IMPs to ROSENKRANZ.

The bleeding had stopped, but only for a moment.

Board 44. N-S Vul.

```
                    ♠ 8
                    ♡ 9 4
                    ♦ A 8 5 3
                    ♣ Q J 10 8 3 2
♠ J 10 6 4                          ♠ 9 3 2
♡ —                    N            ♡ A Q 8 7 5 3
♦ K Q 9 6 2        W     E          ♦ J 4
♣ K 7 5 4              S            ♣ A 9
                    ♠ A K Q 7 5
                    ♡ K J 10 6 2
                    ♦ 10 7
                    ♣ 6
```

Open Room

West	North	East	South
Wold	*Ross*	*Lair*	*Pender*
pass	pass	1♡	1♠
dbl*	2♣	2♡	dbl
redbl	all pass		

Wold's redouble was intended as a rescue attempt, but apparently Lair missed that subtlety. He could not avoid the loss of eight tricks in 2♡ redoubled to finish three down, -1000.

As the cards lie, West does best to escape to 2NT ('Natural — right, partner?'). There are always seven tricks thanks to the favorable position in diamonds, and the defenders need to be careful to avoid conceding an eighth.

Closed Room

West	North	East	South
Wolff	*Rodwell*	*Hamman*	*Meckstroth*
pass	pass	1♡	1♠
dbl*	2♣	2♡	dbl
3♦	dbl	all pass	

Here, too, West decided not to play in 2♡ doubled, relying on South to know what he was doing. North led his spade against Wolff's 3♦ (a rather remarkable call) doubled, and South took three tricks in the suit, North discarding two hearts. The heart switch was ruffed, declarer releasing a club, and back came the ♣Q, declarer winning with dummy's ♣A and accurately playing a second club. South ruffed and played a heart, but declarer ruffed with the nine, and North's ace of trumps was the defenders' last trick. Two down, -300, but 12 IMPs to SHEINWOLD, which extended the lead to 110 IMPs, the high-water mark in the match so far.

For what it's worth, perhaps East should not be so keen to volunteer 2♡ on a minimum hand with a poor internal suit and a terrible holding in his LHO's suit, especially when North is offering to play in one of West's announced suits.

Board 48. E-W Vul.

```
              ♠ J 3
              ♡ J 7
              ◇ 10 9 8 7 6 3 2
              ♣ 9 6
  ♠ K Q 8 7 5 4              ♠ A 10 9 2
  ♡ Q 10 8         N          ♡ A K 6 2
  ◇ K Q       W       E       ◇ A J
  ♣ A 8            S          ♣ J 3 2
              ♠ 6
              ♡ 9 5 4 3
              ◇ 5 4
              ♣ K Q 10 7 5 4
```

Open Room

West	North	East	South
Wold	Ross	Lair	Pender
1♠	pass	2NT[1]	3♣
3♠[2]	pass	3NT[3]	pass
4♣[4]	pass	4NT[5]	pass
5♠[6]	pass	6♣[7]	pass
7♠	all pass		

1. Game-forcing raise.
2. Extras, no shortness.
3. Slam try.
4. Control bid.
5. RKCB for spades.
6. Two keycards + ♠Q.
7. Grand slam try.

Declarer won the club lead, drew trumps and played a high heart from each hand, claiming when the jack fell, +2210.

Closed Room

West	North	East	South
Wolff	*Rodwell*	*Hamman*	*Meckstroth*
1♠	1NT[1]	dbl	3♣
3♠	pass	5♠	pass
6♣	pass	6♠	7♣
dbl	all pass		

1. 15-17 natural, or 'comic' (in the very weak jump overcall family).

Although it was soon clear to everyone that Rodwell was joking, Hamman was unwilling to try for seven without a source of tricks, so SHEINWOLD was going to lose 13 IMPs had Meckstroth passed 6♠. Instead, 7♣ gave Wolff a chance to pass the final word to Hamman, but with a balanced hand and slow values he was unwilling to reopen a partnership discussion that had been mutually concluded. The defense allowed Meckstroth to take a heart trick to escape for seven down, which in the old money in circulation in 1985 was a mere -1300; 14 IMPs to ROSENKRANZ.

The last few results in that set had been positive for the trailing team, who lost the stanza 38-72 and would start the fourth segment 'only' 90 IMPs behind, 89-179.

Set Four (Boards 49-64)

Having witnessed so many dramatic comebacks over the years, experience has taught us that the momentum in a match can change in a heartbeat, and that virtually no lead is safe when strong, tenacious teams are involved. The previous set had ended on a positive note for ROSENKRANZ, so perhaps the tide had started to turn. There was one more segment to play on the first day.

Board 49. Neither Vul.

```
              ♠ K J 10 6 5 4
              ♡ A 6 5
              ◇ A Q 4
              ♣ 3
              ┌──────────┐
              └──────────┘
              ♠ 3 2
              ♡ 9 8 3
              ◇ K J 10 5
              ♣ A K Q 6
```

Open Room

West	North	East	South
Cohen	Pender	Bergen	Ross
	1♠	pass	2◇
pass	3◇	pass	4♣
pass	4♡	pass	4NT
pass	5♠	pass	6◇
dbl	all pass		

The undeniably obscure 6◇ ran into an enterprising double, and, with trumps 5-1 and ♠AQ97 offside, went two down, -300.

Closed Room

West	North	East	South
Martel	Rodwell	Stansby	Meckstroth
	1♠	pass	2♣
pass	2♠¹	pass	4♠
all pass			

1. 6+ spades.

Meckstroth, facing a limited opening bid with long spades, was not tempted to look beyond 4♠. The spade layout that was fatal for 6◇ was not so here, and 4♠ was unbreakable, so +420, 12 IMPs to ROSENKRANZ, 101-179.

There were plenty of opportunities for ROSENKRANZ's gladiators over the next nine deals, but they left a substantial number of IMPs (mostly in the card play, somewhat surprisingly) on the table, SHEINWOLD gaining a net 5 IMPs.

But then ROSENKRANZ rallied. This was a big deal:

Board 60. N-S Vul.

```
                 ♠ K 5 2
                 ♡ K 10 4
                 ◇ Q 6 4
                 ♣ Q J 10 6
   ♠ A 8                          ♠ Q 10 9 6 3
   ♡ Q J 7           N            ♡ 9 8 5 3
   ◇ K J 5 3     W       E        ◇ A 9
   ♣ K 8 4 3         S            ♣ A 2
                 ♠ J 7 4
                 ♡ A 6 2
                 ◇ 10 8 7 2
                 ♣ 9 7 5
```

Open Room

West	North	East	South
Cohen	Pender	Bergen	Ross
1NT[1]	pass	2♣[2]	pass
2◇[3]	pass	3♡[4]	pass
3NT	all pass		

1. 14-16.
2. Stayman.
3. No major.
4. Four hearts and five spades.

North led the ♣Q, and declarer won with dummy's ace, Ross following with the nine, denying the ten and nominally discouraging. With a more fluid entry position, Cohen might have played spades differently, but here had to be content with low to the ace, low to the queen (catering to the extra chance of doubleton jack in South's hand) and a third round, hoping for a 3-3 split, discarding a diamond.

Today, largely thanks to Jean-Marc Roudinesco's *Dictionary of Suit Combinations* and, more recently, Fred Gitelman's monthly feature in *The Bridge World* on card combinations, every interested player knows that, assuming unlimited entries, the correct technical line for four tricks with this combination is to start with dummy's queen, which offers a 40.37% chance for success.

Pender won the third spade with the king and switched to a low diamond, presenting declarer with his ninth trick, +400. As the lead of the ♣Q would most often be from a QJ10 holding, it's surprising that Ross would not encourage a continuation at Trick 1, especially as signaling with the nine could waste a useful card.

Reverse or upside-down carding has become much more popular since then, although some favor different signaling approaches for attitude and count situations. There is a strong case for using standard signals at Trick 1 against notrump contracts (with exceptions when third hand is known to have a long suit): squandering a significant card to send a clear discouraging signal can be costly, and so can retaining a blocking high card in positions such as third hand's A10x on an honor lead from (say) KQ9x with two low in dummy.

Closed Room

West	North	East	South
Martel	Rodwell	Stansby	Meckstroth
1NT[1]	pass	2♣[2]	pass
2♢[3]	pass	2♠[4]	pass
2NT	pass	3NT	all pass

1. 12-14.
2. Stayman.
3. No major.
4. Invitational, 5+ spades.

Martel won the club lead in hand, South giving reverse count with the nine, and played spades the same way that Cohen did at the other table, also releasing a diamond on the third round. However, with the blank ♣A visible in dummy, Rodwell had an easy low-club continuation. Declarer won and cashed the spades, throwing his clubs while South parted with his red deuces to keep the ♣7. North, who was under some pressure, discarded a diamond and a heart in normal tempo. There was no reason for declarer to play for the actual diamond position; when he cashed the ace and finessed the jack he was two down, -100 and 11 IMPs the poorer. In the abstract, North needs to exit with the ♣J or ♣10. Then he can discard two hearts on the spades.

On Board 62, with neither side vulnerable, East was dealt:

♠ A K J 10 9 8 ♡ 8 6 3 ♢ 3 ♣ 10 8 6

Stansby, who was looking at everyone's textbook weak two-bid, opened 2♠. Bergen, who had *at least* one spade more than he could have for one of *his* weak twos (a 2♢ opening would show a weak 2♠), opened 3♢, a two-under transfer preempt in spades. Which of those actions do you like better?

The full deal follows:

Board 62. Neither Vul.

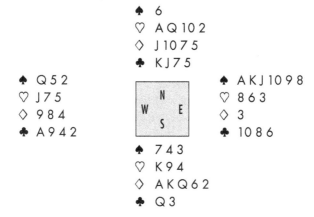

```
                    ♠ 6
                    ♡ A Q 10 2
                    ◇ J 10 7 5
                    ♣ K J 7 5
   ♠ Q 5 2                            ♠ A K J 10 9 8
   ♡ J 7 5          ┌─────────┐       ♡ 8 6 3
   ◇ 9 8 4          │    N    │       ◇ 3
   ♣ A 9 4 2        │ W     E │       ♣ 10 8 6
                    │    S    │
                    └─────────┘
                    ♠ 7 4 3
                    ♡ K 9 4
                    ◇ A K Q 6 2
                    ♣ Q 3
```

Over 3◇ Ross did not have an accurate system bid (double would have been takeout of spades) so he passed, and over Cohen's 3♠ Pender thought he needed a bit more to double, facing a partner who did not act over 3◇. So 3♠ was passed out for two down, -100.

In the other room, over 2♠, Meckstroth risked a 3◇ overcall and soon reached the cold 5◇; +400. That was 7 more IMPs to ROSENKRANZ, who had finished the set on a run of 41 unanswered IMPs, won it 60-24, and trailed at the halfway mark of the match by only 149-203. If it was possible to retire for the night happy to be 54 IMPs behind, ROSENKRANZ's men were all smiles!

Jeff Meckstroth

Set Five (Boards 65-80)

The first deal of the fresh set did not stem the previous evening's tide:

Board 65. Neither Vul.

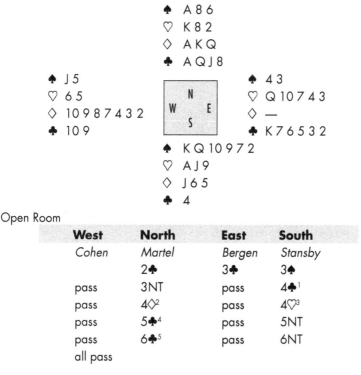

```
              ♠ A 8 6
              ♡ K 8 2
              ◇ A K Q
              ♣ A Q J 8
♠ J 5                        ♠ 4 3
♡ 6 5              N         ♡ Q 10 7 4 3
◇ 10 9 8 7 4 3 2   W   E     ◇ —
♣ 10 9                 S     ♣ K 7 6 5 3 2
              ♠ K Q 10 9 7 2
              ♡ A J 9
              ◇ J 6 5
              ♣ 4
```

Open Room

West	North	East	South
Cohen	Martel	Bergen	Stansby
	2♣	3♣	3♠
pass	3NT	pass	4♣[1]
pass	4◇[2]	pass	4♡[3]
pass	5♣[4]	pass	5NT
pass	6♣[5]	pass	6NT
all pass			

1-5. Control bids for spades.

Bergen's fearless (and spotless) 3♣ did not affect the early auction for North-South, but when Stansby showed interest in a grand slam with his 5NT bid, Martel could hardly do more than cooperate with a six-level try, with the ♣K surely on his left. Perhaps 6♣ should have been enough for Stansby, but the partnership stopped short anyway, +1020 for 6NT+1.

On this auction, 7♠ would be excellent except for the small matter of the possible diamond ruff at Trick 1, but were East to double a putative 7♠, North or South might well run to 7NT. Bergen's 3♣, although it seemed to pinpoint the location of the ♣K, had the effect of wrong-siding his opponents' suit grand slam. Today, we would expect many expert pairs to play transfers over a 3♣ overcall and reach the superior 7♠ from the strong side. Then, absent any bidding by East-West, declarer would try to ruff out the ♣K tripleton before playing hearts for three tricks (here East is caught in a show-up squeeze between hearts and clubs).

Lew Stansby

Closed Room

West	North	East	South
Wolff	Lair	Hamman	Wold
	2NT	pass	4♡[1]
pass	4♠	pass	4NT[2]
pass	5♣[3]	pass	5♡[4]
pass	7♠	all pass	

1. Transfer.
2. RKCB for spades.
3. Three keycards.
4. Grand slam try, all keys plus the ♠Q on board.

Lair won the trump lead, drew a second round, played the ♣A, and ruffed a club, West following nine-ten. When declarer cashed three rounds of diamonds, East, believing his partner's carding indicated a third club, discarded three small clubs. When declarer played the ♣Q he knew the king would appear, and he could claim, +1510, which gave ROSENKRANZ 10 IMPs. Unless declarer convinces himself to do something as drastic as the backward finesse in hearts when East reveals his void, it doesn't matter how East discards: he won't be able to keep the ♣K and three hearts in the endgame.

Board 66. N-S Vul.

```
                    ♠ Q 6 4
                    ♡ K Q J 9 4 3
                    ◇ J 8 3
                    ♣ J
    ♠ A 5 3                        ♠ J 10 8 7 2
    ♡ A                N            ♡ 8 7 6 5 2
    ◇ A K 5 4 2    W       E        ◇ Q 6
    ♣ A 9 6 5          S            ♣ 7
                    ♠ K 9
                    ♡ 10
                    ◇ 10 9 7
                    ♣ K Q 10 8 4 3 2
```

Open Room

West	North	East	South
Cohen	Martel	Bergen	Stansby
		2◇¹	pass
2♡²	pass	2♠³	pass
pass!	3♡	pass	pass
dbl	pass	pass	4♣
dbl	all pass		

1. Transfer preempt in spades.
2. Relay.
3. A bad hand.

Bergen and Cohen described their two-level two-under preempts as: 'five or more cards; 0-11; we use this bid very freely'. Still, it was difficult to anticipate Cohen's decision to quit (very) short of game: apparently Bergen's hand could have been even worse (he had once opened a 4-3-3-3 yarborough with a two-bid in a serious IMP-scored event)! When Martel (who needed a better hand to double the artificial 2♡ response) dared to reopen on the strength of his strong suit, Cohen decided to try for a significant penalty rather than settle for +140-odd in 3♠; bidding game on the rebound was not on his radar. And right he was: 3♡ doubled was going for 800, and when Stansby judged to escape the frying pan, he soon realized that he had stepped into a raging fire. Cohen led the ◇A, and when Bergen risked the queen (something he could not afford were the jack not visible in dummy), Cohen cashed the ♡A, ◇K and ♣A before giving East a diamond ruff. When Bergen returned a heart, Stansby ruffed high; Cohen discarded, establishing a second natural trump trick for himself. That was four down, -1100.

Chip Martel

Closed Room

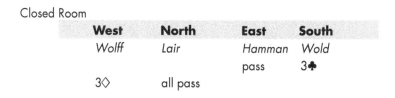

West	North	East	South
Wolff	Lair	Hamman	Wold
		pass	3♣
3◇	all pass		

Wold's 3♣ opening gave Wolff a tricky bidding problem that he resolved with an imperfect overcall (internally weak short suit, heavy hand) that landed him in a makeable contract; 4♠ was not even a mirage on the horizon. Lair led the ♡K and declarer won, cashed the ♣A, and played a second club, discarding a heart from dummy when North ruffed in with the ◇8. Declarer took the ◇5 return with dummy's queen and continued with the ♠J, South following with the nine. Had Wolff played low, he would have been in command, but he took the ace and led a third club. North ruffed in with the ◇J and crossed to South's ♠K for a trump return, which left declarer with two black-suit losers, -50. Although it is comforting to know that nine tricks in the eminently makeable 3◇ would not have saved a single IMP, how much comfort can there be in a 15-IMP loss? Had Wolff opted to overcall 3NT (surely his second choice) only an impossible *low* heart opening lead by North would beat it legitimately.

Perhaps, over 3NT, it would be better for East to try for a major-suit contract, but without a significant sample of deals from actual play or a careful computer simulation, we'd all be relying on personal experience or gut feeling to make that type of decision.

Board 67. E-W Vul.

```
              ♠ A 9 6
              ♡ A J 9 7 5
              ◇ 8 5
              ♣ A Q 4
   ♠ 8 4                        ♠ K J 2
   ♡ 3 2          N            ♡ Q 8
   ◇ A K Q 4 3 2  W   E        ◇ J 10 7 6
   ♣ 8 6 3          S          ♣ K J 10 9
              ♠ Q 10 7 5 3
              ♡ K 10 6 4
              ◇ 9
              ♣ 7 5 2
```

Open Room

West	North	East	South
Cohen	Martel	Bergen	Stansby
			pass
2NT[1]	dbl	4◇	all pass

1. Transfer preempt to diamonds.

Martel's double was takeout of diamonds. Stansby had a promising hand, but felt he needed a second move from partner to have a good play for game. In the event, 4◇ was down one, -50.

Closed Room

West	North	East	South
Wolff	Lair	Hamman	Wold
			pass
pass	1♡	pass	4♡
all pass			

Once Wolff passed in second seat (he did not have a natural weak 2◇ available and 3◇ was not his style), there was no further opportunity to impede North-South. Today, similarly constrained strong clubbers would probably open a 2+ 1◇.

Against 4♡, Hamman led the ♣J, which ran around to the queen. Lair demonstrated that he could make his game without a winning guess in spades (the 75% line of two finesses through West would not work on this layout). He conceded a diamond, took the club continuation, got trumps right, ruffed a diamond and exited in clubs, forcing whoever won to break spades or concede a meaningful ruff and discard. That was +420, and another 8 IMPs to ROSENKRANZ.

ROSENKRANZ also had the best of the next block of deals, and halfway through the set, SHEINWOLD's once-seemingly-unassailable lead had shrunk to just 13 IMPs.

Board 74. Both Vul.

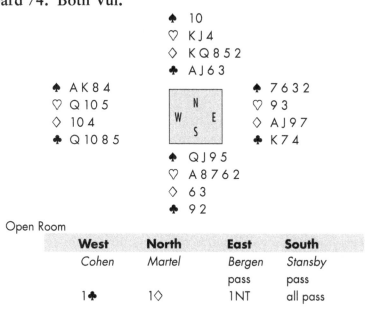

```
              ♠ 10
              ♡ K J 4
              ◇ K Q 8 5 2
              ♣ A J 6 3
♠ A K 8 4                    ♠ 7 6 3 2
♡ Q 10 5           N         ♡ 9 3
◇ 10 4         W     E       ◇ A J 9 7
♣ Q 10 8 5         S         ♣ K 7 4
              ♠ Q J 9 5
              ♡ A 8 7 6 2
              ◇ 6 3
              ♣ 9 2
```

Open Room

West	North	East	South
Cohen	Martel	Bergen	Stansby
		pass	pass
1♣	1◇	1NT	all pass

Bergen's 1NT effectively blocked out South's majors; today, many pairs employ a variant of the responsive double in this position to indicate length in both unbid suits. Stansby led the ◇6 (four, queen, ace). Although the contract can be made at double dummy after the diamond lead with a big view in clubs, there was no reason to find that line and declarer came to six tricks: two spades, three diamonds and a club, -100.

Closed Room

West	North	East	South
Wolff	Lair	Hamman	Wold
		pass	pass
1♠	dbl	2♣	3♡
pass	4♡	all pass	

Wolff's four-card 1♠ opening created a different initial-action scenario for Lair, and, somewhat serendipitously, it was easy for North-South to locate their heart fit after North's routine takeout double. Lair would have been forgiven for passing 3♡, but when things are going well it is intuitive to resolve close decisions optimistically. West led the ♠K: ten, six, five. When he continued with a low spade declarer released a club from dummy and won in hand with the queen. A diamond to the queen held and, when declarer continued with a second round of the suit, East won with the jack and continued with a spade, covered by the jack and ace and ruffed in dummy. Declarer ruffed a diamond with the eight, and West overruffed to switch to the ♣10, effectively 'surrounding' dummy's ♣J had that been important. Wold called for dummy's ♣A, ruffed a diamond with the ace, played a trump to the jack, drew the remaining trumps with the king, and discarded his losing club on the long diamond for a delightful +620 and 11 IMPs to ROSENKRANZ. Only 2 IMPs separated the teams now — from a three-digit lead, SHEINWOLD was now hanging on by a fingernail.

West can do better by switching to a club at Trick 2. The ten is the technical play, but even the five is good enough, East winning with the king when declarer plays low from dummy and returning a club, which leaves declarer with too much to do. If East switches to a club at Trick 5, the defenders will be in control, though that is a tough play to find. However, if declarer discards a diamond from dummy at Trick 2, plays a heart to the jack, and continues with ace and another club, he will have the communications he needs to get home via a combination of a crossruff and the ruffing spade finesse.

Three deals later, ROSENKRANZ had erased the last dregs of the 110-IMP deficit (not without a bit of good luck, as a respectable Hamman-Wolff game failed while Bergen and Cohen's partscore succeeded) and assumed a 5-IMP lead. Would SHEINWOLD ever smile again?

Board 78. Neither Vul.

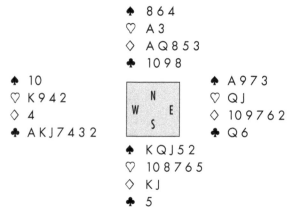

```
              ♠ 864
              ♡ A3
              ◇ AQ853
              ♣ 1098
♠ 10                        ♠ A973
♡ K942          N           ♡ QJ
◇ 4         W       E       ◇ 109762
♣ AKJ7432       S           ♣ Q6
              ♠ KQJ52
              ♡ 108765
              ◇ KJ
              ♣ 5
```

Open Room

West	North	East	South
Cohen	Martel	Bergen	Stansby
		pass	pass
1♣	1◇	1♠	dbl[1]
3♣	all pass		

1. Five hearts, usually tolerance for diamonds.

The communications theme we encountered on Board 74 appeared again on this lively deal. Declarer won the spade lead with dummy's ace and played a heart, North winning and switching to a club. It may not be apparent at first glance, but that shift held declarer to ten tricks: when he won in hand, crossed to dummy with a heart, ruffed a spade, and ruffed the ♡9 with the ♣Q, North discarded his remaining spade, so declarer could not leave dummy without suffering a trump promotion, +130.

Closed Room

West	North	East	South
Wolff	Lair	Hamman	Wold
		pass	pass
2♣[1]	pass	2◇[2]	2♠
3♡	3♠	pass	4♠
5♣	dbl	all pass	

1. Natural, limited.
2. Artificial constructive inquiry.

North led the ♠8. We've seen in the Open Room that starting hearts and taking major-suit ruffs would not see declarer home with eleven tricks: careful defense would lead to North scoring a late trump trick on a promotion.

If declarer assumes North has three spades, he can counter this defense — at Trick 5, after crossing to dummy's high heart, declarer leads dummy's ♠9 (or ♠7, if the ♠8 was led). South must cover, but declarer discards a diamond and now, as South has no more trumps, has the necessary timely transportation to return to hand after taking his heart ruff.

Wolff tried something different by calling for a low diamond from dummy at Trick 2. Wold put up the king and could have defeated the contract by switching to a trump (North plays a second trump when he wins the ♡A). However, as it did not appear that declarer was seeking a ruff in dummy, Wold played a 'safe' second spade; now declarer could ruff, organize a heart ruff, and return to hand later with a diamond ruff to draw trumps for +550 and 9 IMPs to SHEINWOLD.

It appears that a trump lead will defeat 5♣, as when North gets in with the ♡A he can play a second trump. However, declarer can run his trumps to reach this ending:

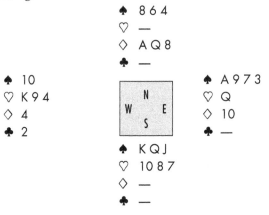

```
              ♠ 8 6 4
              ♡ —
              ◇ A Q 8
              ♣ —
 ♠ 10                        ♠ A 9 7 3
 ♡ K 9 4      ┌─────────┐    ♡ Q
 ◇ 4          │    N    │    ◇ 10
 ♣ 2          │ W     E │    ♣ —
              │    S    │
              └─────────┘
              ♠ K Q J
              ♡ 10 8 7
              ◇ —
              ♣ —
```

South, obliged to look after both majors, has been forced to discard his diamonds. Declarer plays ♠A, spade ruff, heart to the queen, and another spade, which leaves South on play to lead into declarer's heart tenace.

It does not help North to duck the first heart; although this removes an entry to dummy, declarer can cash all his trumps, the last of which will squeeze South, who will be down to ♠KQJ ♡108 and must release a spade, leading to the same endplay.

A note on partner management: some players do not use their time as dummy to relax and save energy, and might well notice on a deal like this one that there is a legitimate line that would work. Some of them would not resist sharing that information before moving on to the next deal, not appreciating that doing so might kill the buzz partner may have been enjoying from perpetrating a successful swindle. You can be sure that this did not happen in the Closed Room. It's obvious that you can't be a bridge expert without technical acumen, but the ability to remain silent is an underrated skill that is rarely mentioned.

Wolff, surely feeling invigorated by that result, on the next deal guessed 4♡ better against softer defense (+420) than Cohen faced in the same contract (doubled, -100) to bring in 11 IMPs. Although SHEINWOLD's troops lost the set by 40 IMPs, 25-65, the late mini-rally left them with a modest 14-IMP lead in the match, 228-214. Had the momentum turned again?

Set Six (Boards 81-96)

Board 83. E-W Vul.

```
                    ♠ K 6
                    ♡ 10 8 7 5 2
                    ◇ Q 10 7
                    ♣ 10 8 7
  ♠ A J 9                            ♠ Q 10 8 7 5 4 3
  ♡ A J 9 3            N             ♡ K
  ◇ 8 6 2         W        E         ◇ A J 4
  ♣ K 9 5             S             ♣ A J
                    ♠ 2
                    ♡ Q 6 4
                    ◇ K 9 5 3
                    ♣ Q 6 4 3 2
```

Open Room

West	North	East	South
Meckstroth	Martel	Rodwell	Stansby
			pass
1◇[1]	pass	1♠	pass
1NT	pass	2♣[2]	pass
2♡[3]	pass	2♠[4]	pass
3NT[5]	pass	4♣[6]	pass
4♠[7]	pass	6♠	all pass

1. Precision, 2+ diamonds.
2, 4, 6. Artificial ask.
3. 13-14 with three spades.
5. Some 4-3-3-3.
7. Two keycards for spades.

Stansby led a club around to the jack, so declarer had two discards for diamond losers and could soon claim, losing only one trick to the king of trumps, +1430.

Would declarer make 6♠ on a more challenging diamond lead? He can get home (and probably would, according to Edgar Kaplan, writing in *The Bridge World*) by combining his chances: ◇A, ♡K, ♣K, ♡A (diamond discard), heart ruff to fell the queen, trump to the ace to discard the remaining diamond loser on the established ♡J. Or he could simply take the spade finesse without risking an overruff in hearts or king-third of spades onside... and go down.

	West	North	East	South
	Ross	Lair	Pender	Wold
				pass
	1NT[1]	pass	2♡[2]	pass
	2♠	pass	4♠[3]	all pass

1. 12-14.
2. Transfer to spades.
3. Mild slam try.

North led a heart and declarer won with dummy's king and took a trump finesse; he had time to ruff out the ♡Q for twelve tricks and +680, but ROSENKRANZ gained 13 IMPs. So much for SHEINWOLD reclaiming the momentum!

Although SHEINWOLD recorded some gains over the course of this set, they were all small ones. In contrast, the runaway ROSENKRANZ express train steamed on with an extended run of major pickups.

Board 85. N-S Vul.

```
              ♠ A Q 9 8 6 4 3
              ♡ Q
              ◇ 5
              ♣ A Q 7 3
♠ K 10 5                         ♠ —
♡ K J 10 5         N             ♡ 9 7 4
◇ J 10 4      W         E        ◇ A Q 9 7 6 3 2
♣ 8 6 5           S             ♣ 10 4 2
              ♠ J 7 2
              ♡ A 8 6 3 2
              ◇ K 8
              ♣ K J 9
```

Open Room

	West	North	East	South
	Meckstroth	Martel	Rodwell	Stansby
		1♠	3◇	dbl*
	4◇	pass	pass	4♠
	pass	4NT[1]	pass	5◇[2]
	pass	5♠	all pass	

1. RKCB for spades.
2. One keycard.

South has a difficult hand to describe over 3◇ and Stansby tried to buy some time without overstating either major; as his 4♠ implied sound values, it was attractive for Martel to move forward by checking on keycards. The one-keycard response highlighted a subtle flaw in the convention: since South's keycard could be the ♠K (so that the red aces would be missing), North had no option but to sign off in 5♠; in the process he missed a 50% slam that was a favorite to succeed after East's preempt. Declarer's technical play in the trump suit — starting with dummy's jack — neutralized the threat posed by West's ten, +680.

Closed Room

	West	**North**	**East**	**South**
	Ross	Lair	Pender	Wold
		1♠	3◇	4♠
	pass	5♣¹	pass	5♡²
	dbl	6♠	all pass	

1-2.   Control bids.

As Wold's 4♠ (jump raise over a weak jump) suggested something more than merely competitive-raise strength, Lair was not inclined to take charge with Blackwood, but moved forward by showing his club control. When Wold cooperated, Lair, with control of the enemy suit, could hardly sign off in the jammed auction. He made his slam by duplicating Martel's textbook play in the trump suit; +1430 and 13 IMPs to ROSENKRANZ, reclaiming the lead, 242-240.

Mark Lair

Board 87. Both Vul.

```
                    ♠ 8 3
                    ♡ A 4 3
                    ◇ J 8
                    ♣ K Q J 10 9 7
    ♠ A 9                           ♠ K Q J
    ♡ Q 8 6 2          N            ♡ K J 10
    ◇ K Q 10 9 5   W       E        ◇ A 7 6 4 3
    ♣ 3 2              S            ♣ 5 4
                    ♠ 10 7 6 5 4 2
                    ♡ 9 7 5
                    ◇ 2
                    ♣ A 8 6
```

Open Room

West	North	East	South
Meckstroth	Martel	Rodwell	Stansby
			pass
1◇[1]	3♣	3◇[2]	5♣
pass	pass	dbl	all pass

1. Precision, 2+ diamonds.
2. Forcing.

Had Stansby not passed originally, Martel's 3♣ would perhaps have been more narrowly defined, but bouncing to the five-level without a fourth trump would always be a questionable strategy. There was nothing to the play in 5♣ doubled, declarer losing a diamond, two hearts and two spades for three down, -800. Not the end of the world if East-West could make a vulnerable game (and Stansby surely thought slam was a live possibility), but both the normal 5◇ and the less-normal 4♡ figured to be defeated without much difficulty.

Closed Room

West	North	East	South
Ross	Lair	Pender	Wold
			pass
pass	3♣	dbl	3◇[1]
dbl	4♣	pass	pass
4♡	pass	5◇	all pass

1. Theoretically natural.

Would Ross's 4♡ have made had Pender passed at his last turn? Not if North led a high club: South would overtake to switch to a diamond, and the diamond ruff would follow later as a matter of course, a second club cashing. However, might North, holding the ace of trumps, have led a spade, preserving South's ♣A as a timely entry to provide a late spade ruff?

We can see that 5◊ is down off the top, but Wold led a spade, hoping to arrange a ruff or two for Lair; now declarer could draw trumps and shake a club loser on a high spade for +600. That was a great result for SHEINWOLD, but even 'great' proved to be not good enough this time; 5 IMPs to ROSENKRANZ, 247-241.

Board 90. Both Vul.

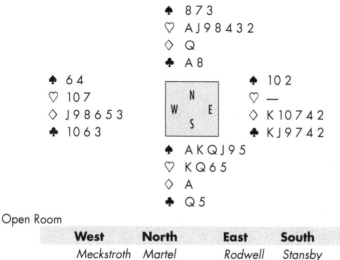

Open Room

	West	North	East	South
	Meckstroth	Martel	Rodwell	Stansby
			pass	2♣¹
	pass	3♣²	pass	3♠
	pass	5◊³	pass	6♠
	all pass			

1. Strong.
2. Four controls (A=2; K=1).
3. Splinter.

The combination of the control-showing auction and North's space-consuming splinter jump to 5◊ left South in the dark about North's heart length, and with duplicated shortage in diamonds he settled for the small slam rather than introduce his second suit; +1460 when West led a diamond.

If South declares 7♠ and East doubles to suggest he can ruff something, West would be hard-pressed to find the killing heart lead, and North might well run to the unbreakable 7NT.

Closed Room

West	North	East	South
Ross	Lair	Pender	Wold
		pass	2♣[1]
pass	2♡	2NT[2]	4NT[3]
5♢	dbl[4]	pass	7♡
all pass			

1. Strong.
2. Minor two-suiter.
3. RKCB for hearts.
4. Even number of keycards.

The natural positive 2♡ response located the optimal North-South fit, but it was not completely safe for Wold to check on keycards with a dangerous club holding, especially as the two-suited hand would be on lead if a club start would set 6♡. Against that, Blackwood would simplify the grand-slam investigation, not to mention that it had become clear to everyone which way the wind was blowing. Plus 2210 gave ROSENKRANZ 13 IMPs and some breathing room at 260-241.

To emphasize the prevailing aura in the match, consider your strategy with this East hand:

♠7652 ♡K 10 ♢KQJ1092 ♣7

Neither side vulnerable. Before it gets to you the bidding has proceeded: (1♡) dbl (3♡). Anything could be right: 4♢, 5♢, 3♠, 4♠, 4♡ or a responsive double.

Pender, for SHEINWOLD, tried a hopeful 4♢, planning 4♠ next if opener continued with 4♡. Indeed, Wold did bid 4♡, but the dread third opponent spoiled the party for Pender: Ross, with:

♠K983 ♡2 ♢A543 ♣AJ109

competed to 5♢, which had to lose two spades and a heart for one down, -50. Rodwell, for ROSENKRANZ, jumped to 4♠ as East, aiming to protect his ♡K and conceal his distribution, the winner on this layout with spades 3-2 with the ace in opener's hand; +420, and 10 IMPs more to ROSENKRANZ, 270-241.

Board 92. E-W Vul.

```
                    ♠ 7 4
                    ♡ Q J 10 3 2
                    ◇ 9 4
                    ♣ K Q 9 5
  ♠ 10 6 5 3                        ♠ K Q
  ♡ 9 6 4          ┌─────────┐      ♡ K 8 5
  ◇ K 10 8 7       │    N    │      ◇ 6 5 2
  ♣ 10 4           │ W     E │      ♣ A 7 6 3 2
                   │    S    │
                   └─────────┘
                    ♠ A J 9 8 2
                    ♡ A 7
                    ◇ A Q J 3
                    ♣ J 8
```

Open Room

West	North	East	South
Meckstroth	*Martel*	*Rodwell*	*Stansby*
pass	pass	1◇*	1♠
pass	2♡	pass	4♡
all pass			

East led the ◇2, which went to the queen and king. Back came the ♣10, ducked to the jack. Martel cashed the ◇A and exited dummy with a club. East took his ace and played a third round of the suit, ruffed low in dummy and overruffed by West. The king of trumps was the setting trick, -100.

The winning line is to play a low heart rather than a second club. If East wins and plays a third club, the ♡A stands guard in dummy, and declarer can ruff, discard a spade on a diamond, cash the ♠A, ruff a spade and draw trumps. Even if East craftily ducks the first trump lead, the remarkably friendly layout permits declarer to succeed without doing anything special.

Closed Room

West	North	East	South
Ross	*Lair*	*Pender*	*Wold*
pass	pass	1NT[1]	dbl
2◇	3♡	pass	3♠
pass	4♣	pass	4♡
all pass			

1. 12-14.

Here too East led the ◇2 to the queen and king. When West returned the ♣10, East took the ace and returned the suit (North's bidding made it very likely that the ♣10 was a singleton), but declarer overtook dummy's jack, ran the ♡10, crossed to the ♡A, cashed two diamonds discarding a spade, played the ♠A, ruffed a spade, and led a third trump with East now marked with 2=3=3=5 distribution. A painless +620 for Lair and 12 IMPs to ROSENKRANZ, 282-241.

If East starts with a top spade declarer is in trouble. His best shot is to duck; then East needs to play two rounds of clubs. Declarer can win and take a heart finesse, but the defenders are sure to score two trump tricks, West being able to ruff a club.

Board 93. Both Vul.

```
                    ♠ Q 10 5 4
                    ♡ Q J 9 4
                    ◇ K 8 4
                    ♣ A 2
   ♠ J 2                              ♠ K 9 6
   ♡ K 10 6          N                ♡ 8 7 2
   ◇ J 7 2        W     E             ◇ Q 6 5
   ♣ Q 7 6 5 3       S                ♣ K 10 8 4
                    ♠ A 8 7 3
                    ♡ A 5 3
                    ◇ A 10 9 3
                    ♣ J 9
```

Closed Room:

West	North	East	South
Ross	Lair	Pender	Wold
	1◇	pass	1♠
pass	2♠	pass	3♣[1]
pass	4♣[2]	pass	4♠
all pass			

1. Artificial inquiry about distribution.
2. Four spades, no short suit.

Ross, on lead, missed the alert to 4♣ and believed it was natural, marking dummy with short hearts. Accordingly, he led the ♠2, trying to stop ruffs.

That didn't look like a good start for the defense, but Wold called for dummy's queen. Had Pender covered, the defense would have still have had time to switch to clubs, but Pender, not surprisingly, followed low. Now Wold could come to the ♠A and play on diamonds (or, alternatively, hearts) to set up a club discard in time for +620.

Peter Pender

In the Open Room North declared 4♠ after a weak notrump and a Stayman auction. Rodwell, East, led a club and the defenders stayed off diamonds, declarer losing a trick in each suit for one down, -100. A further 12 IMPs to ROSENKRANZ, a 47-0 run over four successive deals to make the score 294-241. ROSENKRANZ had outscored SHEINWOLD by 163 IMPs over the previous 48 deals, overturning the 110-IMP deficit to lead by 53 IMPs.

Perhaps hinting that the Great Shuffler has a merciful side, SHEINWOLD gained 9 IMPs at the end of the set, which ROSENKRANZ won convincingly, 80-22. With 32 boards to play, SHEINWOLD trailed by 44 IMPs, 250-294.

Set Seven (Boards 97-112)

Although a 44-IMP difference is hardly conclusive, there also had to be psychological factors in play: could SHEINWOLD recover from some of the worst adversity ever witnessed in a bridge match? There were some opportunities for SHEINWOLD in the early going, but better guessing would have been required. On the first deal, for example, Pender and Ross belatedly reached a marginal 4♡ with these cards:

Board 97. Neither Vul.

	♠ 6 5 4		♠ A K
	♡ K Q 10 6 4	N	♡ J 8 7
	◇ 8 7 5	W E	◇ A J 2
	♣ Q 2	S	♣ K 9 8 7 3

The king-queen of diamonds were in front of the ace-jack, South's clubs were A6 doubleton, but hearts were 4-1. Ross had a chance to make it, but misguessed, not unreasonably, and finished -50. As Meckstroth and Rodwell stopped in 2♡ on a routine transfer auction and recorded +170, ROSENKRANZ gained 6 IMPs, where a more successful line of play would have netted SHEINWOLD those 6 IMPs. The margin was now 50 IMPs.

Board 98. N-S Vul.

```
     ♠ Q8642                      ♠ KJ3
     ♡ A107432        N           ♡ J
     ◇ KJ         W     E         ◇ A7632
     ♣ —              S           ♣ AK73
```

Open Room

West	North	East	South
Meckstroth	Hamman	Rodwell	Wolff
		1◇[1]	2♣
2♡[2]	pass	2NT	pass
3♠	pass	4♣	pass
4◇	pass	5◇	pass
5♡	all pass		

1. 2+ diamonds, 10-15.
2. Not forcing.

Closed Room

West	North	East	South
Ross	Bergen	Pender	Cohen
		1◇	2♣
dbl*	pass	2NT[1]	pass
3♣	pass	3♠	pass
4♣	pass	4◇	pass
4♡	pass	5NT[2]	pass
6♠	all pass		

1. 15+.
2. Pick a slam.

In theory, at least, Meckstroth's first two bids should have come close to describing his hand. Rodwell, who was super-maximum for a non-1♣ opening, seems to have read 3♠ differently. The unlovely 5♡ went down two, -100. When Ross started with a negative double rather than bidding either of his suits, he felt that when he showed both majors via 3♣ he had limited his strength and could issue a couple of below-game slam tries. However, Pender bid an awful lot in that context, and 6♠, which had only one top loser, had far too few winners on the lie of the cards, and drifted three down, -150. 2 IMPs to ROSENKRANZ, a nice surprise for Meckstroth-Rodwell; 302-250.

On Board 100, Ross got away with a questionable bid. With both sides vulnerable, he and Meckstroth were dealt:

♠K Q 9 3   ♡A 10 9   ◇K 8   ♣A 8 4 2

Meckstroth opened a strong notrump, played there and went down four, -400. Ross, a weak notrumper, had to open 1♣; it continued (1♡) pass (2♣) — showing a heart fit. He passed, of course, but when overcaller's retreat to 2♡ came around to him, Ross reopened with 2♠, strongly suggesting a fifth club. He was fortunate that no one doubled the correction to 3♣; only two down, -200, while 2♡ would have been touch-and-go. So 5 'surprise' IMPs to SHEINWOLD , 255-302. The next nine deals featured a number of partscore and overtrick/undertrick swings, SHEINWOLD outscoring ROSENKRANZ 16-12. ROSENKRANZ led by 43, 314-271.

Board 110. Neither Vul.

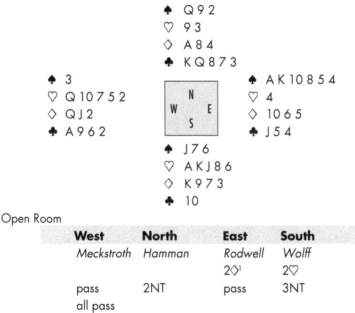

<pre>
                    ♠ Q 9 2
                    ♡ 9 3
                    ◇ A 8 4
                    ♣ K Q 8 7 3
 ♠ 3   ♠ A K 10 8 5 4
 ♡ Q 10 7 5 2   N   ♡ 4
 ◇ Q J 2   W   E   ◇ 10 6 5
 ♣ A 9 6 2   S   ♣ J 5 4
                    ♠ J 7 6
                    ♡ A K J 8 6
                    ◇ K 9 7 3
                    ♣ 10
</pre>

Open Room

West	North	East	South
Meckstroth	Hamman	Rodwell	Wolff
		2◇¹	2♡
pass	2NT	pass	3NT
all pass			

1. Weak two in an unspecified major, no strong option.

Superficially, 3NT has no chance, but Rodwell made the unfortunate choice of the ♣4 as his opening lead. Meckstroth won with the ace (three from declarer) and switched to spades, East clearing the suit. To defeat the contract, West needed to discard a heart and a diamond. That was particularly difficult, looking at dummy, and when he innocently parted with a club, playing Rodwell for 6=1=2=4, declarer had four tricks in clubs and nine in all; +400.

Closed Room

West	North	East	South
Ross	Bergen	Pender	Cohen
		2◇[1]	pass[2]
2♠[3]	pass	pass	3♡
dbl	all pass		

1. Weak two in an unspecified major, with two strong options.
2. 2♡ would have been artificial.
3. Signoff opposite spades; encouraging opposite hearts.

Cohen, whose defense to Multi did not include a natural overcall in a major, faced a difficult decision at his second turn as Ross's 'encouraging in hearts' 2♠ bid did not guarantee or deny a strong holding in hearts. Aware of the danger, Cohen elected to reopen and was not shocked to see a penalty double. West led his spade and East played three rounds of the suit. West ruffed and switched to the ◇Q. Declarer won with the king, took a round of trumps and played his club, which West took with the ace to continue diamonds. Declarer won with dummy's ◇A, discarded two diamonds on clubs, ruffed a diamond and exited with the ♡8 to endplay West for one down, -100. Not too bad, but that was still 11 IMPs for SHEINWOLD, 282-314.

Board: 111. N-S Vul.

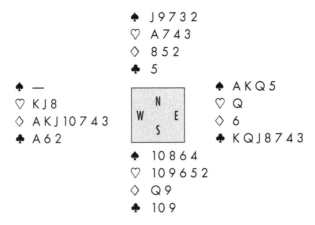

```
              ♠ J 9 7 3 2
              ♡ A 7 4 3
              ◇ 8 5 2
              ♣ 5
  ♠ —                        ♠ A K Q 5
  ♡ K J 8          N         ♡ Q
  ◇ A K J 10 7 4 3  W   E    ◇ 6
  ♣ A 6 2          S         ♣ K Q J 8 7 4 3
              ♠ 10 8 6 4
              ♡ 10 9 6 5 2
              ◇ Q 9
              ♣ 10 9
```

Open Room

West	North	East	South
Meckstroth	Hamman	Rodwell	Wolff
			pass
1♣[1]	pass	2♣	pass
2◇	pass	2♠	pass
3♣	pass	4NT[2]	pass
5♡[3]	pass	6♣	all pass

1. Strong.
2. RKCB for clubs.
3. Two keycards.

Meckstroth, whose honor controls reinforced his view that Rodwell would not be interested in the spade void, simply showed his keycards for clubs and passed 6♣. With the ♡A on lead, six was the right level; +920.

Closed Room

West	North	East	South
Ross	Bergen	Pender	Cohen
			pass
1◇	pass	4NT[1]	pass
5♡[2]	pass	6♣	pass
7♣	all pass		

1. Old-fashioned Blackwood.
2. Two aces.

Lacking the ♣10 in a mere seven-card suit, and with only one ace opposite a simple one-bid, Pender's 4NT was a remarkably committal action, but as he anticipated potential problems in checking on aces if he bid his suits naturally he was willing to gamble a bit. Ross, who sensibly believed his partner was intending to play in *spades*, was in any case not involved with void-showing over Blackwood, but when Pender signed off in clubs, Ross had reason to reconsider the position. Might Pender have the likes of:

♠ K Q J   ♡ A   ◇ x   ♣ K Q J 10 x x x x

(still a risky choice with only one ace)? After considerable thought, Ross decided to gamble that his undisclosed void would be the key to a grand slam.

Over now to Larry Cohen, who had been thinking along with Ross and realized that the unsolicited raise to seven had to be based on a void. But how did that information help with the opening lead decision? The only hard evidence available to Cohen was the absence of a double of 5♡ and he guessed to lead a spade. Pender, perhaps a tad sheepishly, chalked up +1440 and SHEINWOLD gained 11 IMPs where the swing might have been 14 IMPs to ROSENKRANZ. Bergen, as good partners have always been known to do, reproached himself bitterly for not doubling 5♡, but should a player be worrying about his Blackwooding opponents bidding a grand slam off a cashing ace, or a small slam off two fast losers in a suit?

SHEINWOLD won the seventh set 43-20 and trailed now by just 21 IMPs, 293-314, with 16 deals remaining. The atmosphere in the ROSENKRANZ camp had changed dramatically: they had lost more than half of their lead, more than once in strange and unusual ways, and the momentum seemed to have turned against them. Although ROSENKRANZ was still a couple of swings ahead, the score comparison was visibly grim. Not much time to reflect on what might have been. The final segment was about to begin.

Set Eight (Boards 113-128)

These were the North-South cards on Board 114, North-South vulnerable:

```
        ♠  6
        ♡  A K 10 7 4
        ◇  K 8 7 4
        ♣  J 10 6
        ┌─────────────┐
        └─────────────┘
        ♠  A 10 9
        ♡  6 3
        ◇  Q
        ♣  A K 9 5 4 3 2
```

Both Souths, playing strong club systems, opened 2♣: 6+ clubs, limited strength. In the Closed Room, Meckstroth, North, jumped directly to 5♣ after a takeout double on his right. Rodwell, who had no idea whether his partner was bidding to make or gambling with some distribution, had to pass. In the Open Room, Hamman started with a redouble with the North cards, and saw it continue: (2♠) 3NT (4♠), back to him. Wolff's 3NT showed extra length in clubs, a spade stopper, and sound values. What now? Hamman settled for 5♣ (although the partnership employed an Italianate DI 4NT, it's not clear whether that would have applied in this situation) and Wolff needed a better reason to go on to six. Clubs were 2-1 and both declarers took thirteen tricks on a good lie when West did not lead the ◇A. No swing, but a difficult missed opportunity.

Board 115. E-W Vul.

```
                    ♠ A K 5 4
                    ♡ 6
                    ◇ J 10 8 7 5 2
                    ♣ 9 3
  ♠ J 10 9                         ♠ Q 8 7 3
  ♡ A 9 8 5 3         N            ♡ J 7 4
  ◇ —             W       E        ◇ A K Q 9 4
  ♣ A J 8 6 4         S            ♣ 10
                    ♠ 6 2
                    ♡ K Q 10 2
                    ◇ 6 3
                    ♣ K Q 7 5 2
```

Open Room

West	North	East	South
Lair	Hamman	Wold	Wolff
			pass
1♡	3◇	pass	pass
dbl	all pass		

Trading on the vulnerability, Hamman stepped out with an atypical weak jump overcall of 3◇, going for someone's throat. That it might have been his own was suggested to him by the remainder of the auction — imagine how Wold must have felt, looking at those diamonds in a tight match!

Somewhat surprisingly, East did not lead a safe high trump, instead choosing the ♡4 (king, ace, six). Lair, reading the heart position accurately, made the normal switch to the ♠J. Declarer won and played a club to the queen and ace. West continued spades, so declarer won, ruffed a spade, discarded his remaining spade on the ♡Q and tried to cash the ♣K. When Wold could ruff, Hamman was three down, -500.

Both sides could have done better: after the spade switch declarer can play three rounds of the suit, ruffing in dummy, discard a club on the ♡Q, ruff a heart to fell the jack, ruff the last spade safely (as it happens), and pitch his remaining club on the ♡10, escaping for -300. However, the defenders have several ways to restrict declarer to five tricks. For example, if East leads a club on the go, West can win and return a club for East to ruff. A heart to West's ace is followed by a third club and if declarer discards a spade East ruffs with the nine, draws two rounds of trumps and plays a spade for four down, -700 (as it was then).

West	North	East	South
Stansby	Meckstroth	Martel	Rodwell
			pass
1♡	2◇	dbl*	pass
3♣	pass	4♡	all pass

Meckstroth led the ♠A (three, *six*, nine). Although Meckwell use reverse carding almost exclusively, they make an exception for leads showing the ace-king at Trick 1, so Rodwell, despite his powerful trump holding, did what he could to request a spade continuation to score his small trump as soon as possible. Nonetheless, North switched to the ◇10; Stansby won in dummy, discarding a spade, and played the ♣10. When South did not cover, declarer could have made the contract by running it, then playing on crossruff lines, but he went up with the ace of course, ruffed a club, ditched his remaining spade on a diamond and played a low diamond. South ruffed in with the ♡10; declarer overruffed, ruffed another club and played the ◇Q. South ruffed high, then cashed his trump winner and a club for a less-than-comfortable one down, -100; 12 IMPs to ROSENKRANZ, 326-293.

Board: 116. Both Vul.

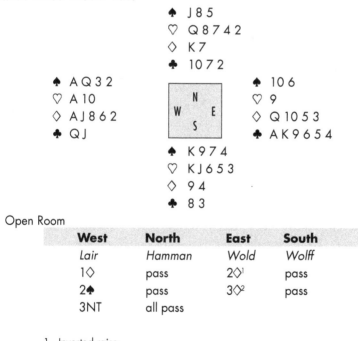

```
                 ♠ J 8 5
                 ♡ Q 8 7 4 2
                 ◇ K 7
                 ♣ 10 7 2
  ♠ A Q 3 2                    ♠ 10 6
  ♡ A 10              N        ♡ 9
  ◇ A J 8 6 2     W     E      ◇ Q 10 5 3
  ♣ Q J              S         ♣ A K 9 6 5 4
                 ♠ K 9 7 4
                 ♡ K J 6 5 3
                 ◇ 9 4
                 ♣ 8 3
```

West	North	East	South
Lair	Hamman	Wold	Wolff
1◇	pass	2◇[1]	pass
2♠	pass	3◇[2]	pass
3NT	all pass		

1. Inverted raise.
2. Minimum for 2◇.

Lair's 3NT was not at all secure at single dummy after North led a heart, but declarer won, cashed the ♣Q, overtook the jack and could claim his contract when the suit divided, +600. Had clubs not behaved, declarer had the diamond finesse in reserve.

Closed Room

West	North	East	South
Stansby	Meckstroth	Martel	Rodwell
1◇	pass	2♣	pass
2♠	pass	3◇	pass
3♡	pass	4♣	pass
4♠	pass	4NT¹	pass
6♣	pass	6◇	all pass

1. DI (general slam try).

The contract of 6◇ was excellent: declarer lost only the trump king for +1370 and 13 IMPs, SHEINWOLD reclaiming with interest the points lost on the previous deal; 306-326. Martel's 2♣ response (a more attractive choice than an inverted raise when facing a balanced 15+ or an unbalanced hand with diamonds) really helped Stansby revalue his hand accurately.

Board 117. N-S Vul.

```
              ♠ A J 10 9
              ♡ A K Q
              ◇ 8 7 6
              ♣ K 8 5
♠ Q 8 7 5 4 2              ♠ K
♡ 9 8 7          N         ♡ J 4 3
◇ Q J        W     E       ◇ K 10 9 5 4 3 2
♣ A 9           S          ♣ 4 3
              ♠ 6 3
              ♡ 10 6 5 2
              ◇ A
              ♣ Q J 10 7 6 2
```

Open Room

West	North	East	South
Lair	Hamman	Wold	Wolff
	1NT	3◇	3NT
4◇	dbl	all pass	

West	**North**	**East**	**South**
Stansby	Meckstroth	Martel	Rodwell
	1NT	3◇	3NT
all pass			

With favorable vulnerability, both Easts were willing to risk a less-than-sound 3◇ with a poor suit and some defensive bits and pieces. As they hoped, that set a real problem for South that both Wolff and Rodwell solved with a stab at 3NT.

Lair, whose diamonds and fast side trick suggested that 4◇ would not be expensive and might even make, did not pass. Hamman, despite his maximum, was not interested in seeing 4NT from Wolff and doubled 4◇, a practical battlefield decision. South led the ♣Q and declarer won with dummy's ace to play a spade. North went in with the ace and cashed the ♡K (four, five, seven) then the ♡A (jack, six, eight) — Wolff assuming that declarer held the ♡Q. When North switched to a trump, South won with the ◇A and continued with the ♣10, overtaken by North, who played a second trump. That allowed declarer to discard a heart on dummy's ♠Q to escape for two down, -300. Had Hamman switched to the *queen* of hearts, Wolff would have signaled with the six to give a legible count; here it seems that Hamman played his partner to have played five-six from ♡106532.

Stansby, who liked his chances of beating 3NT if Martel led his own long suit, remained silent. Indeed, Martel led a diamond and dummy's bare ace was exceptionally good news for the defense. Meckstroth had to go after clubs and was soon three down, -300 and 12 more IMPs for SHEINWOLD, reducing the margin to just 8 IMPs, 318-326.

On the cards, 5♣ is laydown (and even 4♡ is cold as the cards lie), but the well-timed 3◇ had done its job, depriving South of the opportunity to investigate fully the best strain and level.

These were the North-South cards on Board 119, both vulnerable:

```
              ♠  J
              ♡  Q J 8 4
              ◇  K Q 7 6 4 2
              ♣  A K
              ┌──────────┐
              └──────────┘
              ♠  A Q 9 7
              ♡  A
              ◇  A J 10 3
              ♣  10 5 4 2
```

Both Hamman-Wolff and Meckstroth-Rodwell reached the excellent 7◊ after long (five and eight rounds, respectively) cuebidding and Blackwood sequences; no swing at +2140 but plenty of anxiety until each auction reached its conclusion.

On Board 120, neither vulnerable, Wold, East, was dealt:

♠ 6 5 4 2   ♡ A J 10 2   ◊ J 9 8   ♣ 7 2

and saw Lair open a strong notrump. Whether you believe that the 'normal' pass will work better than Stayman (with a weak pass-or-correct 2♡ over an unwelcome 2◊ reply) seems to be a function of personal experience. Wold tried to improve the contract and had to wriggle over 2◊, finishing in 2♡, one down, -50. In the other room, playing weak notrumps, Martel got to try for hearts by responding 1♡ to 1♣, and was committed to passing Stansby's 15-17 1NT rebid; that yielded +150 against gentle defense, so SHEINWOLD gained 5 IMPs, inching closer at 323-328, with half the set still to play.

Board 121. E-W Vul.

```
                    ♠ A K J 8 5
                    ♡ 10
                    ◊ K J 7 3
                    ♣ A 6 3
    ♠ Q 9 6 2                         ♠ 10
    ♡ 5 4 3            N              ♡ A Q J 9 8
    ◊ A 10 8 5     W       E          ◊ 9 6 4 2
    ♣ 9 4              S              ♣ J 8 2
                    ♠ 7 4 3
                    ♡ K 7 6 2
                    ◊ Q
                    ♣ K Q 10 7 5
```

Open Room

West	North	East	South
Lair	Hamman	Wold	Wolff
	1◊¹	pass	1♡
pass	2♠²	pass	4♠
all pass			

1. Possible canapé, less than 17 points.
2. Longer spades than diamonds, maximum strength.

Declarer lost a heart, a diamond and a spade (he did not 'deep-finesse' the eight on the second round) and scored +420.

A historical note: in 1985 there was still some respect for a one-level overcall at unfavorable vulnerability; without commenting on the merits, we are confident that today a 1♡ overcall would be at least an 85% expert action with the East hand.

Closed Room

West	North	East	South
Stansby	Meckstroth	Martel	Rodwell
	1♣[1]	1♡	2♣
pass	2♠	pass	2NT[2]
pass	3♣	pass	3♠[3]
pass	4♣[4]	pass	4♡[5]
pass	4NT[6]	pass	5♡[7]
pass	5♠	all pass	

1. Strong, artificial, at least 16 points.
2. Worse than honor-third or four small in spades.
3. Three small spades.
4. RKCB for clubs.
5. 1 keycard.
6. Asks for the ♣Q.
7. ♣Q plus ♡K

It's usually uncomfortable to try for slam and stop in five of a major or four or five notrump, contracts that offer no extra reward but often incur additional risk. Against the fragile 5♠ (it looks like North was especially aggressive here), Martel found the imaginative lead of a club, which was subtly excellent for the defense. Meckstroth won in hand, cashed the ♠K and led his heart. East went up with the ace and continued with the ♣8, declarer winning in dummy to lead the ♠7. With no need to take a chance that declarer would run the seven, Stansby carefully covered with the nine. Meckstroth finessed the jack successfully, but with no way to return to dummy he had to lose a trump trick and the ◇A to go one down, -50. Those 10 IMPs gave SHEINWOLD back the long-lost lead, 333-328.

Board 123. Neither Vul.

```
                    ♠  —
                    ♡  Q J 7 6 5 3
                    ◇  9 8 7 6
                    ♣  10 9 2
  ♠  10 8 6 5 4                      ♠  7 3 2
  ♡  9 2           ┌─────────┐       ♡  A K 10
  ◇  A K J         │    N    │       ◇  10 5
  ♣  K 4 3         │  W   E  │       ♣  A Q J 7 6
                   │    S    │
                   └─────────┘
                    ♠  A K Q J 9
                    ♡  8 4
                    ◇  Q 4 3 2
                    ♣  8 5
```

Open Room

West	North	East	South
Lair	Hamman	Wold	Wolff
			1♠
pass	1NT	2♣	2♠
2NT	pass	3NT	all pass

Facing a limited hand that would often have a longer suit than spades, it's easy to see why Hamman did not pass 1♠. Wolff's free bid of 2♠ was not what Hamman wanted to see, but nothing bad happened. He led a diamond against 3NT, and Lair took the first ten tricks, +430.

Closed Room

West	North	East	South
Stansby	Meckstroth	Martel	Rodwell
			1♠
pass	1NT[1]	2♣	2◇
2NT	pass	3NT	dbl
all pass			

1. Forcing.

Meckstroth's strategy was more about theft than improving the contract, and here, too, South volunteered a second bid over 2♣, but then he went a step further and doubled 3NT. Alas, Meckstroth had no spade to lead, and Stansby took the same ten tricks as Lair, +650; 6 IMPs for the insult to SHEINWOLD, who led now by 11, 339-328.

The South players had a chance on Board 125. With both sides vulnerable they held:

♠ 7　♡ 6 5 3 2　♢ Q 10 2　♣ K Q 9 6 5

Their opponents cruised into 3NT with neither clubs nor hearts mentioned and dummy known to have five spades. Both Wolff and Rodwell led the ♡6, which troubled neither declarer. A low club would have been no better, but a club *honor* would have given the defense realistic chances.

It's interesting that opening lead strategy has attracted so much coverage in the trade literature in recent years, and that where once low from that club holding would have been routine, there has been a strong movement towards the honor lead — the queen emerging as the expert choice when leading high (the king would deliver a strong KQ or AK holding).

When a match is desperately close, every deal with an ounce of potential in it can be stressful. For example, on Board 126, with neither side vulnerable, both North-South pairs stopped sensibly in 2NT and made an overtrick, which was always possible on a good lie of the cards. That was a flat board but created plenty of worry for both pairs lest their aggressive counterparts were to bid and make a game.

On Board 127, Stansby and Martel reached an unpleasant 2NT after Stansby opened:

♠ K J 9 3　♡ 10 7 4　♢ K 10　♣ K J 7 2

with a weak notrump in second seat at favorable colors — four undertricks tricks worth of unpleasantness, to be precise — but, mercifully, that was only -200 and a 4-IMP loss when Lair finished -50 in a safer 2♣.

ROSENKRANZ trailed by 7 IMPs, 332-339. There was one deal remaining in this nerve-wracking, gut-wrenching, mind-bending, character-testing match:

Board 128. E-W Vul.

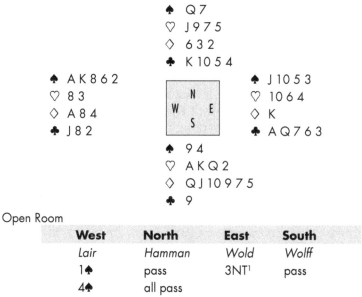

Open Room

West	North	East	South
Lair	Hamman	Wold	Wolff
1♠	pass	3NT[1]	pass
4♠	all pass		

1. 10-12, spade raise with unspecified shortness.

It was surprising at the prevailing vulnerability to see Wolff pass over 3NT, but it seems certain that he knew exactly what he was doing. Hamman led a club, which set an immediate problem for Lair, who could not afford to play low from dummy if the lead was a singleton, but he eventually got it right; he took the ♣9 with the jack, cashed the top spades and played a club to the queen, and set up a long club for a heart discard, +680. That was a good but not abnormal result for ROSENKRANZ, and indeed, it was a quietly dangerous deal for SHEINWOLD.

Closed Room

West	North	East	South
Stansby	Meckstroth	Martel	Rodwell
1♠	pass	3♠	dbl
pass	4♡	4♠	all pass

When Martel decided his cards merited only a limit raise, it seemed that the door had been left ajar for ROSENKRANZ, as Stansby was not going to bid game with his eight-loser minimum. All Rodwell had to do to win the match was duplicate the normally-aggressive Wolff's pass (over 3NT) in the other room, but of course, the circumstances were different: where Wolff knew he could not buy the contract cheaply as his opponents were committed to game, Rodwell could not be sure that the hand did not belong to his side, or whether both sides could take ten or eleven tricks. His takeout double located the eight-card heart fit that would produce seven or eight tricks, depending on the defense. What seemed to be the central issue, now that East-West had clearly voted *not* to bid game, was whether East-West would double 4♡ and find the diamond ruff for 500, enough to secure a 4-IMP victory for SHEINWOLD; a 300-point set (or failing to double), however, would give ROSENKRANZ an unbelievable 1-IMP win.

And why should Martel do anything over 4♡ if his game-invitational raise had described his hand accurately? Sure, his weak heart length would often be facing shortage and he had a decent five-card suit he had not yet mentioned, but was that enough to justify bidding a double-clutch 4♠ in front of his partner, who might have a better idea of what to do? Indeed, had Martel passed 4♡, Stansby might have doubled with ace-king-ace, albeit with no expectation of taking a second spade trick. A double by Martel would have been penalty and not 'equity protection' for the spade partscore, but passing out 4♡ had to be a prime choice.

Remarkably, Martel bid 4♠, and did so quite promptly. You may feel that 4♠ was the practical bid, and who could argue with you? Now all Stansby had to do was make it. The defenders cashed and continued hearts; Stansby got the trumps right, but lost a club trick for +620, and a 2-IMP loss.

So Team SHEINWOLD won the 1985 Team Trials by 5 IMPs, 339-334, and would represent USA in the 1985 Bermuda Bowl in São Paulo, Brazil, seeded into the semifinals.

Hamman and Wolff thought they were underdogs before the comparisons, with three poor results and several questionable positions. But Stansby and Martel had done very well at their table, and the shootout ended with one team slightly ahead of the other, just as it had figured to end before a single card had been played!

In between, however, there had been some remarkable happenings. This match might well have been the most exciting in bridge history: it featured two magnificent comebacks, plenty of luck, some unbelievable emotional swings, some barely credible swings in momentum, and some courageous performances by all the players.

We'd like to think that the title of this chapter is particularly appropriate.

5. 1985 The Real Boys from Brazil

São Paulo, Brazil 1985; the Bermuda Bowl semifinal between underdog Brazil and mighty USA — the same team we have just seen emerge from a thrilling Team Trials final. I[‡‡] have friends on both teams, but I am here with Brazil.

When the host country's lead pair is disqualified for a technical offense after winning the Brazilian Trials, some delicate internal political issues can only be resolved by replacing the star players with a pair that had not participated in the Trials. The Selection Committee chooses Claudio and Fabio Sampaio, both only twenty-one years old with no international experience, which is how I come to be in Rio de Janeiro two weeks before the Bermuda Bowl for my first professional coaching gig. Ernesto d'Orsi, a good friend and Brazil's Godfather of bridge, keen to see his country make a good showing, believes I might be able to help prepare the Sampaio brothers for the big stage and get the two more experienced pairs to settle down emotionally and focus on their partnerships.

I am well acquainted with three of the other four team members — Sergio Barbosa, Gabino Cintra and Marcelo Branco, so I am comfortable when we meet at a noisy Rio restaurant. Pedro Branco, Marcelo's brother, is a wild card for me, though, as we have never met, and I know he is a proud guy, with the 1976 Olympiad title under his belt. I will never forget his reaction when the introductions were made: 'Who is this guy and what can he do for me — I am a World Champion?' Ernesto, the sweetest man you could ever hope to meet, is visibly horrified, but before he can react, the other guys laugh and tell Pedro he would see soon enough. They let him know that he is doing his best to give Brazilian hospitality a bad reputation. It would be of some comfort to me that when our training sessions conclude, Pedro becomes one of my best friends in Brazil, which is saying something. Gabino and I, who share the same birthday and the roller-coaster emotional experience of the 1978 World Open Pairs final, have remained close since then. (Peter Nagy and I were leading after each of the first four final sessions. We were about average in the fifth and last session with a number of tops and bottoms, but Cintra-Branco had something like 70% to pass us at the very end.) We visited Brazil and Argentina earlier that year for some invitational tournaments; Cintra

---

‡‡   Primary author Eric Kokish

was our host for some social events and we were very friendly. It is a small miracle that Gabino is even playing in the Bermuda Bowl, as he has gone through a long recovery process after a nearly-fatal car accident.

Pedro Branco

My schedule in Rio is a strange one, as job commitments mean most of the players will not be available until the late afternoon. With lots of time on my hands, I enjoy Rio's beaches, take long walks, sample the offerings of many of the excellent *churrascarias*, take naps. I wander over to the bridge club where I spend a few hours discussing bidding and defensive principles with the Sampaios, who speak virtually no English but are eager to develop their bridge 'language' and understandings. They are 2/1 players with many of the standard Brazilian agreements, so we have a sound base to work with, and can spend more time on judgment and competitive bidding. With the other four, the main tasks are to eliminate the need for immediate emotional gratification, instill a sense of calm, and create an atmosphere in which accepting responsibility for unilateral actions is the norm. Easier said than done, of course, but once our practice matches and bidding sessions reveal what needs to be worked on, progress is remarkably quick.

The club has a good kitchen and there are regular breaks for the after-office-hours players to have a late lunch or a snack. The bottom line is that our sessions often end at 3 a.m., after which we all go out for 'dinner' and music. That lifestyle might horrify purists, but it suits the Brazilian personality perfectly, and I soon discover that I am an honorary Brazilian for life. I can appreciate how coaching visits like this one might help me experience parts of the world and cultures that I would probably never be able to manage otherwise. I don't know it yet, but this will be the springboard for training missions in over twenty different countries in the coming years.

When we fly from Rio to the tournament venue in São Paulo, I am pleased to find that my wife Beverly is waiting at the hotel after a long flight. She used to hate flying when we first got serious about our relationship, but has been all over the world since those early days and has adapted well. Despite the warm hospitality of the Brazilians, I confess to being lonesome after two weeks away from family. Not that a bridge tournament is the ideal place for a couple to enjoy themselves, even if they're both players. The stress can get to you, especially when everyone else is experiencing some of their own. São Paulo is not Rio, but we have a couple of days to share and are glad to have them.

By now, all three Brazilian partnerships are quietly confident that they will hold their own in the Round Robin stage and not disappoint the strongly partisan Brazilian supporters. Nonetheless, they surprise virtually everyone by convincingly winning the seven-team round robin (USA and the European champions Austria have been pre-seeded into the semifinals), with the Sampaio brothers playing their share and contributing quality sessions. The team has found its best form as the Round Robin progresses and is in a position towards the end to give the veteran players opportunities to get some rest for the impending long knockout match.

(Left to right) Barbosa, C Sampaio, Kraft, Kokish, P Branco, Cintra

As Israel has also survived the first stage, the semifinal draw is forced: Israel will face Austria to avoid an all-Zone 1 final, which is a tough break for Brazil, who will have to contend with the Zone 2 champion, USA: Peter Pender/Hugh Ross, Chip Martel/Lew Stansby, Bob Hamman/Bobby Wolff, with NPC Alfred Sheinwold.

After 80 of the 160 deals, Brazil leads by 45 IMPs, but the Sampaio brothers have not yet seen action, a questionable strategy chosen by their notoriously risk-averse NPC, Serge Apoteker. Playing four-handed begins to take its toll and USA eventually overtakes Brazil, winning the eighth set 49-3 to lead by 21 IMPs.

The script seems all too familiar, but Brazil, willed on by a spectacularly vocal partisan audience, rallies to win Session 9 by a score of 55-36 and trails USA by just 2 IMPs, 309-311, with one more 16-deal session to play.

SESSION 10 (Boards 145-160)

On seven of the first eight deals of Session 10, the contract is the same at both tables. The Americans double their lead to 4, 330-326, despite losing 13 IMPs on Board 149, a vulnerable slam zone deal that is roughly an even-money proposition.

```
♠ —
♡ K 7 5 4 3
♢ A K Q 10 7 3
♣ 10 4
┌──────────┐
└──────────┘
♠ K Q J 7 4 3
♡ A 6
♢ 8
♣ A K Q 5
```

Both Martel and Marcelo open the North hand 1♢ and bid their hearts twice, but Branco's hand is limited by his failure to start with a strong club while Martel's has a much higher maximum. Consequently, Pedro only invites slam with a natural 4NT, and they play there, but Stansby drives to 6NT. The slam needs diamonds to run, roughly a 52% chance, but with jack-fourth offside, Stansby is obliged to concede one down, -100.

Lew Stansby

One of the prettiest deals of the match involves only a single IMP...

Board 153. E-W Vul.

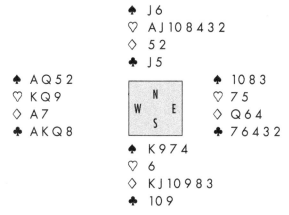

```
                    ♠ J 6
                    ♡ A J 10 8 4 3 2
                    ◇ 5 2
                    ♣ J 5
  ♠ A Q 5 2                        ♠ 10 8 3
  ♡ K Q 9          N               ♡ 7 5
  ◇ A 7         W     E            ◇ Q 6 4
  ♣ A K Q 8        S               ♣ 7 6 4 3 2
                    ♠ K 9 7 4
                    ♡ 6
                    ◇ K J 10 9 8 3
                    ♣ 10 9
```

At both tables, North opens 3♡ and West protects with a heavy but practical 3NT. The blocked club suit and unfriendly diamond position seem to leave declarer with an uphill struggle, but both Cintra and Hamman make it look easy, albeit in different ways.

In the Open Room, Martel leads the ♡J forcing Cintra to decide whether hearts are 7-1 (take the trick) or 6-2 (duck the jack). Cintra goes with the odds, takes his king, cashes four rounds of clubs, and leads the ♠Q, which will see him home if South holds at least four spades headed by the king (or KJx) together with the ◇K and only one heart. Stansby prefers to take his poison by winning the ♠K to play a diamond, but Cintra lets that run to the queen for +630.

In the Closed Room, Marcelo opts to stay off hearts altogether and attacks with the ♠J. Hamman wins with the queen and, somewhat ironically, advances the ♡K, aiming for the same sort of endplay achieved by Cintra. Marcelo wins and continues spades; Hamman ducks, but wins the third round and cashes clubs. Pedro sees that he will be endplayed with the master spade, so he disposes of it, stifling the tiniest of smiles. Hamman scores the ♠5 for his ninth winner, but must lose the last two tricks, +600. The saved overtrick will forever be known in Brazilian folklore as Pedro's Trick. USA 330-327.

Differences in system play a role in the next three deals. Brazil takes the lead on Board 154, thanks to a not-quite-random system choice. Wolff and Barbosa, vulnerable, are dealt:

♠7 5 3 2   ♡A 9 6   ◇ J 9   ♣A K 8 5

That is an easy, if ugly, 1♠ for Wolff, which gets him to 3♠ opposite Hamman's straightforward limit raise, down one for -100. Barbosa, whose choices are a 13-15 1NT or 1◊, normally at least four cards, prefers to pass, but is later willing to reopen over his LHO's weak 2♡ with a double to finish in 2♠, for +110. These 5 IMPs make it 332-330, Brazil.

Board 155. Neither Vul.

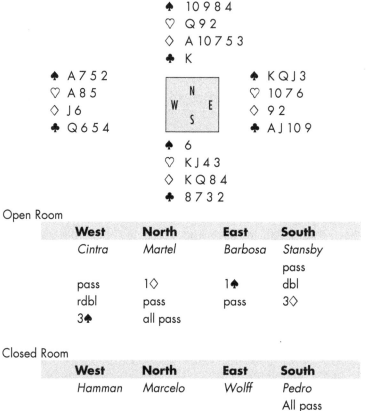

                  ♠ 10 9 8 4
                  ♡ Q 9 2
                  ◊ A 10 7 5 3
                  ♣ K

♠ A 7 5 2
♡ A 8 5
◊ J 6
♣ Q 6 5 4

                            ♠ K Q J 3
                            ♡ 10 7 6
                            ◊ 9 2
                            ♣ A J 10 9

                  ♠ 6
                  ♡ K J 4 3
                  ◊ K Q 8 4
                  ♣ 8 7 3 2

Open Room

West	North	East	South
Cintra	*Martel*	*Barbosa*	*Stansby*
			pass
pass	1◊	1♠	dbl
rdbl	pass	pass	3◊
3♠	all pass		

Closed Room

West	North	East	South
Hamman	*Marcelo*	*Wolff*	*Pedro*
			All pass

Not everyone would open the North hand in third seat, or overcall 1♠ rather than double 1◊ for takeout with the East hand, but both those actions locate their side's best strain. As North-South can make 4◊ without breathing hard, the Brazilian 3♠, which yields an easy +140 despite the 4-1 trump break, is a fine result.

When Marcelo does not open in third seat it is mildly surprising to see Wolff throw it in, but had he opened 1♠, Pedro would have doubled, and North-South might well have competed to 4◊, so perhaps passing it out saves USA 3 IMPs after all. In the end it is 4 IMPs to Brazil, 336-330.

Board 156. N-S Vul.

```
              ♠ Q6
              ♡ K43
              ◇ QJ106
              ♣ A1094
  ♠ A9843                    ♠ KJ105
  ♡ 95          N            ♡ A6
  ◇ 53       W     E         ◇ A984
  ♣ K763        S            ♣ QJ2
              ♠ 72
              ♡ QJ108 72
              ◇ K72
              ♣ 85
```

Open Room

West	North	East	South
Cintra	Martel	Barbosa	Stansby
pass	pass	1NT	pass
2♡[1]	pass	3♠	pass
4♠	all pass		

1. Transfer to spades.

Martel, despite holding two chunky four-card suits, is understandably reluctant to open a weak notrump at unfavorable vulnerability, so his opponents have the auction to themselves, which is not necessarily to their advantage (see the Closed Room). As Barbosa has a maximum for a 13-15 notrump, he is willing to super-accept Cintra's transfer, which is precisely what is needed to reach the nothing-wasted 22-point game. It is only a small anti-climax for Barbosa to get the trumps right, generating a fresh extended wave of cheering from the VuGraph audience.

Closed Room

West	North	East	South
Hamman	Marcelo	Wolff	Pedro
pass	1◇	1♠	dbl
4♠	all pass		

As Marcelo can open with a suit bid, he has less reason to pass in second seat, but his 1◇ merely convinces Wolff, facing a passed partner, to overcall on his four-card spade suit rather than try 1NT. Had he overcalled 1NT Hamman might have transferred to spades and passed 2♠ (with a minimum, Wolff would not super-accept the transfer despite his four-card support) rather than stretch for the non-vulnerable game bonus. Perhaps a better strategy over a 1NT overcall would be Stayman, intending an invitational 2♠ over a red-suit reply, or a game raise if East shows four spades. Having probably saved the board for his team, Wolff completes the mission by finding the queen of trumps, for a most distinguished push.

Bobby Wolff

With both sides vulnerable on board 157, Cintra and Hamman both double a weak(ish) notrump, holding:

♠A5 ♡AKQ864 ◇KJ5 ♣96

and must contend with an escape to 2♣ when it comes back to them. Barbosa's pass is forcing, though not necessarily very strong, but Cintra takes a shot at 4♡ though he knows 3NT might be the only viable game. Hamman, facing a less meaningful pass from Wolff, settles for 2♡, and then contents himself with 3♡ over Wolff's 2♠. As 3♡ is the limit of the hand, +140 and +100 give USA 6 IMPs, which ties the match at 336 with three deals to play.

The bad news on Board 157 quietens the audience a bit, but not for long!

Board 158. Neither Vul.

	♠ AK9853	
	♡ —	
	◇ A96432	
	♣ Q	
♠ 74		♠ 106
♡ AKQ1052	N	♡ J7
◇ QJ105	W E	◇ K7
♣ 4	S	♣ AKJ10987
	♠ QJ2	
	♡ 98643	
	◇ 8	
	♣ 6532	

Open Room

West	North	East	South
Cintra	Martel	Barbosa	Stansby
		2♣	pass
4♡	5♡	pass	5♠
all pass			

The 2♣ opening is natural and limited. Cintra does well to bid what he thinks he can make and then, showing healthy respect for Martel's strong bidding, sell out to 5♠, despite his substantial values and shortage in his partner's long suit. Stansby ruffs the heart lead, plays the ◊A, ruffs a diamond, then plays a club to create a late safe entry to dummy. He wins the trump switch, arranges a second diamond ruff in hand, finishes drawing trumps, and concedes a diamond to establish the long cards while maintaining trump control, +450.

Closed Room

West	North	East	South
Hamman	Marcelo	Wolff	Pedro
		2♣	pass
2◊[1]	2♠	3♣	3♠
4♡	4♠	pass	pass
dbl	all pass		

1. Artificial inquiry.

Hamman prefers to learn more about opener's hand via an artificial 2◊ response to the natural 2♣ opening, and Marcelo starts slowly, expecting more bidding. That works well for him when Pedro volunteers a spade raise, and Hamman, unsure which side owns the hand, doubles 4♠ to protect his side's equity. Wolff leads the ♣K and switches to a trump. Marcelo takes two diamond ruffs and concedes a diamond for eleven tricks and +690. Brazil's 6-IMP gain unties the match, 342-336. The VuGraph theater is not a good place for someone with a headache seeking peace and quiet. Between screams of 'Bra-zeel, Bra-zeel' and 'Bran-co, Bran-co' and a seemingly coordinated wave of foot-stomping, the room is unmistakably shaking, as if a freight train were rumbling by.

Board 159. N-S Vul.

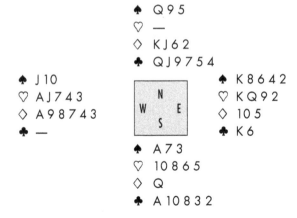

```
              ♠ Q 9 5
              ♡ —
              ◇ K J 6 2
              ♣ Q J 9 7 5 4
♠ J 10                          ♠ K 8 6 4 2
♡ A J 7 4 3         N           ♡ K Q 9 2
◇ A 9 8 7 4 3   W       E       ◇ 10 5
♣ —                 S           ♣ K 6
              ♠ A 7 3
              ♡ 10 8 6 5
              ◇ Q
              ♣ A 10 8 3 2
```

When this deal appears on the screen, the Closed Room is a bit ahead of the Open Room, but the results in the Austria-Israel semifinal are known, one of which is +1540 for 6♣ doubled, Israel's Sam Lev taking the trump finesse to get home. When Marcelo bravely risks a 2♣ overcall with the North hand at unfavorable vulnerability, it is inevitable that his side will reach a high club contract, but will it end at 5♣ or 6♣, or will East-West buy the contract in hearts?

Closed Room

West	North	East	South
Hamman	*Marcelo*	*Wolff*	*Pedro*
			pass
1♡	2♣	4♡	5♣
5♡	pass	pass	6♣
pass	pass	dbl	all pass

Pedro could reasonably try 6♣ over 4♡, as Marcelo's heart void seems a near certainty, but at the table he allows himself to be pushed into it after his opponents compete further. This two-step strategy has the effect of convincing Wolff to double on the theory that Pedro would not have bid only 5♣ if he thought he could make six, and that Hamman might well have been making 5♡. Now Marcelo needs only to make 6♣ doubled to leave Brazil in the catbird seat.

Marcelo ruffs the heart lead, and it seems likely he will get the trumps right, given his opponents' willingness to compete to 5♡ with only nine combined trumps, but nothing is happening quickly. Marcelo asks Wolff whether Hamman's pass to 6♣ is forcing; Wolff replies that it is not, but

Marcelo can't imagine East-West selling out to 6♣ undoubled in this scenario. When the ♣Q is not covered, Marcelo calls for the ace to go one down, -200.

Later, Marcelo would reveal that he had allowed Wolff's answer to his question to steer him away from the winning line, and regretted asking the question when his first thought — a strong one — had been to finesse.

Marcelo Branco

That is a disappointing result for Brazil, to be sure, but there is still the Open Room to be heard from.

Open Room

	West	North	East	South
	Cintra	Martel	Barbosa	Stansby
				pass
	pass	pass	1♠	pass
	2♡	pass	4♡	pass
	5♣	pass	5♡	all pass

The auction there is of an entirely different species, with East-West having a free run after both West and North decline the opportunity to open in second and third position. Cintra's best-guess 'prepared' 2♡ locates the best fit for his side but has the effect of convincing Barbosa to overbid to game, not expecting Cintra to be able to bid again. Cintra, with the material to take a reasonable shot at six, contents himself with 5♣, passing 5♡ when Barbosa does not bid 5◇. The 4-0 trump break is an obstacle, and when Cintra takes the diamond lead with his ace to lead a trump to the king, he is in trouble. He concedes a diamond to the jack, but Martel plays a third round, ruffed with the nine and overruffed. Stansby underleads the ♣A; Cintra ruffs, ruffs a diamond high, finesses against the ♡8, finishes drawing trumps and eventually gets spades right for one down, -50, 6 IMPs to USA. Small potatoes, given what might have been!

Almost impossibly, the match is tied again at 342, with only the final deal to play. (More than 30 years later I get shivers down my spine every time I think of the atmosphere in the Vugraph theater, where it seemed that the entire country was present, chanting and screaming in support of their heroes. Picture a soccer match in a 100,000-seat stadium and you'll have an idea what it was like.)

The last deal, unless overtime is needed to break a tie, looks like a quiet partscore, and in the Open Room, that's what it is.

Board 160. E-W Vul.

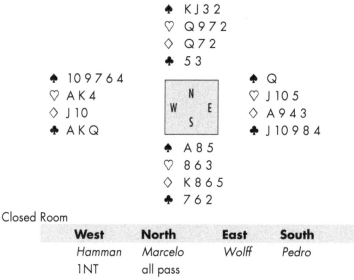

```
                    ♠ K J 3 2
                    ♡ Q 9 7 2
                    ◇ Q 7 2
                    ♣ 5 3
    ♠ 10 9 7 6 4              ♠ Q
    ♡ A K 4          N        ♡ J 10 5
    ◇ J 10      W       E     ◇ A 9 4 3
    ♣ A K Q         S        ♣ J 10 9 8 4
                    ♠ A 8 5
                    ♡ 8 6 3
                    ◇ K 8 6 5
                    ♣ 7 6 2
```

Closed Room

West	North	East	South
Hamman	Marcelo	Wolff	Pedro
1NT	all pass		

Deterred by the poor quality of his spades, Hamman rejects the idea of starting with a strong 1♣ and opens 1NT, normally 15-17 but occasionally 13-14 with clubs the only suit in a balanced hand. Wolff, blessed with a wealth of intermediate cards, might well invite game, vulnerable, but takes the conservative position by passing. Marcelo leads a heart against 1NT, and with a little help from the defenders, declarer emerges with ten tricks. With the normal heart lead rather than an entry-killing diamond lead and continuation, Hamman is always going to take at least nine tricks, but +180 seems like a plus position for USA. To have a match like this one decided by an overtrick would be harsh, but that possibility is very much in play now.

Pedro is the first player from the Closed Room (which finishes before the other) to enter the VuGraph auditorium, triggering a new round of applause. He is exhausted, but appears hopeful, as he can see that his teammates might well bid and make 3NT.

Open Room

West	North	East	South
Cintra	Martel	Barbosa	Stansby
1♣[1]	pass	1◇[2]	pass
1♠	pass	2NT	pass
3NT	all pass		

1. Strong.
2. 0-8.

If Cintra elects to rebid 1NT (16-19), he will almost surely finish in 3NT with North to lead. A heart would hand him a ninth trick, but a spade lead would give the defenders a chance, as South would know that declarer had a concealed five-card spade suit.

However, Cintra rebids 1♠, reasoning that facing a negative response, it might be important to stop in a partscore with a trump suit. When Barbosa announces his considerable values with a natural 2NT, the auditorium erupts in joy, as it seems initially that the ensuing 3NT will make... however, it soon becomes clear that the spectators' elation is premature. With East declarer, South can lead any of his thirteen cards, and there is no way to generate a ninth trick with accurate defense. When South finds the best lead of a diamond, effectively removing the only entry to declarer's long club winners, making even eight tricks becomes impossible. Declarer takes North's ◇Q with the ace and exits with the ♠Q. North wins, and the defenders continue with two more rounds of diamonds, declarer winning the third round to take the losing heart finesse. That is two down, -200, 9 IMPs to USA, who win the last set 40-33 and the match, 351-342.

Bridge can be cruel. Brazil played the entire match with four players, coming within an eyelash of upsetting a mighty American team that had not been obliged to play for eight days to reach the semifinals. The Brazilian dream had died, not on a momentous deal requiring great skill or a tactical coup, but on a choice-of-opening-bids decision that could have gone either way. Why did it have to be such an exquisitely painful dream?

The Real Boys from Brazil
(Standing) Pender, Cintra, Stansby, Martel, Ross, Wolff, Jimmy Oritz-Patino (WBF President)
(Bottom Row) Hamman, M Branco, Apteker, F Sampaio, P Branco, C Sampaio

Epilogue

USA, greatly relieved to have survived the battle with Brazil, advanced to the final against Austria, and won convincingly. Indeed, anyone who had watched the last set of USA-Brazil believed the final would be the anti-climax it proved to be.

Team USA, Bermuda Bowl, 1985
(l-r) Sheinwold, Hamman, Wolff, Martel, Ross, Stansby, Pender

6. 1986 Miami Vice

September 13-27, 1986, the Sheraton Bal Harbor Hotel, Bal Harbor, Florida: pink flamingos, stone crabs, strawberry daiquiris, little Havana, various forms of Miami vice. The world bridge community has descended upon Miami Beach for the Seventh World Bridge Championships, formerly known as the Pairs Olympiad.

It was only in 1978 that a teams event was added to the schedule at these quadrennial championships. It is for the third edition of the Rosenblum Knockout Teams that we are here (Poland won the first in New Orleans in 1978, France the second in Biarritz in 1982).

The Rosenblum, for all its prestige, is a weird event in 1986. Each country is allowed a generous quota for the teams event, but not all entrants are permitted to start in the knockout phase. In fact, the first session reduces the knockout field to what has become the usual three 32-team brackets. Nominally these brackets comprise Europe, North America, and 'Rest of the World', but this breakdown applies only to the top group of seeds in each bracket; it is the random distribution of the unseeded teams from other parts of the world that determines the true strength of each bracket. Meanwhile, many other teams start the event in the parallel Swiss — so near, yet so far from the knockout. There, they will be frequently inundated by a rolling wave of knockout losers who arrive with a splash and a huge chunk of carryover victory points.

Here's a question for the Ultra edition of Trivial Pursuit: which country won the first two Rosenblum Swisses? Right — Canada, both times after reaching the final knockout round in its bracket. For one of those 'triumphs' the WBF awarded Canada the bronze medal, which was an unkind cut to the losing Knockout semifinalists, though perhaps a not unrealistic reward for a team surviving the 'never-ending' Swiss.

I[§§] am in Bal Harbor to play (we will play a lot of matches in the Swiss this time to finish ninth overall), but at the same time I am planning to do some research for the World Championship book that will be written in the next few months. I have done a large part of the analysis for these annual reports since 1979 and always enjoyed the challenge. To my dismay, there is a note waiting for me at the front desk of the hotel from ACBL President Tom Sanders informing me that my services would not be required for this year's World Championship book. Was it something that I said, I wonder?

---

§§ Primary author Eric Kokish.

It takes some doing, but eventually I discover that an Austrian player has indeed taken exception to something accurately and objectively described in my report on the 1985 Bermuda Bowl final. He has threatened the ACBL with a lawsuit if I am not relieved of my position.

I had reported the facts of an Austrian defense including the long tempo break before a switch to a doubleton around to dummy's KQJxxx suit. The winning defense was neither to duck the ace from Axx, nor to take the ace and return the suit for a ruff: it was to take the ace and switch through dummy's king-third in a side suit, which is what would have happened in due course had the doubleton holder simply defended passively. The incident was clearly shown in real time on the closed-circuit TV in the VuGraph theater and discussed disparagingly and openly by the live commentators. I saw it all from a good seat, too. Perhaps our Austrian gentleman was miffed that I had described his partnership's successful defense as 'very efficient'.

As Henry Francis, the editor of the 1985 book, had seen no reason to revise or exclude the impugned passage, it's difficult to see why ACBL would give in to the vengeful threat, and in almost any other walk of life I am sure this sort of thing couldn't happen. In the bridge world, however, a lot of bad things have been overlooked after the possibility of legal proceedings has been raised. The ACBL has decided to bite the bullet more than once when players accused of serious improprieties have turned around and brought potentially difficult-to-defend unrelated charges of their own against the League. However, this episode has politics written all over it (the Austrian player was also a high-ranking WBF and EBL official who had contributed to both organizations in different ways for many years).

Well, how long can a guy play in the dirty laundry of the world's great players anyway? It is not particularly gratifying to be privy to every slopped undertrick of bridgedom's matinee idols. Sure, it's fun to try to capture the essence of a bridge match, trick by trick, but maybe it's time that I found another line of work. Shall I send flowers and a thank-you note to Vienna?

Both the Knockout and Swiss segments bump and grind through three tumultuous days, upsets abounding in the short matches (32 boards in the knockout matches, 7 in the Swiss), and reach the first critical juncture.

In the Knockout, each of the three brackets is won by an American team. BECKER (Mike Becker/Ronny Rubin, Jeff Meckstroth/Eric Rodwell, Mike Lawrence/Peter Weichsel) wins the North American bracket. TOUCHTIDIS (Stelios Touchtidis/Jim Robison, Ross Grabel/Jon Wittes, Robert Radwin/Stanford Holtzberg) emerges from the European bracket. ROBINSON (Steve Robinson/Peter Boyd, Kit Woolsey/Eddie Manfield, Bobby Lipsitz/Neil Silverman) is the last team standing in the 'Rest of the World' bracket.

These three winners are safely through to the Rosenblum semifinals, and will enjoy their reward of a welcome day off while the three losing bracket finalists go into the 'Mini-Knockout' stage, in which they are joined by the five teams who have clawed their way with varying degrees of tenacity to the top of the Swiss standings. Those eight Mini-KO teams will destroy themselves in pitifully short matches (16, then 20, then 24 boards) to produce the fourth Knockout semifinalist. In the end, four tired but smiling Pakistanis (Zia Mahmood/Jan-E-Alam Fazli, Nishat Abedi/Nisar Ahmed) have come back from the dead to earn the long day's prize, the right to play at least one 'real' match of 64 boards with the Rosenblum title in sight. PAKISTAN will face the winner of their original bracket, which happens to be BECKER. That leaves ROBINSON to play TOUCHTIDIS in an all-American match in the other semifinal.

PAKISTAN team, 1986
(Left to right) Mazhar Jafri (WBF), Nisar Ahmed, Nishat Abedi, Zia Mahmood, Jan-E-Alam Fazli, Tom Sanders (ACBL president)

Meanwhile, the teams in the Swiss struggle on. The losing Mini-KO semifinalists are booked to enter or reenter the Swiss (with a few tons of carryover), and the Swiss winner, as in 1982, will win the Rosenblum bronze medal. The team summoning the greatest resolve to earn the bronze in the much-despised Swiss proves to be SWEDEN (Bjorn Fallenius/Magnus Lindkvist, Mats Nilsland/Anders Wirgren), but for the time being, all eyes are trained on the Rosenblum semifinals.

We are going to focus on the match between BECKER and PAKISTAN. Let's meet the players.

Mike Becker and Ronny Rubin are two guys who love action, with equally serious interests in casino gambling and options trading. In all these aspects of their lives, they look for a percentage edge, and in their bridge system — the Ultimate Club — they feel that they have that vital advantage. Mike, who has inherited from his dad, the legendary B.J. Becker, a conservative bent and immaculate technique, can surprise you by stepping out of character on occasion. Ronny, perhaps less orthodox in his approach and often giving you the impression that he is daydreaming, is nevertheless invariably tuned to the same frequency as his partner. They know their stuff, which is saying a lot; their strong-club system (four-card majors, strongish notrumps) is a complex, relay-infested creature that is particularly effective in the slam zone.

Jeff Meckstroth and Eric Rodwell also play a strong club system (R-M Precision: five-card majors, strongish notrumps except first or second position at favorable vulnerability when they're 10-12, lots of specialized treatments, a constant state of flux) but their style is much more aggressive than that of Becker and Rubin. The thoroughness of their preparation, their ferocity and stoic demeanor at the table are among their greatest strengths.

Michael Lawrence and Peter Weichsel, two of America's most successful players for many years in other partnerships, seem to have made a good marriage. They use an Eastern Scientific approach (five-card majors, strong notrumps, strong two-over-ones) and rely more on their abilities and individual experience than a well-annotated partnership history.

Zia Mahmood, who divides his time between Karachi, London and New York, has risen quickly to the forefront of World Bridge. His playboy lifestyle and flashy approach to the game has made him a darling of the media, and he attracts an entourage wherever he goes. He is deadly serious about his bridge, though, and hopes to win a world title playing for his country. Although he is really the only acknowledged star in the Pakistani ranks, he is the first to sing the praises of many of his less-illustrious countrymen. Zia is a man with a mission. In truth, he is not so unlike the legendary American football coach Knute Rockne. 'Give it your best, Chance,' he says to the appropriately-nicknamed Nisar. 'Think of how proud your son will be when he learns you've won the World Championship.' Zia cajoles, he needles, he pleads. He is a master of inspirational rhetoric.

Zia's regular partner (Salim Masood) was unavailable for this tournament, so he has conscripted Jan-E-Alam Fazli, one of the most genuine and sympathetic characters in the world of bridge. Zia is not the easiest guy to play with, as he is always busy in the bidding and defense, and you've got to try to keep up with him, but the new partnership has been a force here in Bal Harbor. Primarily weak notrumpers, with four-card majors, they use a couple of Zia wrinkles — a 3◊ opening to show a weak preempt in one of the majors, and an allegedly completely random 3♣ opening in third seat at favorable vulnerability. At least some of the effectiveness of those opening bids is their unfamiliarity and the lack of opportunity for opponents to devise a defense against them.*¶¶

¶¶ It would be years before the WBF developed a Systems Policy that would restrict the use of such Brown Sticker conventions (the choice of a 'fecal' color designation may not have been a complete coincidence) to events that require pre-filing in advance of the tournament, and even then they are permitted only for relatively long matches.

Nisar 'Chance' Ahmed and Nishat Abedi, who have played together for many years, are both good card players and defenders. The urbane Nisar is wildly aggressive in the bidding, and the partnership is not at all easy to play against.

The Pakistanis, who have made lots of friends and earned the respect of the world bridge community since their surprise silver medal in the Bermuda Bowl in Port Chester in 1981, seem to be the sentimental favorites on the Americans' home turf. Now, isn't that something?

First Quarter (Boards 1-16)

The match is interesting from the outset...

Board 1. Neither Vul.

```
              ♠ 9653
              ♡ AJ
              ◇ AK87
              ♣ 1043
♠ J842                    ♠ KQ107
♡ KQ8          N          ♡ 943
◇ 106       W     E       ◇ Q543
♣ J752         S          ♣ 96
              ♠ A
              ♡ 107652
              ◇ J92
              ♣ AKQ8
```

Open Room

West	North	East	South
Becker	Fazli	Rubin	Zia
	1NT[1]	pass	2◇[2]
pass	2♠	pass	2NT
pass	3◇	pass	3NT
all pass			

1. 12-14.
2. Game-forcing Stayman.

Zia elects to conceal his fifth heart, and against North's 3NT, Rubin chooses to start with the ♡3. This is not a big success, as Fazli is able to play on hearts and finishes with ten tricks, +430.

	West	North	East	South
	Nishat	Meckstroth	Nisar	Rodwell
		1◊[1]	pass	1♡[2]
	pass	1♠	pass	2♣[3]
	pass	2NT	pass	3NT
	all pass			

1. 2+ diamonds, 10-15.
2. 3+ hearts.
3. Fourth-suit forcing.

With spades bid on his right, Nisar does well to lead the suit, choosing the king, and Nishat encourages with the eight under dummy's ace. Meckstroth decides not to attack hearts, which would require not only a miracle in the suit itself (7.1% chance of four tricks) but also something good to happen in spades. He runs the ◊J around to Nisar's queen. If Nisar cashes out the spades now, Nishat will be squeezed in the rounded suits on the fourth diamond. Nisar sees this, and shifts to a heart (the ♡4), knowing that declarer holds at most two cards there. Now, when Meckstroth wins the ♡A and runs the diamonds, Nishat can spare a spade and the ♡8, and the defenders can take five tricks for down one, -50. A 10-IMP jump start for PAKISTAN.

Board 3. E-W Vul.

```
              ♠ 9 4
              ♡ J 7 6 2
              ◊ K 10 9 5 2
              ♣ 7 6
♠ K Q                      ♠ 7 3
♡ A K Q 5 4       N        ♡ 10 9 3
◊ Q J 7 6    W       E     ◊ 4
♣ Q 4            S         ♣ A 10 9 8 5 3 2
              ♠ A J 10 8 6 5 2
              ♡ 8
              ◊ A 8 3
              ♣ K J
```

	West	North	East	South
	Becker	Fazli	Rubin	Zia
				1♠
	1NT	pass	3NT	all pass

Ronny Rubin

Becker elects to overcall Zia's 1♠ with a heavy but soft 1NT, and Rubin wagers that his clubs will produce enough tricks in time to secure the vulnerable game bonus. Fazli duly leads a spade against 3NT, ducked to the queen. Becker cashes two high hearts and then tries for the contract by running the ♣Q. Now he can be prevented from taking another trick (he is squeezed on the run of the spades) for -600, but Fazli parts with his heart threat one trick too early, so Becker scores a diamond in the end for -500, a truly modest triumph that reminds me of one of my own favorite bridge experiences.

In 1968, at my second Nationals, my partner, Joey Silver, fixed me up with one of my heroes, Marshall Miles, for a pairs event. When we encountered Peter Nagy and Allan Graves, who would respectively be my partner and my teammate for many years, Peter overcalled my weak notrump opening with 2♡. Marshall's 3NT ended the auction, and Peter led the doubleton jack of spades through dummy's king-and-one to Alan's ♠AQ10xxx. When spades were finished, Alan led his doubleton ♡J through my king-and-one, and Peter claimed. Down nine, -450. Marshall, who had been following the discards carefully as dummy, took only a moment to announce that this 'should be nearly average, partner; they can make 4♡ or 4♠ with an overtrick'. It takes a special player to believe that a bad result is not a bad result until the scores are posted.

Closed Room

West	North	East	South
Nishat	Meckstroth	Nisar	Rodwell
			1♠
2♡	pass	4♡	4♠
dbl	all pass		

Nishat, who settles for a simple 2♡ rather than 1NT, is bumped all the way to 4♡ by Nisar, whose imagination is purring in fifth gear. This bullies Rodwell into 4♠, which Nishat is pleased to double. He cashes a high heart and elects to continue the suit. Rodwell ruffs and plays the ace of trumps and another trump.

Nishat seems to be endplayed: a high heart establishes the jack and lets Rodwell guess clubs for his tenth trick, and a high diamond is no good either if Rodwell divines the position. Meanwhile, if he plays a club, he will later be squeezed in the red suits... but something is nagging at me about this last scenario — what if East ducks that club shift? Now the count has not been rectified for the squeeze, but declarer still has a chance — he runs spades, forcing West down to three diamonds and the ♡Q; he can't retain his second club. Now declarer leads a low diamond, forcing West to split his honors. Declarer wins with the ♢K and plays the ♡J, discarding his remaining club as West wins the ♡Q and is obliged to lead from his guarded diamond honor. Wouldn't that be something?

In the event, Nishat switches to a low diamond, and with three diamonds and six spades on top, Rodwell has time to build a club trick for +590.

A trump switch at Trick 2 appears to be the most effective defense, leaving Nishat a timely heart exit when he wins his trump trick. If declarer keeps a trump, he has to go to the ♢K to establish his ninth trick in clubs, but the defenders must then come to a trick in each suit; if he plays his last trump, West bares the ♣Q and declarer can lead the ♣K from hand, but West makes a second heart trick. In the end, 3 IMPs to BECKER, tying the match.

I'm sure Marshall Miles would have been the first to announce that Becker's -500 might gain a few IMPs for his team. A bad result is not a bad result until the scores are posted!

BECKER is 5 IMPs ahead on the strength of an unsuccessful speculative double by Zia when Board 6 appears.

Board 6. E-W Vul.

```
                    ♠ A 5
                    ♡ K 9 6 5 3
                    ♢ Q 9 4 3 2
                    ♣ A
      ♠ K J 7                          ♠ 10 9 8
      ♡ J 8 7          N               ♡ A
      ♢ A 7 6 5     W      E           ♢ K J 8
      ♣ J 8 2          S               ♣ K 10 9 5 4 3
                    ♠ Q 6 4 3 2
                    ♡ Q 10 4 2
                    ♢ 10
                    ♣ Q 7 6
```

West	North	East	South
Becker	Fazli	Rubin	Zia
		pass	pass
pass	1♡	2♣	3♡
pass	4♡	all pass	

Rubin is the only player in the two semifinal matches not to open the East hand (a 2♣ opening would show a better suit), and his side is never really in the running to do anything but defend 4♡. He leads the ♠10, which runs to the ace. Fazli leads a diamond towards the ten in dummy, and Rubin puts in the jack to continue with the ♠8. Becker wins the ♠J and continues with the king, Fazli judging to ruff with the ♡9. Although a low trump brings the ace, Fazli can no longer complete the process of leading good spades through Becker while ruffing diamonds to reenter dummy. Becker ruffs in with the ♡8, and the defense must come to either a second trump winner or a diamond trick. One down, -50. To make the hand legitimately, Fazli must return a spade at Trick 2, a counter-intuitive play.

The notion that a singleton ace of trumps can be a dangerous card to hold is illustrated here: if declarer had ruffed the third spade low he would have survived. By the same token, if East leads the ♡A on the go, and then switches to a spade, declarer should go down, as when West gets in with the ♠J, he can return a second trump, leaving declarer a trick short. The contract will also fail if East switches to the ♡A when in with ◊J at Trick 2, before exiting with anything but a club.

West	North	East	South
Nishat	Meckstroth	Nisar	Rodwell
		1♣	pass
1◊	1♡	2♣	3◊*
4♣	4♡	pass	pass
dbl	pass	5♣	pass
pass	dbl	all pass	

In the Closed Room, where East-West compete more vigorously, Nisar seems willing to let Meckstroth play in 4♡. It is not at all clear why he then elects to overrule Nishat's more forceful decision to defend, but the mercurial Chance is an instinctive player who is not afraid to back his judgment at the risk of looking foolish. In 5♣ doubled, he loses a spade, the ace of trumps and two diamond ruffs for -500. So 11 IMPs to BECKER, 26-10.

A few moments later, we are treated to a deal with enormous entertainment value.

Board 8. Neither Vul.

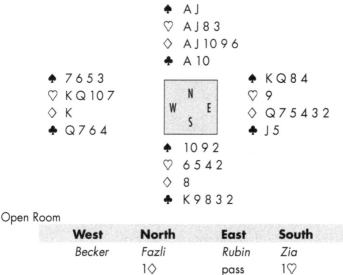

                ♠ A J
                ♡ A J 8 3
                ◊ A J 10 9 6
                ♣ A 10

♠ 7 6 5 3   ♠ K Q 8 4
♡ K Q 10 7   N   ♡ 9
◊ K   W   E   ◊ Q 7 5 4 3 2
♣ Q 7 6 4   S   ♣ J 5

                ♠ 10 9 2
                ♡ 6 5 4 2
                ◊ 8
                ♣ K 9 8 3 2

Open Room

West	North	East	South
Becker	Fazli	Rubin	Zia
	1◊	pass	1♡
pass	2♠	all pass	

Fazli opens normally enough with 1◊. Zia chooses to respond 1♡, which is the way bridge is being played these days. As Fazli apparently does not have an accurate balanced game raise in his toolkit, he improvises with a forcing 2♠, where Zia leaves him to rot; a mere three down, -150.

Closed Room

West	North	East	South
Nishat	Meckstroth	Nisar	Rodwell
	2NT[1]	pass	3♣[2]
pass	3◊[3]	pass	3♠[4]
pass	4♡	dbl	all pass

1. 20-21.
2. Puppet Stayman.
3. No five-card major.
4. Four hearts.

Meckstroth prefers to open 2NT (nominally 20-21+ HCP), Rodwell elects to move forward and a Puppet Stayman sequence lands Meckstroth in 4♡. The fierce Nisar doubles this, expecting a bad lie for declarer, and leads the ♠K.

Meckstroth takes the ♠A and returns the jack, Nisar winning to play a third spade. Now a trump, low from Nishat... eight. Nisar gratefully wins the nine, and Nishat must take two more trump tricks for one down, -100. Just 2 IMPs to BECKER, 28-10. Meckstroth curses himself (well, mildly) for not putting in the jack of trumps.

Then, a partscore with several points of interest...

Board 10. Both Vul.

```
                    ♠ K J 6 3
                    ♡ A Q 4
                    ◇ A 7 4
                    ♣ Q 6 2
    ♠ A Q 4 2                        ♠ 9 8 7
    ♡ 6 5 3           N              ♡ K 10 9 8 7 2
    ◇ Q 6 2      W         E         ◇ J 8
    ♣ A K 3           S              ♣ 8 5
                    ♠ 10 5
                    ♡ J
                    ◇ K 10 9 5 3
                    ♣ J 10 9 7 4
```

Open Room

West	North	East	South
Becker	Fazli	Rubin	Zia
		pass	pass
1NT	pass	2◇[1]	pass
2♡	all pass		

1. Transfer.

Do you think that Zia should reopen against 2♡? This is not the sort of action that has great appeal for successful rubber bridge players, but it would probably have netted his side +110 or +100 this time. Against Becker's 2♡, Fazli finds the best lead, a small club. Becker wins, leads a trump to the king, and then the ◇J. Zia's king holds the trick, and he switches to the ♠5, catering mainly to some ace-jack holding in Fazli's hand. When Becker ducks the spade to the jack, Fazli continues the suit, and Becker has eight tricks; +110.

If Fazli first cashes his trump winners, and exits with a club, Becker can still prevail by ruffing a club and running trumps to reduce to the ♠AQ and ◇Q. If he reads the ending correctly, he will catch Fazli in a strip-squeeze and endplay.

West	North	East	South
Nishat	Meckstroth	Nisar	Rodwell
		pass	pass
1NT	dbl	2♡	all pass

Meckstroth's double of Nishat's strong notrump (perhaps he mistakes it for a weakie) seems especially aggressive, as he has no source of tricks, minimum point count and lots of jeopardy. When Nisar scampers out to 2♡, Rodwell contributes a forcing pass (or so says his convention card). Meckstroth refuses to be forced, however, and the Pakistanis steal a partscore. It looks as if 2♡ is scheduled to go down on a club lead, but that's not what happens...

Nisar wins with the ♣A in dummy and tries a diamond to the jack and king. Rodwell returns the ◇10 and Nisar covers, ruffs the third diamond, crosses to dummy in clubs, and leads a heart to his king. Meckstroth wins the trump continuation, cashes his remaining trump winner and exits with his last safe card, a club. Nisar ruffs and leads the ♠9: ten, queen, king. Meckstroth is endplayed; +110. No swing.

With East declarer, a spade lead is the killer, preventing the endplay.

Board 11. Neither Vul.

```
                    ♠ K 9 3
                    ♡ A 8 6 5
                    ◇ A 7
                    ♣ K J 10 8
  ♠ A 10 7 6 5 4 2           ♠ Q
  ♡ K J 10 7         N       ♡ Q 4
  ◇ 4            W       E   ◇ K 10 9 8 2
  ♣ 6                S       ♣ Q 7 5 4 2
                    ♠ J 8
                    ♡ 9 3 2
                    ◇ Q J 6 5 3
                    ♣ A 9 3
```

West	North	East	South
Becker	Fazli	Rubin	Zia
			pass
pass	1♣	pass	1◇
2♠	dbl[1]	pass	2NT
pass	3NT	all pass	

1. 'Strong', balanced.

Neither West elects to open in second seat, perhaps because there is no opening bid that accurately describes his hand. Meanwhile, 1♠ would get plenty of expert support today, and in the UK in any era.

Becker's passed-hand jump overcall might imply that he has a secondary heart suit. Fazli doubles this to show a strong notrump type (probably stronger than this, however), and when Zia gropes with 2NT (minors?), Fazli finds a 'raise' to 3NT, which tells us that he does not have a handle on the meaning of 2NT. Becker starts with the ♡10, which holds, and he continues with the ♡7, ducked to the queen. Rubin's switch to the ♠Q runs to dummy's king, and Zia calls for the ◇7. Rubin rushes up with the king and exits with the ◇2. Zia advances the ♣J from dummy, and Rubin, picturing Becker with the ♣A and Zia with the ♠A for his notrump bid, decides to go in with the queen. Suddenly, Zia has nine winners: four clubs, three diamonds, and one of each major. A rather spectacular +400.

It would not have helped East to withhold the ♣Q, but retaining the ◇K would have left declarer with no route to nine tricks.

Closed Room

West	North	East	South
Nishat	Meckstroth	Nisar	Rodwell
			pass
pass	1NT	pass	2♣[1]
pass	2◇[2]	pass	2♡[3]
3♠	all pass		

1. Puppet Stayman.
2. No five-card major.
3. No four-card major or only four spades.

I'll give long odds that you will never again see an auction in which someone makes a jump overcall at his *third* turn in a live auction, but I recognize I might have to pay off if Nisar and Nishat hang around for a while. With the friendly spade position, there are only four losers in 3♠, so +140 and 11 IMPs to PAKISTAN, now 12 IMPs behind, 21-33.

Board 12. N-S Vul.

```
                        ♠ 2
                        ♡ A 5
                        ◇ K Q 8 7 5 3
                        ♣ K 10 9 3
        ♠ A J 10 9 6              ♠ K Q 7 4
        ♡ 7 6 2          N         ♡ K J 9 8 4
        ◇ J 10        W     E      ◇ —
        ♣ A 8 2          S         ♣ Q J 6 5
                        ♠ 8 5 3
                        ♡ Q 10 3
                        ◇ A 9 6 4 2
                        ♣ 7 4
```

Open Room

West	North	East	South
Becker	Fazli	Rubin	Zia
pass	1◇	1♡	1NT
dbl[1]	2◇	2♠	pass
pass	3♣	pass	3◇
3♠	all pass		

1. Normally clubs and spades.

Zia leads the ♣7, ducked to the king, and Fazli switches to the ◇K. When declarer ruffs, I suspect Fazli thinks, 'Ah, of course!' Rubin cashes two rounds of trumps, ruffs a diamond, plays a club to the ace, draws the outstanding trump and plays a heart to the king for eleven tricks, +200.

Rubin's 2♠ looks like a serious underbid to me, but perhaps there is some doubt about the nature of Becker's double of 1NT. Zia gets some brownie points in my ledger for his tactical notrump, which seems to have played a part in the American misjudgment at his table.

Closed Room

West	North	East	South
Nishat	Meckstroth	Nisar	Rodwell
pass	1◇[1]	1♡	pass
1♠	2◇	4♠	all pass

1. 2+ diamonds, 10-15.

It is rarely easy to find a paying sacrifice at unfavorable vulnerability, and it is easy to see why Rodwell does not go on to 5◇ over 4♠. He is hurt a bit by his system, unable to raise diamonds (which may be nonexistent) over 1♡, while the price is right.

In 4♠, Nishat gets hearts right for +450, and 6 IMPs to PAKISTAN. The American lead is down to 6 IMPs, 33-27.

BECKER builds the lead to 18 with a couple of well-judged competitive decisions, but Pakistan ends the first quarter on a positive note...

Board 16. E-W Vul.

```
                    ♠ J 7 4
                    ♡ A Q
                    ◇ 6 4
                    ♣ A 10 6 5 4 2
     ♠ A 8                            ♠ K Q 9
     ♡ K J 9 5          N             ♡ 6 4 3 2
     ◇ K Q J 10 9   W       E         ◇ 8 5 3
     ♣ Q 9              S             ♣ K J 3
                    ♠ 10 6 5 3 2
                    ♡ 10 8 7
                    ◇ A 7 2
                    ♣ 8 7
```

Open Room

West	North	East	South
Becker	Fazli	Rubin	Zia
1◇	2♣	dbl*	pass
3♡	pass	4♡	all pass

Two trump losers and two aces: -100.

Closed Room

West	North	East	South
Nishat	Meckstroth	Nisar	Rodwell
1◇	2♣	2◇	pass
3◇	pass	3NT	all pass

Nisar must choose from among pass, 2◇, 2NT, and a penalty double of 2♣. He opts for 2◇ (his partnership plays four-card majors, so missing a heart fit is not such a big concern). Nishat raises himself to 3◇, suggesting a suit of quality, and Nisar accepts the invitation with an easy (well, easier) 3NT. Plus 600. Hearts are never a factor, and it's 12 IMPs to PAKISTAN. You can decide for yourself whether that big swing to PAKISTAN is well earned or simply a matter of luck.

BECKER leads 45-39 at the end of the set, but it is shaping up as a close match.

Second Quarter (Boards 17-32)

Lawrence and Weichsel come in for Becker and Rubin to face Nisar and Nishat, while Meckstroth and Rodwell take on Zia and Fazli.

Board 17. Neither Vul.

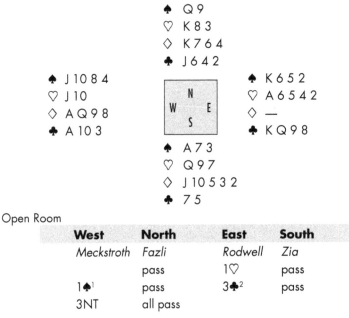

♠ Q 9
♡ K 8 3
◇ K 7 6 4
♣ J 6 4 2

♠ J 10 8 4
♡ J 10
◇ A Q 9 8
♣ A 10 3

♠ K 6 5 2
♡ A 6 5 4 2
◇ —
♣ K Q 9 8

♠ A 7 3
♡ Q 9 7
◇ J 10 5 3 2
♣ 7 5

Open Room

West	North	East	South
Meckstroth	Fazli	Rodwell	Zia
	pass	1♡	pass
1♠[1]	pass	3♣[2]	pass
3NT	all pass		

1. Possibly only three spades.
2. Short diamonds, three or (more often) four spades.

When Meckstroth responds 1♠, Rodwell's jump to 3♣ confirms diamond shortness. With all that diamond duplication and with such lovely notrump cards in the other suits, Meckstroth tries 3NT. As his 1♠ might have been a three-card suit in the partnership methods, Rodwell is in no position to return to 4♠. Against 3NT, Fazli starts a diamond to the ten and queen, dummy parting with a spade. He covers Meckstroth's ♠J with the queen, and Zia takes the king with the ace and returns a diamond to the eight and king, dummy throwing a heart. Fazli switches to the ♡K. Meckstroth ducks, then ducks again on the continuation of the ♡3. Zia wins with the queen, and switches to the ♠3, so Meckstroth is faced with a guess for the contract. Perhaps convinced from the early defense that hearts are not about to break evenly, he puts in the ♠8. Fazli's ♠9 is the setting trick. Rather well done by the Pakistanis.

Closed Room

West	North	East	South
Nishat	Weichsel	Nisar	Lawrence
	pass	1♡	pass
1♠	pass	4◇*	pass
4♠	all pass		

How aggressive is that Nisar person? Enough to splinter to 4◇ over a 1♠ response to his 1♡. Although lesser players might wait for an extra ace-king for such a big bid, it is not Nisar's style to worry about high cards. Nishat realizes this, and signs off in 4♠ with a hand that seems worth at least one move. High enough. A club is led, and Nishat wins the ten and starts with a low trump: nine, king, ace. Lawrence returns his remaining club, and Nishat continues with the ♠10. Weichsel wins and does not give Lawrence his club ruff as that will obviate the need for Nishat to draw a third round of trumps and the hearts will come home in due time. Instead, Weichsel switches to a diamond, hoping to force dummy and ruin the transportation. Nishat can draw the last trump now and lose a trick in the wash for +420. PAKISTAN takes the lead with this 10-IMP pickup, 49-45.

Nisar Ahmed

Watch closely now, and you will see some of the more unusual things that seem to be part of the game today.

Board 18. N-S Vul.

```
                    ♠ 9 4
                    ♡ 9 3 2
                    ◇ A J 9 5 2
                    ♣ A J 5
   ♠ 8 7                              ♠ A Q 6
   ♡ 10 8 7 5 4      ┌─────────┐      ♡ 6
   ◇ K 3            │    N    │      ◇ 10 7 6 4
   ♣ Q 10 8 6       │ W     E │      ♣ K 9 4 3 2
                    │    S    │
                     └─────────┘
                    ♠ K J 10 5 3 2
                    ♡ A K Q J
                    ◇ Q 8
                    ♣ 7
```

Open Room

West	North	East	South
Meckstroth	Fazli	Rodwell	Zia
		pass	1♠
1NT*	dbl	2♣	2♡
pass	2NT	pass	4♠
all pass			

Is Meckstroth's 1NT overcall a pure psych? Well, maybe. Meckstroth and Rodwell play a 'comic' notrump overcall that purports to deliver a weak one-suiter when it not strong; is this such a hand? Rodwell runs when 1NT is doubled, allowing the vulnerability to influence him in identifying the psychist. In 4♠, Zia loses two trump tricks — East rises with the ace on the first round of the suit, and later Zia lays down the king, for +650.

Closed Room

West	North	East	South
Nishat	Weichsel	Nisar	Lawrence
		pass	1♠
pass	1NT*	2♣	2♡
4♣	dbl	all pass	

Nisar comes charging in with 2♣. Why this should be sensible, I can't begin to fathom. The suit is terrible; there is playability in another strain; two-thirds of the high cards live in a suit bid by an offside opponent; partner has not acted; RHO has at least temporarily denied a fit; no bidding space is being stolen. Nishat is willing to offer a jump raise to 4♣, where the Pakistanis are doubled.

South starts with two rounds of hearts and declarer ruffs to play a diamond to the king and ace. North returns the ♠9: queen, king. Declarer wins the spade return with the ace and exits with his remaining spade, pitching dummy's diamond. South exits with the ◇Q, and declarer ruffs in dummy, ruffs a heart, ruffs a diamond (South throwing a heart), and ruffs a heart with the ♣9. When South can't overruff, declarer ruffs a diamond with the ♣Q, but North overruffs with the ace, and returns the ♣J, pinning dummy's ten and leaving his ♣5 to beat the ♣4! If you've been keeping track of the trick totals you will know that Nisar has gone down only three, merely -500, so PAKISTAN actually gains 4 IMPs, extending their lead to 8 IMPs, 53-45.

Then, a lead problem.

Board 19. E-W Vul.

```
              ♠ Q 9 4 3 2
              ♡ Q J 10 9 5
              ◇ 7
              ♣ Q 8
  ♠ J 7 5                      ♠ K 10 8
  ♡ 7 2            N           ♡ A 8 4
  ◇ K J 10 3 2  W   E         ◇ 9 8 5
  ♣ 10 6 3         S           ♣ A J 9 7
              ♠ A 6
              ♡ K 6 3
              ◇ A Q 6 4
              ♣ K 5 4 2
```

Open Room

West	North	East	South
Meckstroth	Fazli	Rodwell	Zia
			1♣
pass	1♡	pass	1NT[1]
pass	2♣[2]	pass	3♡
pass	4♡	all pass	

1. 15-17.
2. Checkback.

It's standard practice to respond 1♠ with 5-5 in the majors, but on certain one-bid hands it can work well to bid 1♡, intending to rebid a good five-card suit if necessary. Fazli sees merit in that idea on this deal, then finds himself badly placed on the second round. He gets lucky when Zia shows a maximum with heart support.

Rodwell's low-trump lead is deadly, as he can lead two more rounds when he gains the lead in spades; down one, -50.

Closed Room

West	North	East	South
Nishat	Weichsel	Nisar	Lawrence
			1NT
pass	2♣	dbl	pass
pass	2♡[1]	pass	3♡
pass	4♡	all pass	

1. Hearts and spades, non-forcing.

Nisar's diamond lead fares less well. Weichsel wins the ace and plays on spades. He accepts the diamond force, ruffs the spades good, and plays trumps. Forced again in diamonds, he needs some luck, and gets it. When he finishes with his spade winners and plays a club, he finds the opponent with the ♣A is out of diamonds, so can't be prevented from scoring his tenth trick in clubs. That's 10 IMPs to BECKER, back in the lead, 55-53.

Board 20. Both Vul.

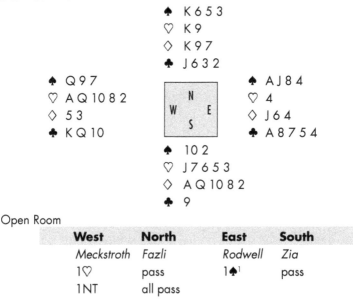

Open Room

West	North	East	South
Meckstroth	Fazli	Rodwell	Zia
1♡	pass	1♠[1]	pass
1NT	all pass		

1. Possibly only three spades.

Fazli leads a club, and Meckstroth wins with the ten, unblocks the ♣KQ, and plays the ♠Q, covered by the king and ace (South has already pitched the ♠10), so declarer cashes two more clubs and three more spades before playing a heart to the queen. North wins with the king, and the defenders score the last three tricks with diamonds, +150.

Closed Room

West	North	East	South
Nishat	Weichsel	Nisar	Lawrence
1♡	pass	1♠	pass
2♠	pass	3◇	pass
4♠	all pass		

A question of evaluation, after a raise to 2♠ (potentially three-card support). Nisar tries for game with 3◇ (help suit) and Nishat, perhaps feeling that this sequence suggests a fifth spade, jumps to game.

Lawrence starts with his singleton club and Nisar wins dummy's king to advance the ♠Q, a fine start. If Weichsel covers, the defense might have a chance, but he doesn't, naturally enough. Nisar continues with the ♠9 to his jack, and notes with hope the appearance of the ten (although he knows that Lawrence, who has written a book with that title, is certainly capable of falsecarding). Now a club to the queen and the ♣10. Weichsel has no good answer. He elects to cover, but Nisar wins the ace, goes to the ♡A, finesses the ♠8 (Weichsel actually puts up his ♠K, but Nisar is wide awake and captures it), draws the last trump, and finishes the clubs for ten tricks, and a spectacular +620. That's 10 IMPs to PAKISTAN, who now lead 63-55.

Peter Weichsel

Board 25. E-W Vul.

```
              ♠ 6 5 2
              ♡ 8
              ◇ A K J 8 6 4 3
              ♣ J 7
♠ A J 9                        ♠ K Q 10 8 4
♡ A 9 4 3          N           ♡ Q 10 7 6 5
◇ Q 10 9 2      W     E        ◇ —
♣ 9 3              S           ♣ 10 4 2
              ♠ 7 3
              ♡ K J 2
              ◇ 7 5
              ♣ A K Q 8 6 5
```

Open Room

West	North	East	South
Meckstroth	Fazli	Rodwell	Zia
	2◇[1]	pass	2NT[2]
pass	3NT[3]	all pass	

1. Weak.
2. Inquiry.
3. Excellent suit for notrump.

Rejecting 2♣ (either strong and artificial or a diamond preempt) Fazli starts with a weak 2◇. Convinced that East-West would do well in a major, Zia makes a semi-psychic response, which leads to an unlikely game that can be made if he gains the lead soon enough. Meckstroth, whose diamond holding suggests that he might have time to recover from a misguess, starts with a low heart. Zia tests diamonds early and soon takes ten tricks, +430.

Closed Room

West	North	East	South
Nishat	Weichsel	Nisar	Lawrence
	3◇	all pass	

Weichsel's 3◇ promises a good suit, but Lawrence really has no reason to move forward. East leads the ♠K, and West overtakes to switch to the ◇2. Declarer puts in the jack (the eight would be the true safety play) to retain the possibility of ruffing his third spade if necessary. When East discards, declarer can no longer claim, but when he plays a heart to the jack and ace, the contract is secure. If Nishat does not cash a second spade to continue trumps, declarer will make four, discarding one spade on the ♡K and another on a high club as West ruffs with his trump trick. Nishat sees this, offers a little shrug, and cashes the ♠J, holding Weichsel to +110. BECKER had been ahead 69-64, but the 8-IMP swing on this deal gives PAKISTAN a 3-IMP lead, 72-69.

Board 26. Both Vul.

```
               ♠ A Q 7 6 2
               ♡ 9 5 3
               ◇ 5 4 2
               ♣ A 5
 ♠ 4                          ♠ 10 9 8 5 3
 ♡ A J 10 6        N          ♡ 8 7 4
 ◇ A Q J 10 9 7  W   E        ◇ —
 ♣ K J            S           ♣ Q 10 8 6 4
               ♠ K J
               ♡ K Q 2
               ◇ K 8 6 3
               ♣ 9 7 3 2
```

Open Room

West	North	East	South
Meckstroth	Fazli	Rodwell	Zia
		pass	pass
1♣*	1♠	pass[1]	2♠
dbl	pass	3♣	pass
3◇	all pass		

1. 0-4.

North leads his lowest trump, and declarer wins with the seven, cashes the ace and continues with the queen. South takes the king and switches to the ♣2. North takes declarer's king with the ace and returns a club. That allows declarer to win in dummy, pitch a spade on the ♣10, as North follows helplessly, and play a heart, +130.

It would be better for North to duck the ♣K, but then declarer draws the last trump and plays a black card. As South has only two spades, declarer will eventually come to a position in which he can exit with a middle heart to endplay South. Only an inspired low spade lead and club switch (North must duck if West plays the king, but win if West plays the jack) would set 3◇. Even Zia, whose tactical raise to 2♠ gave the defense a theoretical chance, is not prepared to fault Fazli... too harshly... for not finding the optimum lead.

West	North	East	South
Nishat	Weichsel	Nisar	Lawrence
		pass	1◇
pass	1♠	pass	1NT
all pass			

Lawrence's 1◇ is natural, 3+ diamonds. Nishat doesn't have a natural diamond overcall available, but after the 1NT rebid, both a double (takeout of spades rather than a diamond trap, intending to convert clubs to diamonds) and a natural 2◇ are viable alternatives to his hopeful pass. Nishat leads the ◇Q, and Lawrence has only to unblock spades and knock out the ♡A for seven tricks. A happy +90.

If West starts with the ◇A (lose to the blank ◇K just *once* in your life and you will never again lead the queen when you have a sure side entry), and East discards a discouraging heart, do you think West could justify a switch to the ♣K at Trick 2?

BECKER gains 6 IMPs, back in front now, 75-72.

Board 27. Neither Vul.

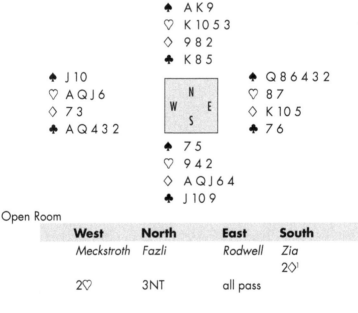

```
              ♠ A K 9
              ♡ K 10 5 3
              ◇ 9 8 2
              ♣ K 8 5
♠ J 10                      ♠ Q 8 6 4 3 2
♡ A Q J 6          N        ♡ 8 7
◇ 7 3          W     E      ◇ K 10 5
♣ A Q 4 3 2        S        ♣ 7 6
              ♠ 7 5
              ♡ 9 4 2
              ◇ A Q J 6 4
              ♣ J 10 9
```

Open Room

West	North	East	South
Meckstroth	Fazli	Rodwell	Zia
			2◇[1]
2♡	3NT	all pass	

1. Weak.

After a lively, imaginative auction, Rodwell leads the ♡8 against Fazli's bold 3NT. Do we think he expects Zia to have the sort of hand Fazli held for 2◇

on Board 25? Meckstroth takes the ace and switches to the ♣3, which runs to dummy's ten. Fazli is cold for ten tricks now on the lie of the cards, for a 'wow' +430. Go bid that one, friends!

Closed Room

West	North	East	South
Nishat	Weichsel	Nisar	Lawrence
			pass
1♣	dbl	1♠	2◊
pass	pass	2♠	3◊
3♠	all pass		

Nisar does not sell out without a fight, but 2♠ convinces Nishat to compete to 3♠ — not that 3◊ is in any jeopardy. After Lawrence's heart lead, Nisar loses a heart, three diamonds and two spades for two down, -100, but that is 8 IMPs to PAKISTAN, ahead now, 80-75.

Board 28. N-S Vul.

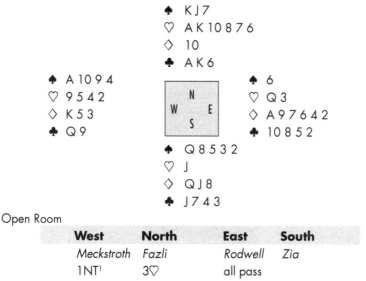

```
              ♠ K J 7
              ♡ A K 10 8 7 6
              ◊ 10
              ♣ A K 6
♠ A 10 9 4              ♠ 6
♡ 9 5 4 2         N     ♡ Q 3
◊ K 5 3        W   E    ◊ A 9 7 6 4 2
♣ Q 9            S      ♣ 10 8 5 2
              ♠ Q 8 5 3 2
              ♡ J
              ◊ Q J 8
              ♣ J 7 4 3
```

Open Room

West	North	East	South
Meckstroth	Fazli	Rodwell	Zia
1NT[1]	3♡	all pass	

1. 9-12, balanced.

When Meckstroth opens a mininotrump, Fazli, worried about a long diamond suit, opts for a 'strong' jump overcall of 3♡ rather than a penalty double, and Zia can't find a reason to go on. Meckstroth wins the spade lead with the ace as Fazli contributes the jack. He switches to a trump, ducked to the queen, and now Rodwell underleads his ◊A for a spade ruff. Cute, but +140 for Fazli.

Closed Room

West	North	East	South
Nishat	Weichsel	Nisar	Lawrence
pass	1♡	3◊	pass
4◊	dbl	pass	4♠
all pass			

Nishat leads a straightforward low diamond, but now the defense can't play diamonds twice to force dummy as declarer has a diamond winner. Lawrence has tricks to burn in the rounded suits and loses only two trump tricks for +620. That's 10 IMPs to BECKER, 85-80; yet another lead change!

Declarer might well make 4♠ anyway, but it would be more interesting on the lead of the ◊K from West, the sort of lead that would become much more common in the next millennium. Declarer would ruff the second diamond and play the ♠K. West wins and returns a diamond, forcing declarer to ruff with the ♠J, but because declarer can cash three hearts, ruff the fourth in hand, and cash both high clubs, he reduces to Q85 of trumps while West has 1094. Declarer ruffs a plain card with the eight or five and West is endplayed when he overruffs.

Those on Zia's speed-dial list can expect an unwelcome early-morning call (jet lag makes him an early riser) challenging them with this lead problem, to be followed by an expletive-filled lament of how unlucky Pakistan was that Zia was not in the West seat. Only after his captive audience acknowledges the brilliance of the ◊K lead would The Great Zia explain how he would still make 4♠ if *he* were in declarer's seat.

Zia Mahmood

Board 31. N-S Vul.

```
                    ♠ 9 8 6 4
                    ♡ —
                    ◇ Q J 5 3 2
                    ♣ A K 10 4
    ♠ Q J 5 2          ┌──────────┐      ♠ K 10 7 3
    ♡ Q 8 3 2          │    N     │      ♡ A J 10 5 4
    ◇ 10 7 6           │ W     E  │      ◇ A 8
    ♣ 8 5              │    S     │      ♣ 7 2
                       └──────────┘
                    ♠ A
                    ♡ K 9 7 6
                    ◇ K 9 4
                    ♣ Q J 9 6 3
```

Open Room

West	North	East	South
Meckstroth	Fazli	Rodwell	Zia
			1♣
pass	1◇	1♡	2◇
3♡	4♡	pass	5◇
all pass			

In this room, where Zia and Fazli contrive to miss their club fit, Rodwell leads the ♡A, and Fazli ruffs, draws trumps, and concedes a spade for +600.

Closed Room

West	North	East	South
Nishat	Weichsel	Nisar	Lawrence
			1♣
1NT[1]	2♣[2]	pass	2♡
pass	3♣	dbl[3]	pass
3♠	dbl	all pass	

1. 15-18 or 'comic', apparently some nonspecific weak hand.
2. Stayman, at least one major.
3. Takeout.

In this room, there is some confusion about the bidding and East-West's explanations. In theory, the defenders can collect 500 — a high club lead (South following with the queen) and a diamond switch, South giving North two or three heart ruffs, but that doesn't happen. A heart ruff disappears and Nishat escapes for two down, -300. The Americans feel they have not been given timely complete information, but when the director disagrees and the case goes to appeal, the score stands, and PAKISTAN gains 7 IMPs to reclaim the lead, 88-85, which is how the first half concludes.

There is a rumor that Nishat's book on the comic notrump is an overnight sensation in Karachi. Perhaps it is Zia's empathetic foreword that is the catalyst.

Third Quarter (Boards 33-48)

It's Fazli and Zia versus Weichsel and Lawrence in the Open Room, with Rubin and Becker against Nisar and Nishat in the Closed Room.

On the second deal of the set, East-West are faced with these hands, East dealer, North-South vulnerable:

♠ 8 4		♠ A Q 9 7 6
♡ K 10 8 6 2		♡ A 3
◇ K Q J 10 7 2		◇ 9 4 3
♣ —		♣ K 5 4

Lawrence, West, buries his hearts, and uses an invitational sequence in diamonds after Weichsel's 1♠ opening, responding 2◇ and bidding 3◇ over 2♠. Weichsel tries 3NT, which Lawrence removes to 4♡, giving a good picture of his hand. Weichsel converts to 5◇. Lawrence takes a straightforward line but can't make the contract, -50.

At the other table, Nisar opens the East hand with a weak notrump, and Nishat uses Stayman with the West hand. Over 2♠, he tries 3♡, invitational, and there he plays. He attacks diamonds early, and is pleased to learn later that his careful play for +140 has earned him 5 IMPs.

Board 37. N-S Vul.

```
        ♠ A 9 7
        ♡ A Q 2
        ◇ J 4 2
        ♣ K 9 7 6
        ▭▭▭▭▭
        ♠ 5 4
        ♡ J 8
        ◇ A K 6 5 3
        ♣ A Q 3 2
```

Where would you like to play these North-South cards? Zia and Fazli bid 1NT-3NT, which is cold on an average lie of the cards, +600.

Rubin is obliged to open the North hand with 1◇, and is treated to a weak jump overcall of 2♠ by Nisar, who holds:

♠ K Q 10 6 3   ♡ 9 5 3   ◇ Q 10 9 7   ♣ 10

Over Becker's 3♠ cuebid, Nishat raises to 4♠ on:

♠ J 8 2   ♡ K 10 7 6 4   ◇ 8   ♣ J 8 5 4

Rubin is happy to double this, and the price is 700. Probably not a phantom save as Rubin figured to rebid 3NT over 3♠, but it's easy to imagine North-South getting too high in a minor. In the event, 3 IMPs to BECKER, trailing now by 5, 89-94.

The following is a true story. None of the names have been changed to protect the guilty.

Board 41. E-W Vul.

```
              ♠ J 10 8 7 5
              ♡ 9 4 3 2
              ◇ Q
              ♣ J 10 9
♠ 6 4                          ♠ K 3 2
♡ A K J 10 7      N            ♡ Q 5
◇ 9 6 3       W       E        ◇ K 10 8 5 4 2
♣ 8 3 2           S            ♣ 7 6
              ♠ A Q 9
              ♡ 8 6
              ◇ A J 7
              ♣ A K Q 5 4
```

Open Room

West	North	East	South
Nishat	Rubin	Nisar	Becker
	1♠!	1NT¹	dbl
pass	2♣	pass	pass
2NT	pass	3◇	pass
3♡	all pass		

1. 16(15)-18 or comic, apparently some nonspecific weak hand.

No one knows the score, of course, but the match is actually tied at this point. Rubin can't resist opening the bidding, and he chooses 1♠. Perhaps a tad husky for a psych, but picking up a bad hand in first seat at favorable vulnerability is not so unlike contemplating an overture towards an attractive member of the appropriate sex: seduction is seduction. Just ask Nisar, East, who rather remarkably counters with a psychic of his own. Oh, his 1NT is described as potentially 'comic' on his system card, but he is vulnerable against not, after all! Will his foil, Nishat, figure this one out?

That remains unclear when Nishat rejects both a sensible business redouble and a sensible runout to 2♡ when Becker doubles for penalty. However, Rubin can't stand it (had he passed, even the intrepid Nisar would not have sat for it: the number would have been 1700 or so) and starts with a wriggle to 2♣, perhaps only a moment before the imaginative Nisar would have started a deceptive escape strategy with the same 2♣ bid! Well, now Nisar can see good things on the horizon, so he rejects the cheap opportunity to show his diamonds. Becker knows that Rubin has psyched, and expects a far less useful hand than he holds, so he decides to pass. Poor Nishat really can't be sure what is happening, but can't assume Nisar does not have a real notrump. He tries 2NT, continuing his middle-of-the-road approach with a hand that could easily be deemed suitable for more of a commitment. When Nisar removes to 3◊, Nishat begins to have his doubts, but he converts to 3♡ just the same. Now it is up to Becker on the way out. He has lots of high cards, but can hardly expect to defeat 3♡ opposite a yarborough, so he passes. The defense is good, and Nishat makes only his five trump tricks, which leaves him down a cool 400 points.

Closed Room

	West	North	East	South
	Lawrence	Fazli	Weichsel	Zia
		pass	pass	2NT
	pass	3♣	pass	3◊
	pass	3♠	pass	4◊*
	pass	4♠	all pass	

Fazli doesn't have much, but must force to game, fending off Zia's (natural) lead-dissuading slam try. Nonetheless, Weichsel leads a diamond lead through the ace-jack. Declarer goes up with the ace and calls for the ♠Q, aiming to keep control as much as possible. If Weichsel wins and plays on hearts now, Fazli will be able to ruff high and overtake the ♠9, but Weichsel continues trumps, and Fazli takes his ten winners in top cards. That translates to one strange, wretched IMP to PAKISTAN, who take the lead by that very margin!

Isn't bridge fun?

Board 42. Both Vul.

```
              ♠ 10 8 5 4 3
              ♡ J 10 8 5 3
              ◇ Q
              ♣ A J
    ♠ K 2                      ♠ J 6
    ♡ A K 2            N       ♡ 9
    ◇ A 7 2        W       E   ◇ 10 9 8 6 5 4
    ♣ K Q 10 6 5       S       ♣ 9 7 4 2
              ♠ A Q 9 7
              ♡ Q 7 6 4
              ◇ K J 3
              ♣ 8 3
```

Open Room

West	North	East	South
Nishat	Rubin	Nisar	Becker
		pass	1♡
1NT[1]	3♡	all pass	

1. 16-18 balanced or a random hand.

Nishat could not be accused of overbidding this time. Becker has to go one down in 3♡ after the ♣K lead, losing two hearts and one of each remaining suit, for -100.

Closed Room

West	North	East	South
Lawrence	Fazli	Weichsel	Zia
		pass	1NT[1]
dbl	2♡	3◇[2]	pass
3NT	dbl	rdbl[3]	all pass

1. 12-14.
2. Alerted, interpreted as showing values.
3. Intended as showing doubt.

Lawrence and Weichsel are on different frequencies regarding the strength of 3◇ as they skate into 3NT, then stick it out, redoubled, for the wrong reason. Fazli elects to lead a spade, and Zia plays the ace and queen. Lawrence wins, and leads the ♣Q to Fazli's ace. Fazli cashes his spades, Zia unblocking the nine. Lawrence keeps all his clubs and gets out for just one down one when the ♣K fells the jack, -400. That triumph holds the American loss to 11 IMPs, leaving PAKISTAN ahead by 12, 106-94.

Board 43. Neither Vul.

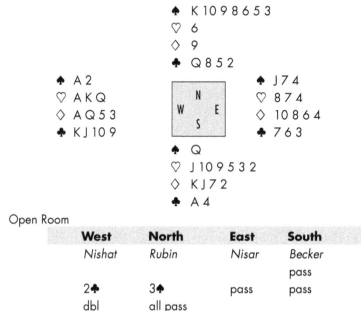

```
                    ♠ K 10 9 8 6 5 3
                    ♡ 6
                    ◇ 9
                    ♣ Q 8 5 2
   ♠ A 2                              ♠ J 7 4
   ♡ A K Q              N             ♡ 8 7 4
   ◇ A Q 5 3        W       E         ◇ 10 8 6 4
   ♣ K J 10 9           S             ♣ 7 6 3
                    ♠ Q
                    ♡ J 10 9 5 3 2
                    ◇ K J 7 2
                    ♣ A 4
```

Open Room

West	North	East	South
Nishat	Rubin	Nisar	Becker
			pass
2♣	3♠	pass	pass
dbl	all pass		

Becker elects to pass that peculiar South hand, but although Rubin is full value for 3♠, that just helps him hold down the American loss when Nisar judges wisely to pass Nishat's reopening (balanced hand) double, -300.

Closed Room

West	North	East	South
Lawrence	Fazli	Weichsel	Zia
			2♡
dbl	pass	2NT[1]	pass
3NT	all pass		

1. Lebensohl.

Although neither 1♡ nor 2♡ is perfect, passing as dealer does not figure to leave you with a clean action on the next round, and Zia's heavy weak two-bid strikes me as the intuitive choice. Weichsel goes three down in 3NT for -150: after a heart lead, he plays ace-queen of diamonds, and Zia gets his hearts going. If declarer plays on clubs instead of diamonds, he might well do three tricks better and make the contract! That's 10 more IMPs to PAKISTAN, ahead now by 22, 116-94.

Board 44. N-S Vul.

```
                 ♠ A 10
                 ♡ A 10 9
                 ◇ J 9 6 5 3
                 ♣ 9 8 6
   ♠ 9 3                        ♠ Q 8 7
   ♡ J 6 4         N            ♡ K Q 8 7 5 2
   ◇ A K 8 4    W     E         ◇ Q 7 2
   ♣ A K Q 5       S            ♣ 4
                 ♠ K J 6 5 4 2
                 ♡ 3
                 ◇ 10
                 ♣ J 10 7 3 2
```

Open Room

West	North	East	South
Nishat	Rubin	Nisar	Becker
1◇	pass	1♡	2♠
dbl[1]	pass	4♡	pass
pass	4♠	dbl	all pass

1. At least strong-notrump values.

At this table, Rubin's curiously-timed sacrifice at unfavorable vulnerability, after allowing his opponents to find their fit and level, achieves -500 on four rounds of clubs, East overruffing dummy's ten and returning a diamond.

Closed Room

West	North	East	South
Lawrence	Fazli	Weichsel	Zia
1NT	pass	4◇[1]	pass
4♡	all pass		

1. Transfer to hearts.

If the defenders start with three rounds of spades, declarer will need to ruff with the ♡J, but Fazli leads a diamond. If declarer wins and plays off the top clubs, pitching spades, he will come to eleven tricks, but after taking the trick with dummy's ◇Q, declarer plays a heart to the jack. North wins with the ace and switches to ace and another spade, South cunningly overtaking the ten with the *king* to play a third round of the suit. As Fazli can ruff or overruff, Zia's play doesn't make a difference, but it's always useful to let your opponents know that you're ready to create a problem for them. So 11

IMPs more to PAKISTAN, whose 32 unanswered IMPs over the last three deals have blown open the tight match. PAKISTAN leads by 33, 127-94.

However, on Board 46, where strong notrumpers Becker and Rubin bid and make a routine 3NT, +400, after bidding 1NT-3NT, Zia and Fazli pay a price for their four-card majors/weak notrump approach. Zia opens a systemic 1♡ on:

♠ J 9 7 6   ♡ K Q 6 4   ◇ A 10 5   ♣ A K

and feels himself unable to continue comfortably after Fazli's competitive raise to 2♡ over a 1♠ overcall. He scores +140 in his 4-3 heart fit, so BECKER recoups 6 IMPs.

It is not the weak notrump that is to blame in this case; if a raise is the *worst* thing that can happen to you after opening in a major, it must be better to open in a minor.

And on Board 48, after (1♠) - 1♡ - (1♠), Zia raises Fazli to 4♡ at favorable vulnerability on:

♠ Q 9 5   ♡ 9 8 7 6 4   ◇ 9 6 4   ♣ 10 3

only to find that the opponents have no game. The price in 4♡ doubled is 300, which wipes out an excellent +130 by Nishat and Nisar. That's 5 IMPs to BECKER, now 22 IMPs behind, 105-127.

Fourth Quarter (Boards 49-64)

For the final set, Weichsel and Lawrence stay in the Open Room, East-West, where they face Nishat and Nisar. Meckstroth and Rodwell occupy the North-South seats in the Closed Room to take on Fazli and Zia.

To preserve the spirit of the match, we'll deal with the boards in the order that they are presented to the VuGraph audience. Boards 62, 63, and 64 are played first in one room to provide comparisons with the other room as play progresses on the Bridgerama screen.

Board 62. Neither Vul.

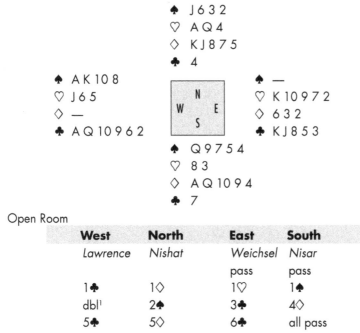

Open Room

West	North	East	South
Lawrence	Nishat	Weichsel	Nisar
		pass	pass
1♣	1◇	1♡	1♠
dbl¹	2♠	3♣	4◇
5♣	5◇	6♣	all pass

1. Three-card heart support.

I'm not sure why Nishat does not double 1♣ for takeout, but his 1◇ overcall should help Nisar gauge his defensive prospects. I am even more surprised that Nishat does not jump-raise spades, but he does go on to the five-level later. The defense can take six tricks against 5◇ doubled by arranging two spade ruffs, for 700, but Weichsel has no way to know the penalty would be so substantial, so goes on to 6♣, which might be cold, or might be a cheap save against 5◇ or 5♠; it feels like an action with very little downside. With the ♡Q onside and hearts 3-2, 6♣ is easier to make than to bid, but the fine +920 is partly neutralized by events at the other table:

Closed Room

West	North	East	South
Zia	Rodwell	Fazli	Meckstroth
		pass	pass
1♣	dbl	1♡	4♠
dbl	pass	5♣	dbl
all pass			

After doubling a contract that proves cold for an overtrick, South can console himself by imagining that his teammates might save the day by bidding their slam. That's +650 for Zia, but 7 IMPs to BECKER, closing to within 15 at 112-127.

Board 63. N-S Vul.

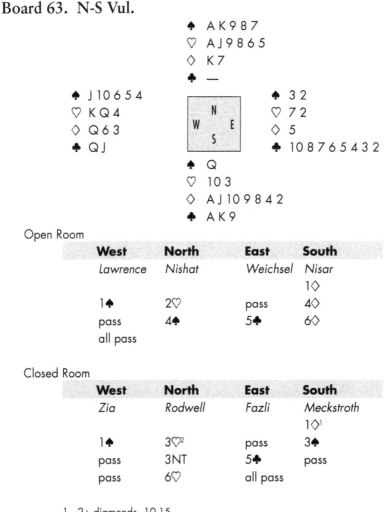

```
                        ♠ A K 9 8 7
                        ♡ A J 9 8 6 5
                        ◇ K 7
                        ♣ —
        ♠ J 10 6 5 4            ♠ 3 2
        ♡ K Q 4          N      ♡ 7 2
        ◇ Q 6 3      W       E  ◇ 5
        ♣ Q J            S      ♣ 10 8 7 6 5 4 3 2
                        ♠ Q
                        ♡ 10 3
                        ◇ A J 10 9 8 4 2
                        ♣ A K 9
```

Open Room

West	North	East	South
Lawrence	Nishat	Weichsel	Nisar
			1◇
1♠	2♡	pass	4◇
pass	4♠	5♣	6◇
all pass			

Closed Room

West	North	East	South
Zia	Rodwell	Fazli	Meckstroth
			1◇[1]
1♠	3♡[2]	pass	3♠
pass	3NT	5♣	pass
pass	6♡	all pass	

1. 2+ diamonds, 10-15.
2. 6+ hearts, game-forcing; 2♡ would be non-forcing.

Neither Weichsel nor Fazli is shy about introducing his topless eight-card suit at the five-level, but both North-South pairs are undeterred. Both slams are easy to make, but 6♡ is a lot worse than 6◇, and perhaps worse than 7◇. BECKER is fortunate to gain 2 IMPs for 1430 versus 1370, cutting PAKISTAN's lead to 13.

Board 64 is flat, and PAKISTAN leads 127-114, with thirteen boards (Boards 49-61) remaining.

Board 49. Neither Vul.

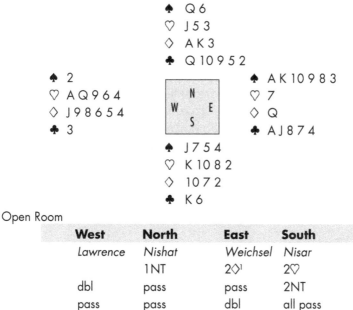

```
                    ♠ Q 6
                    ♡ J 5 3
                    ◇ A K 3
                    ♣ Q 10 9 5 2
     ♠ 2                             ♠ A K 10 9 8 3
     ♡ A Q 9 6 4        N            ♡ 7
     ◇ J 9 8 6 5 4   W     E         ◇ Q
     ♣ 3                 S           ♣ A J 8 7 4
                    ♠ J 7 5 4
                    ♡ K 10 8 2
                    ◇ 10 7 2
                    ♣ K 6
```

Open Room

West	North	East	South
Lawrence	Nishat	Weichsel	Nisar
	1NT	2◇¹	2♡
dbl	pass	pass	2NT
pass	pass	dbl	all pass

1. Spades and another suit.

Nisar, always busy, is caught speeding when he needlessly gets involved after Nishat's weak 1NT opening. His opponents do very well to come after him, and it soon gets very ugly. Lawrence's penalty double of 2♡ is aggressive, but makes it easy for Weichsel to double Nisar's escape to 2NT. Nishat goes four down after the lead of the ♠K,-700.

Mike Lawrence

Closed Room

West	North	East	South
Zia	Rodwell	Fazli	Meckstroth
	1◊[1]	1♠	dbl*
pass	1NT	2♣	all pass

1. 2+ diamonds, 10-15.

When Fazli introduces his clubs, Zia, whose black-suit preferences are largely unprintable, elects to pass before the doubling starts. Clubs is the defenders' best suit, and Fazli goes down two, -100, but this is a lucky board for PAKISTAN because both pairs have poor results on the same deal, holding the loss to a mere 13 IMPs. Suddenly, the match is tied at 127.

A brief diversion: the devil is out collecting souls again on Board 50. The East players hold in first seat, at favorable vulnerability:

♠ 9 8 2 ♡ 10 9 8 6 4 ◊ 6 3 ♣ 9 7 5

In the all-American semifinal, Stevie Robinson elects to open with a weak 2♡; Jim Robison chooses to begin with a strong notrump! You can understand Robison's position, perhaps, but Robinson's team is far ahead in the match — perhaps Steve thought a disaster wouldn't matter. Neither bid has much effect, though, North-South reaching their cold vulnerable 3NT.

In our featured match, both Easts manage to resist temptation, and West is left to open in third seat, holding:

♠ J 10 5 4 ♡ K Q ◊ 10 4 ♣ K Q J 8 2

Lawrence settles for a normal 1♣ and defends an equally normal 3NT, which yields 630. Zia, however, opens 3♣, which is described on his system sheet as 'anything, third seat, with favorable vulnerability'. It is not at all clear whether this characterization is simply 'full disclosure' or something designed to keep the opponents on edge. Here, Rodwell doubles for takeout with a balanced 23-count, and Meckstroth, attempting to flush out the bluffer, passes with ace-ten-third of clubs and out. Zia, with nothing better to do, stands his ground. Best defense (leading trumps, South ducking, and subsequently playing two more rounds of the suit) nets 700, but Rodwell starts with a high spade from an honor sequence, which costs a tempo, and the price is only 500 points, so PAKISTAN not only survives but actually gains 4 IMPs in (dare we say) bizarre fashion. PAKISTAN leads now by those 4 IMPs, 131-127.

BECKER runs into bad luck on Board 51, where Meckstroth and Rodwell find their way to 4♠ with this combination:

```
            ♠ K 5 3 2
            ♡ —
            ◊ 5 4 3
            ♣ Q J 9 8 6 3
            ▭
            ♠ A 8 6 4
            ♡ A K J 10 7
            ◊ 10 6
            ♣ A 10
```

Although the ♣K is onside, the contract goes one down on a 4-1 trump break. It's not that game is so wonderful, but 4♠ deserves a better fate than the less attractive 2♡ reached by Nishat and Nisar (1♡-1NT; 2♡-pass), which also goes one down. No swing.

Board 53. N-S Vul.

```
                        ♠ A J 10 5 4 2
                        ♡ 5 4
                        ◊ A K 10 8 2
                        ♣ —
   ♠ K 8 6 3                              ♠ —
   ♡ K 3              ┌─────────┐         ♡ Q 8 7
   ◊ Q 9 6 5         │    N    │         ◊ J 4 3
   ♣ A 10 8          │ W     E │         ♣ Q J 9 7 5 4 3
                      │    S    │
                      └─────────┘
                        ♠ Q 9 7
                        ♡ A J 10 9 6 2
                        ◊ 7
                        ♣ K 6 2
```

Open Room

West	North	East	South
Lawrence	Nishat	Weichsel	Nisar
	1♠	3♣	3♡
5♣	5◊	pass	5♠
all pass			

Closed Room

West	North	East	South
Zia	Rodwell	Fazli	Meckstroth
	1♠	3♣	3♡
pass	4◊	pass	4♠
pass	5♣	pass	5♠
all pass			

Zia's decision not to increase the preempt with his balanced hand and defense-suitable cards leaves his opponents plenty of room to investigate slam, and they stay out. Lawrence's more active, less-than-obvious 5♣ puts it squarely to Nishat and Nisar, but they too manage to stop short of slam. Both declarers take eleven tricks, a push at +650.

Board 54. E-W Vul.

```
              ♠ Q 10 8 6 3 2
              ♡ J 5
              ◇ Q 7 2
              ♣ 10 6
  ♠ 4                        ♠ A K 5
  ♡ Q 8 7         N          ♡ 6 3 2
  ◇ K 8 4 3    W     E       ◇ A J 6 5
  ♣ A Q J 9 8     S          ♣ 7 4 3
              ♠ J 9 7
              ♡ A K 10 9 4
              ◇ 10 9
              ♣ K 5 2
```

Open Room

West	North	East	South
Lawrence	Nishat	Weichsel	Nisar
		pass	1♡
pass	1♠	pass	2♠
all pass			

Closed Room

West	North	East	South
Zia	Rodwell	Fazli	Meckstroth
		pass	1♡
pass	1♠¹	pass	1NT
pass	2♠	all pass	

1. At least three spades.

When neither Weichsel nor Fazli opens his spotless five-control hand and neither Lawrence nor Zia volunteers a dangerous 2♣ overcall, both pairs sell out to 2♠ when they can make a vulnerable 3NT. It would be easier for Zia to protect than for Lawrence to enter a live auction. The resulting 2♠ is booked for two down with accurate defense, but neither table yields that result.

Rodwell calls for the king on Fazli's lead of the ♣4, and Zia takes two club tricks before switching to a trump, Fazli playing three rounds as Zia discards two clubs. The defense is right on track, but as neither opponent seems to hold both high diamonds, Rodwell has reason to place the ♡Q with West, as Fazli would have opened the bidding with that card. Rodwell decides to cash two more trumps and sees Fazli discard his remaining club and a diamond, Zia a diamond and a crafty heart, trying to look like a man with four. Rodwell leads the ♡J to the ace, ruffs dummy's remaining club, sees Fazli show out, and leads the ♡5 to the king, felling the queen to chalk up a delightful +110.

Eric Rodwell

Nishat fares three tricks worse, trying to make 2♠. After a similar start, he does not draw the same inference about the red-suit honors and leads an early heart to dummy's ten. The defenders have two clubs, two trumps, the ♡Q and three diamond tricks now: that's -150, and 6 IMPs to BECKER, back in front by 2 IMPs, 133-131.

The session is taking forever, but the match has had so many fascinating twists that no one wants to leave the VuGraph theater. After the next three deals are quiet, BECKER's lead is still 2 IMPs with four boards to play.

Board 58. Both Vul.

```
                  ♠ 7 4 3
                  ♡ J
                  ◇ Q J 8 5 3
                  ♣ K 7 3 2
  ♠ J 9 6                        ♠ K 10 8 5
  ♡ A 9          ┌─────────┐     ♡ K 10 8 7 6 3
  ◇ 10 9 6 4     │    N    │     ◇ 2
  ♣ A 8 5 4      │ W     E │     ♣ 9 6
                 │    S    │
                 └─────────┘
                  ♠ A Q 2
                  ♡ Q 5 4 2
                  ◇ A K 7
                  ♣ Q J 10
```

Open Room

West	North	East	South
Lawrence	Nishat	Weichsel	Nisar
		pass	1♡
pass	1NT	pass	2NT
all pass			

Again, PAKISTAN turns in a poor result after opening a strong balanced hand with a four-card major, but as Nishat would normally raise himself to 3NT facing 18-19, his apparently conservative pass suggests there is some doubt about the minimum strength required for that raise to 2NT. Nishat scores +180 in 2NT, and all eyes turn to the other table.

Nishat Abedi

Closed Room

West	North	East	South
Zia	Rodwell	Fazli	Meckstroth
		pass	1♣*
pass	1◊¹	1♡	1NT
2♡	3NT	all pass	

1. 0-7.

Meckstroth and Rodwell roll briskly into 3NT after a strong club and negative 1◊ response, South showing 18-19. Fazli gets his long suit into the game, so Zia leads the ♡A and ♡9. Fazli overtakes with the ten, and Meckstroth ducks, attempting to cut communications should hearts be 5-3 with the ♣A in the West hand. Back comes a low spade. If the hearts are indeed 5-3, it is imperative to put in the queen, lest the defenders get three hearts, a spade and the ♣A, but after considerable thought, Meckstroth plays low on the spade. With hearts 6-2, there are no further problems and he scores up +600. That is 9 IMPs to BECKER, now ahead by 11, 143-132, with three boards to play.

Meckwell

By now, Lawrence-Weichsel and Nishat-Nisar have finished play and have emerged from the Open Room. The scuttlebutt strongly suggests a victory for BECKER. There are no bad results on the American pair's card, and the deals seem to be less than lively. The VuGraph crowd starts to thin out.

Bad idea, crowd members.

Board 59. Neither Vul.

```
                  ♠ K J 7
                  ♡ K J 10 9 4
                  ◇ J 10 6
                  ♣ K 5
   ♠ Q 8 6 5 4              ♠ 9
   ♡ A 7 2          N       ♡ Q 8 6 5 3
   ◇ 9 4 2      W       E   ◇ A 7 3
   ♣ 8 6            S       ♣ A Q 9 4
                  ♠ A 10 3 2
                  ♡ —
                  ◇ K Q 8 5
                  ♣ J 10 7 3 2
```

Open Room

West	North	East	South
Lawrence	Nishat	Weichsel	Nisar
			1♣
pass	1♡	pass	1♠
pass	2◇¹	pass	3◇
pass	3NT	all pass	

1. Fourth suit forcing.

Closed Room

West	North	East	South
Zia	Rodwell	Fazli	Meckstroth
			1◇¹
pass	1♡²	pass	1♠
pass	2♣³	pass	3♡⁴
pass	3NT	all pass	

1. 2+ diamonds, 10-15.
2. Three or more hearts.
3. Artificial force.
4. Short hearts.

The play starts the same way at both tables. East leads the ♡5; West wins with the ace and returns the ♡7 to the jack and queen (dummy discarding a club and a spade). At this point, it is vital for East to play on clubs, lest declarer guess the ♠Q after knocking out the ◇A. Weichsel switches to the ♣9, Fazli the ♣4. Dummy's jack holds as West gives count. Now the declarers play on diamonds, but when East wins the ◇A, he cashes the ♣A, felling the king, and the ♣Q is the setting trick. An honorable push, thanks to strong defense by the East players. Still BECKER by 11 IMPs, with two boards to play.

Board 60. N-S Vul.

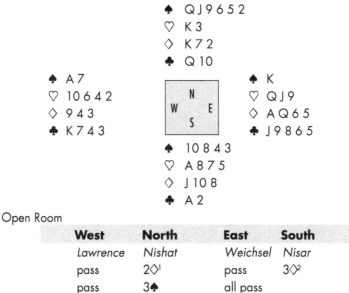

Open Room

West	North	East	South
Lawrence	Nishat	Weichsel	Nisar
pass	2◇¹	pass	3◇²
pass	3♠	all pass	

1. Multi: weak in a major or strong in a minor.
2. Bid your major at the three-level.

Nishat feels that the North cards merit a weak two-bid in second seat at unfavorable vulnerability, so starts with a Multi 2◇, as he must. He finishes in 3♠, and the defenders get all five of their tricks, -100. There doesn't seem to be too much trouble available to BECKER on this one, but...

Closed Room

West	North	East	South
Zia	Rodwell	Fazli	Meckstroth
pass	1♠	dbl	4♠
dbl	all pass		

Rodwell starts with a light 1♠ (although no one would do so in real life, is it unspeakable to pass that North hand?) and Fazli throws in an ugly takeout double that seems to have 'Hail Mary' written all over it, even at favorable. Now Meckstroth could offer various non-forcing raises (2NT or 3♡), but he opts for an atypical (lots of defense, not much shape) 4♠, hoping to encourage a phantom sacrifice at the prevailing vulnerability. No, Zia is there with a double that is not described as responsive, and Fazli is going nowhere. Here too the defenders get all their tricks, and the price is 500 points, 9 IMPs from nowhere to PAKISTAN, trailing now by just 2 IMPs with one fateful deal to play.

Good friends run to drag good friends back to the VuGraph theater.

The deal flashes up on the VuGraph screen. The commentators savor the moment, and set the scene for the audience. The closed-circuit TV cameras pan in turn to each of the bone-weary gladiators, none of whom seems to be smiling... it is high drama indeed in Miami Beach.

Board 61. Both Vul.

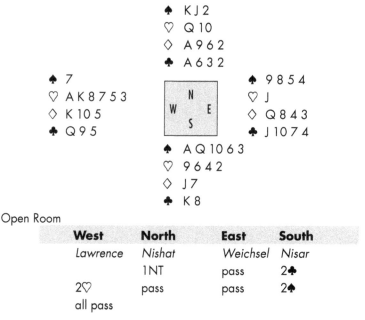

♠ K J 2
♡ Q 10
◇ A 9 6 2
♣ A 6 3 2

♠ 7
♡ A K 8 7 5 3
◇ K 10 5
♣ Q 9 5

♠ 9 8 5 4
♡ J
◇ Q 8 4 3
♣ J 10 7 4

♠ A Q 10 6 3
♡ 9 6 4 2
◇ J 7
♣ K 8

Open Room

West	North	East	South
Lawrence	Nishat	Weichsel	Nisar
	1NT	pass	2♣
2♡	pass	pass	2♠
all pass			

After the weak-notrump opening, Nisar's sequence is invitational, and Nishat has to decide how far to go, with a potentially useless ♡Q in an otherwise promising hand. He makes the ultraconservative choice, passing 2♠. This, please note, is not what Nisar would have done had the partnership hands been switched. Lawrence leads ace, king and another heart, innocently enough. Nisar ruffs high and draws trumps, claiming ten tricks (the ♡9 is high), +170.

The only result BECKER *cannot* afford now is a minus from Meckstroth-Rodwell, presumably in 4♠. Not that anyone expects them to stay out of game. And it is not going to be so easy to defeat it.

Closed Room

West	North	East	South
Zia	Rodwell	Fazli	Meckstroth
	1◇¹	pass	2♠²
pass	4♠	all pass	

1. 2+ diamonds, 10-15.
2. Five spades, at least four hearts, invitational.

It doesn't take long to advance the drama to its climax. Sure enough, the American pair, with no reason to devalue any of their high cards, cruises into game, but the auction is peculiar, and the Pakistani silence and the vagaries of the bidding have created an entirely different set of conditions.

Zia, with known heart length on his right, judges to start a club. Meckstroth sets out to score as many trump tricks as possible, and starts with three rounds of clubs, ruffing the third low. Now a low heart towards dummy. Zia goes up with the ♡K, crashing the jack, and switches to his trump. Meckstroth wins in dummy to lead the ♡Q, hoping that Fazli will not ruff.

But Fazli does ruff, and his trump return gets the job done; there is no squeeze either, and Meckstroth is a trick short and goes one down, -100. So 7 IMPs to PAKISTAN.

The match is over. PAKISTAN has won by 5 IMPs at the very end, 148-143.

Epilogue

ROBINSON prevails over TOUCHTIDIS in the other match, 180-112.

The euphoria of their stunning semifinal does not sustain the Cinderella Pakistanis, and over 128 boards, they bow to ROBINSON by a wide margin, 207-357. ROBINSON goes home with the Rosenblum Cup, but PAKISTAN finishes no worse than tied for first in the hearts of the world bridge community.

ROBINSON team, winning the Rosenblum Cup, 1986
(Left to right) Silverman, Manfield, Boyd, Robinson, Lipsitz, Woolsey

7. 2001 La Vie Parisienne

The 2001 World Bridge Championships are unique in several ways. When the 9/11 terrorist attacks make it impossible to play the event as planned in Bali, the President of the World Bridge Federation, José Damiani, manages in the space of three short weeks to relocate the Championships to Paris. This logistical miracle requires the first week's play to take place in the depths of the Stade de France, better known as a soccer, rugby and concert venue, before moving to the Hotel Concorde Lafayette for the second week.

Players are shuttled between the stadium and designated collection points and are inevitably exhausted by the conclusion of play each day, but, hey, we are in Paris in autumn. As beautiful as Bali was going to be, two weeks in this wonderful city is a remarkable consolation prize for the players.

I[***] am in Paris as coach of USA 1 in the Bermuda Bowl (Don Krauss, NPC: Nick Nickell, Dick Freeman, Bob Hamman, Paul Soloway, Jeff Meckstroth, Eric Rodwell) and part-time VuGraph commentator, working with Lucky Dana, Pierre-Yves Guillaumin and Jean-Paul Meyer. I am counting on my infrequently-used French (I was born and raised in Montreal) to help me communicate and avoid misinterpreting what my colleagues are saying in their own language. I needn't have worried, as their English is excellent.

Many of our sessions prove to be memorable, including two of the six sets of the USA 1-Italy Bermuda Bowl quarterfinal, which are decidedly one-sided. The match is virtually even with two sets to go, but Italy wins those 57-0 and 67-9. Amazingly, there is enough in those deals that the match might have gone the other way had the cards been dealt slightly differently. Most of the USA 1 players book flights home the next day. 'Time to get outta Dodge,' is Hamman's usual parting shot. I stay on to cover the semifinals and finals and enjoy my down time exploring the city.

*** Primary author Eric Kokish

The final of the Venice Cup between France and Germany is historic as it marks the first occasion that an American team has not contested the final. It proves to be a classic, and during the final session, the overflowing VuGraph theater features football-style chanting accompanied by the cheering of every point scored, reminding me of the electricity-charged Brazil-USA Bermuda Bowl semifinal in 1985. The final act of this play is a gripping spectator spectacle, just the sort of session that could sell bridge as a sport.

All three French pairs (Bénédicte Cronier and Sylvie Willard, Véronique Bessis and Catherine d'Ovidio, Catherine Fishpool and Elizabeth 'Babette' Hugon), play 'Standard French': five-card majors, strong notrump. Their NPC is the irrepressible Patrick Grenthe.

Germany's roster is comprised of Daniela von Arnim and Sabine Auken, using their strong club system with its four-card majors canapé approach and a mini notrump; Beate 'Pony' Nehmert and Andrea Rauscheid, playing four-card majors and a variable 1NT; Barbara Stawowy Hackett and Katrin Farwig, using methods much like those played by the French pairs; and Christoph Kemmer, NPC.

France, starting with a 5.5 IMP carryover lead (we'll round that up to 6.0 for convenience), is in great form from the outset, winning the first set by 40 IMPs to lead 82-36. The French take a quiet second set, 27-15, to make the score 109-51 but lose the next, another low-scoring session, to lead 124-74. In the fourth set, Germany makes a strong move, winning it 68-29 to trail only narrowly at 142-153, but France hits back in the penultimate set, outscoring Germany, 61-27 to go into the last 16 deals in a strong position, ahead by 47 IMPs, 214-167.

Germany, needing to gain an average of 3 IMPs per board with only 16 deals to play, faced a steep uphill struggle against the hometown favorites.[†††]

Set 6 (Boards 81-96)

The VuGraph room is packed, and just as in Brazil, in 1985, the large home contingent is noisy and boisterous. They are expecting a coronation, and are here to cheer the French women to the title. This is the first deal:

[†††] There are many things one can do to try and overturn a sizeable deficit, and before the last session of play, Sabine and I discuss strategy in the Bulletin Room. (As a former NPC of the German Women's Team, I know all their pairs well.) The things I emphasize most are that it is no use recovering all the points if you give away too many by being overly aggressive, and that playing at home the French women might just become a little nervous if they feel they have lost some ground in the early stages. *Mark Horton*

Board 81. Neither Vul.

```
                    ♠ 4 2
                    ♡ 9 5 4
                    ◇ A 8 5 3 2
                    ♣ A Q 10
    ♠ K Q 8                        ♠ 7 6 5 3
    ♡ K Q 3 2          N           ♡ A J 10
    ◇ Q J 10       W       E       ◇ 6
    ♣ K 6 4            S           ♣ J 8 7 3 2
                    ♠ A J 10 9
                    ♡ 8 7 6
                    ◇ K 9 7 4
                    ♣ 9 5
```

Open Room

West	North	East	South
Bessis	Auken	d'Ovidio	von Arnim
	1NT¹	pass	pass
dbl	rdbl²	2♣	2♡³
2NT	pass	3NT	dbl
pass	pass	4♣	pass
pass	dbl	all pass	

1. 10-12.
2. A five-card suit other than clubs.
3. Pass or correct to your five-card suit.

North's specialized redouble makes it clear to South that selling out to 2♣ is bound to be wrong as East-West will have at least eight combined trumps; her 'pass-or-correct' 2♡ implies that she is prepared to go the three-level in diamonds, but does not say anything yet about spades. Bessis' voluntary 2NT reveals that she has missed the inferences available from the 2♡ bid, and d'Ovidio, sensibly expecting roughly a 20-count, raises to game. When South doubles, East does well to reconsider and 'escapes' to 4♣, but now North has enough to double for penalty.

Von Arnim leads the ◇4, low from two or four cards (if not a singleton) in her methods. Auken wins with the ace and is certain that the lead must be from a four-card holding, as South was prepared to play in 3◇ if that were North's suit. With no possibility of a second diamond trick or diamond ruff, North switches to the ♠2. South ducks to dummy's queen. When declarer continues with the ♣4, North goes in with the queen and continues with her remaining spade to arrange her ruff for two down, -300.

West	North	East	South
Rauscheid	Cronier	Nehmert	Willard
	pass	pass	pass
1NT[1]	all pass		

1. 14-16.

The defenders start with three rounds of diamonds, South returning the nine and unblocking the seven. Rauscheid uses dummy's heart entries to play spades towards her hand. South wins the second spade and plays back her remaining diamond, but when North follows with the deuce under the four, the club switch leaves declarer one down, -50; 6 IMPs to Germany, 173-214.

Board 82. N-S Vul.

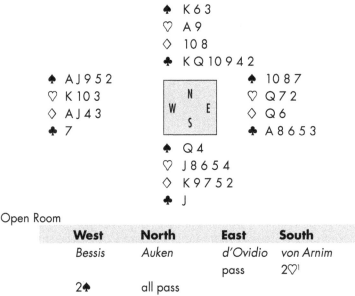

```
              ♠ K 6 3
              ♡ A 9
              ◇ 10 8
              ♣ K Q 10 9 4 2
♠ A J 9 5 2            ♠ 10 8 7
♡ K 10 3       N      ♡ Q 7 2
◇ A J 4 3    W   E     ◇ Q 6
♣ 7            S      ♣ A 8 6 5 3
              ♠ Q 4
              ♡ J 8 6 5 4
              ◇ K 9 7 5 2
              ♣ J
```

Open Room

West	North	East	South
Bessis	Auken	d'Ovidio	von Arnim
		pass	2♡[1]
2♠	all pass		

1. Either a weak one-suiter with spades or a weak two-suiter with hearts and a minor.

We are treated early to one of the North-South pair's specialized two-way two-bids, which can easily lead to some guessing by both sides. Not here, however, as Bessis has a fairly comfortable natural 2♠ overcall available. Auken has a method to compete to 3♣ without inviting correction or showing strength, but decides against it — wisely as it turns out, as 3♣ doubled would cost at least 500. East, with no trump honor and questionable assets in the red suits, takes the low road. North leads the ◇10 against 2♠ (queen, king, ace). Declarer cashes the jack and leads a third diamond, ruffing in dummy when North discards a club. A heart to the king loses to the ace, and North switches to the ♠3. Declarer takes South's queen with the ace, plays a club to the ace, and ruffs a club before leading her last diamond. North pitches her remaining heart and declarer ruffs, and ruffs another club. North is sure to score both her trumps, but declarer has ten tricks, +170.

Closed Room

West	North	East	South
Rauscheid	Cronier	Nehmert	Willard
		pass	pass
1♠	2♣	pass	pass
dbl	pass	2♠	all pass

Playing four-card majors, Nehmert does not raise directly, but it is surprising that she does not do more when Rauscheid shows sound values and suggests club shortness. Cronier leads the ♣K, and declarer wins with dummy's ace and leads the ◇Q, which Willard does not cover. Declarer continues with a diamond to the jack, and tries to cash the ace. North ruffs low, so declarer overruffs, ruffs a club, and ruffs her last diamond, North discarding the ♡9. The ♡Q goes to North's ace, and declarer ruffs the club return to play the ♡K, which costs a trick, as North ruffs it and forces declarer with another club, +140 and an IMP for France. France now lead by 42: 215-173.

Pony Nehmert

Board 83. E-W Vul.

```
                        ♠ K J 8 4
                        ♡ 9 6 4
                        ◇ K 5
                        ♣ 9 8 6 2
    ♠ A 9 7 2                          ♠ 10 5 3
    ♡ 7 2              ┌─────────┐     ♡ A K Q J 8
    ◇ A Q 10 8 4       │    N    │     ◇ J 3 2
    ♣ K 3              │  W   E  │     ♣ A 10
                       │    S    │
                       └─────────┘
                        ♠ Q 6
                        ♡ 10 5 3
                        ◇ 9 7 6
                        ♣ Q J 7 5 4
```

Closed Room

West	North	East	South
Rauscheid	Cronier	Nehmert	Willard
			pass
1◇	pass	1♡	pass
1♠	pass	2♣[1]	pass
2NT	pass	3NT	all pass

1. Fourth-suit forcing and artificial.

The East-West hands fit well and, absent a spade lead, a slam in either red suit is an excellent proposition. Even with a spade lead, a slam is playable if the diamond finesse is onside. Against 3NT, North leads the ♣8, and the ◇K is the defenders' only trick, +690.

Open Room

West	North	East	South
Bessis	Auken	d'Ovidio	von Arnim
			pass
1◇	pass	1♡	pass
1♠	pass	2◇[1]	pass
3◇	pass	3♡	pass
4♡	all pass		

1. Artificial game force.

East takes some time before her final pass, as well she might. South leads the ♣J against 4♡ so there is no swing.

North reveals later that if East-West had reached 6♡ she planned to double, hoping that her partner would find the essential spade lead. It might not have come to that, however, for North might well have had the chance to double a spade cuebid.

Board 84. Both Vul.

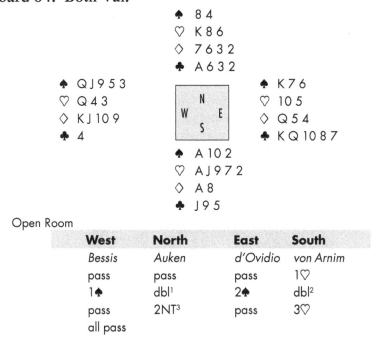

```
              ♠ 8 4
              ♡ K 8 6
              ◇ 7 6 3 2
              ♣ A 6 3 2
♠ Q J 9 5 3              ♠ K 7 6
♡ Q 4 3         N        ♡ 10 5
◇ K J 10 9   W     E     ◇ Q 5 4
♣ 4             S        ♣ K Q 10 8 7
              ♠ A 10 2
              ♡ A J 9 7 2
              ◇ A 8
              ♣ J 9 5
```

Open Room

West	North	East	South
Bessis	Auken	d'Ovidio	von Arnim
pass	pass	pass	1♡
1♠	dbl[1]	2♠	dbl[2]
pass	2NT[3]	pass	3♡
all pass			

1. Useful values.
2. Any maximum.
3. Asks for further description.

Pairs who play four-card majors quite often bid optimistically in competitive auctions when they have opened a five-card major on a sound hand. Von Arnim has just that kind of hand, and with the likelihood of some sort of fit facing a hand with one or two spades and some values, she thinks it worthwhile to take some action over d'Ovidio's raise to 2♠. This time it would have been easier to achieve a plus on defense, as we'll soon see. The French, 'following the Law', decline to bid again at the three-level with only eight trumps and the likelihood that North-South are similarly endowed. Von Arnim faces an uphill struggle to bring home 3♡.

West leads the ♣4, which smells like a singleton, as a spade lead figures to be safe from any holding on the auction. Declarer takes dummy's ace. (Curiously, it might be better to duck, in case East has better diamond intermediates or two spade honors, which would guarantee an entry before declarer can arrange her spade ruff in dummy and allow the defenders to promote a trump trick.) A spade to the ten loses to the jack, and West switches to the ◊J, which is permitted to hold. Declarer takes the ◊9 continuation with the ace, and takes a few moments to verify her read on the deal. West's distribution appears to be 5=3=4=1, East's 3=2=3=5; it seems likely that East has only one spade honor (else she would have played one on the first round) and one diamond honor in addition to the ♣KQ — with the ♡Q as well, East would surely have opened in third seat. If this is the layout, there is only one chance left for the contract. Von Arnim backs her judgment by leading the ♡J and running it when West follows with the three. When the ♡J holds, declarer ruffs a spade in dummy, cashes the ♡K, returns to hand with a diamond ruff and draws the outstanding trump for a superb +140. Even the very partisan French spectators in the VuGraph theater acknowledge the beauty of declarer's play, albeit with restrained applause.

Daniela von Armin

Closed Room

West	North	East	South
Rauscheid	*Cronier*	*Nehmert*	*Willard*
pass	pass	pass	1♡
1♠	2♡	2♠	all pass

After a heart lead to the ace, Willard switches to ace and another diamond. When declarer wins in hand and and tries a club, North goes up with the ace and gives her partner a diamond ruff, -100. That is 1 IMP to Germany, 174-215, where it would have been 5 IMPs the other way had von Arnim done a trick worse.

Board 85. N-S Vul.

```
                    ♠ A K
                    ♡ 10 9 5
                    ◇ K J 9 8 6 5 4
                    ♣ J
   ♠ 10 4                          ♠ 9 8 7 6 3 2
   ♡ 8 7              N            ♡ K Q 6
   ◇ A 3          W     E         ◇ Q 7 2
   ♣ A Q 8 6 5 4 2    S            ♣ 10
                    ♠ Q J 5
                    ♡ A J 4 3 2
                    ◇ 10
                    ♣ K 9 7 3
```

Open Room

West	North	East	South
Bessis	Auken	d'Ovidio	von Arnim
	1◇[1]	pass	1♡[2]
2♣	2◇	2♠	dbl
3♣	3◇	all pass	

1. Limited, no four-card major unless maximum and intending to reverse.
2. Natural, or a relay with at least invitational strength.

As the East hand is inappropriate for either a weak jump overcall (in the French methods) or a simple overcall (of the day), d'Ovidio sticks to the system by passing at her first turn. Although she competes later, the possible benefits accruing from immediate obstruction have faded. South's 1♡ response is either a natural bid or a relay with at least invitational values, balanced or with a long minor suit. North's 2◇ promises a minimum hand, while a double of 2♣ would indicate a better 2◇ bid; given their tendency to open light, this is a subtly close decision for Auken.

As von Arnim's competitive double of 2♠ still does not clarify that she has hearts, Auken rebids her diamonds one more time, judging game unlikely if South can't move on. The 3◇ contract has the advantages of being cold and being very easy to play after a club lead to the queen and a spade switch; +110. A heart lead or switch at Trick 2 would be more challenging, but neither play is particularly obvious.

Looking back at this deal more than fifteen years later, it seems to me that it would be useful for a double of 3♣ to be reserved for hands with three-card heart 'support' willing to compete to 3◇.

West	North	East	South
Rauscheid	Cronier	Nehmert	Willard
	1◇	1♠	2♡
3♣	3♡	all pass	

Nehmert, less constrained by style and system, tries 1♠, rejecting a weak jump overcall not so much because of her woeful suit as because she has a potentially good dummy for hearts and doesn't want to make it difficult for her partner to introduce the suit. Here, however, the gentler action leaves the French just enough room to find *their* heart fit, limit their hands, and stop in what seemed to be a makeable contract.

By contrast, 4♡ is reached at both tables in the Bermuda Bowl final, and is defeated in a hurry: the defense starts with ace and another club, which leads to two ruffs or overruffs for East as West regains the lead in diamonds. In fact, Chip Martel, who overcalls 2♠, doubles 4♡ to get partner Lew Stansby to lead his own (club) suit.

It's curious that the defense that would beat 4♡ off the top would also make it very easy for declarer to claim nine tricks. Against 3♡, Rauscheid leads her partner's suit — spades. Willard wins in dummy, passes the ♣J to West's queen, wins the spade continuation, and calls for a low diamond (as the cards lie, playing on hearts is best). It is not clear to Nehmert to go in with the queen, and when she follows low, declarer's ten forces West's ace. The switch to the ♡7 is covered by the nine, queen and ace. As the ♣10 has appeared on the first round, the ♣K9 are equals against the ace, so declarer can succeed by playing a second trump. When, instead, she ruffs a club low, East overruffs dummy with the six, cashes the ♡K, and exits with a spade; West's ♣A is the setting trick. Willard is -100, and Germany adds 5 more IMPs, 179-215.

Two deals later, with France's IMP total at 216, the trailing team has another opportunity...

Board 87. Both Vul.

```
              ♠ K 7 5 3 2
              ♡ A K J 9
              ◇ J 4
              ♣ J 10
  ♠ A 9 8                    ♠ 4
  ♡ Q 10          N          ♡ 5 4 3
  ◇ A 9 8 3 2   W   E        ◇ K Q 5
  ♣ K 6 5         S          ♣ Q 9 8 7 4 2
              ♠ Q J 10 6
              ♡ 8 7 6 2
              ◇ 10 7 6
              ♣ A 3
```

Open Room

West	North	East	South
Bessis	Auken	d'Ovidio	von Arnim
			pass
1◇	1♠	pass	3◇[1]
pass	3♠	all pass	

1. Distributional raise with some defense.

East leads the ◇K, and declarer loses two diamonds, a club and the ace of trumps: +140.

Closed Room

West	North	East	South
Rauscheid	Cronier	Nehmert	Willard
			pass
1NT[1]	pass	3♣[2]	pass
3NT	all pass		

1. 14-16 HCP.
2. Invitational, long weak suit.

With strong intermediates and a fair five-card suit, Rauscheid upgrades to a 14-16 1NT, and when Cronier settles for a remarkably conservative pass, Nehmert stretches to invite game, with the potential upside of stealing a partscore. West likes her fitting card in clubs and takes a shot at game, which incidentally deprives us of the opportunity to learn whether North would reopen with a double over 3♣.

Cronier leads the ♡A against the fragile 3NT, and when Willard follows with the encouraging seven (the French have a strong bias towards count, but apparently this is an attitude situation), North continues hearts from the top, South playing the two, six and eight (which does *not* suggest a spade switch), while declarer parts with a club and a spade from hand and a club from dummy. A spade now would lead to down 300, but North, relying on South's heart carding, switches to a diamond. Now, declarer can win and knock out the ♣A to escape for one down, -100, recovering the IMP lost on the previous deal, 180-216.

Later, Cronier shares her reservations about the diamond switch: 'I should shift to a spade because at worst that would give away only the eighth trick.'

Benedicte Cronier

Board 88. Neither Vul.

```
                   ♠ A K J 6
                   ♡ 3 2
                   ◇ 10 9 5 4
                   ♣ A 10 8
    ♠ 9 5 3                        ♠ Q 10 8 4 2
    ♡ A K 10          N            ♡ 9 8 6 5
    ◇ A K Q 2     W       E        ◇ 8 6 3
    ♣ Q 6 2           S            ♣ 4
                   ♠ 7
                   ♡ Q J 7 4
                   ◇ J 7
                   ♣ K J 9 7 5 3
```

Open Room

West	North	East	South
Bessis	Auken	d'Ovidio	von Arnim
1◇	1♠	pass	2♣
dbl	3♣	all pass	

Bessis cashes the ◊A and ◊K, d'Ovidio following three-eight to suggest a preference for spades over hearts. Declarer takes the spade switch with dummy's ace, plays a heart (eight, queen, king), puts in the jack on the spade return, and ruffs away East's queen. The ♡4 is taken by West's ten, and declarer discards a heart on the spade continuation to dummy's king.

Although declarer still needs a heart ruff in dummy, there is also the matter of finding the queen of trumps, which can be achieved on this layout via diamond ruff, ♣J, heart ruff, ♣A, diamond ruff, ♣K. Von Arnim must decide whether Bessis holds 4=4=4=1, 3=4=4=2, or the even-less-attractive 3=3=4=3 for her exposed-position takeout double with only one unbid suit. In the first case, a club finesse through East would be the winning play, but in the other two cases, West, with a balanced hand, would hold the ♣Q, because without it she would have opened 1NT. East's red-suit count cards figure to be reliable, which also supports finding the winning play in trumps, but after due deliberation, von Arnim misguesses, going one down: -50.

Closed Room

West	North	East	South
Rauscheid	Cronier	Nehmert	Willard
1◊	all pass		

Cronier and Willard overcall freely in good four-card suits at the one-level and all three of Cronier's counterparts in the finals are willing to come in with 1♠, which argues that the North hand is indeed appropriate for such an action. Cronier's silence, then, suggests that she (and perhaps the whole team) may have committed to a consistently conservative approach for at least the first part of the final segment. When she passes 1◊, so do Nehmert and Willard, neither of those actions being entirely routine.

Cronier cashes the ♠A, Rauscheid following with the five, which makes it more difficult to read the spade layout and find the strongest defense (♠K, spade ruff, club to North for a fourth spade to ruff with the ◊J for an uppercut; declarer would discard her heart loser). North switches to the ◊4, which goes to the jack and king. Declarer exits with a club, Willard winning to play a second trump. Rauscheid wins, ruffs a club (Cronier keeping her ace), comes to the ♡A and leads a spade. On the actual lie of the cards this is enough to get home as Willard is out of trumps. Cronier wins, cashes the ♣A, and leads a heart to the jack and king. Rauscheid cashes the ◊A, finesses the ♣10 and cashes the ♣Q, her eighth and final winner, making two: +90. Germany gains an IMP, 181-216. Halfway through the set, the 47-IMP French lead has been reduced to 35 IMPs, but the boards are threatening to run out for Germany.

Board 89. E-W Vul.

```
                    ♠ —
                    ♡ A 8 7 6 3
                    ◇ A J 6
                    ♣ 10 8 7 5 3
  ♠ A K 8 6 5 2                      ♠ Q J 7
  ♡ 10             ┌─────────┐       ♡ Q J 9 5 2
  ◇ 8 7 4 3        │    N    │       ◇ K Q 2
  ♣ 6 2           W│ W     E │E      ♣ K 9
                   │    S    │
                   └─────────┘
                    ♠ 10 9 4 3
                    ♡ K 4
                    ◇ 10 9 5
                    ♣ A Q J 4
```

Open Room

West	North	East	South
Bessis	Auken	d'Ovidio	von Arnim
	1♡	pass	1♠
2♠	2NT¹	4♠	dbl
all pass			

1. Minimum opening with 5+ hearts and at least four cards in a minor.

Passing as dealer at favorable vulnerability with hands like North's is not part of the German approach. Bessis, keen to get her spades into the picture as economically as possible, risks an understrength natural overcall in the suit bid on her right. Similarly concerned about the auction escalating before she has a chance to finish showing her hand 'safely', Auken makes a statement about her hand type with a conventional 2NT. However, since Auken had not been able to name her second suit without misdescribing her shape, her partner is left with an awkward guess over d'Ovidio's raise to 4♠. Facing a probable spade void, it is surely tempting for von Arnim to compete further with an artificial 4NT, but as that might well be a serious misjudgment opposite a red two-suiter, she doubles for penalty, which achieves a superb result when Bessis misjudges the play.

Auken leads the ♡A and continues with the ♡8, backing her view that shortage in her long suit motivates von Arnim to double 4♠ with such weak spades. It would be best for Bessis to follow low from dummy, although doing so would not secure the contract because she will run out of trumps before she can establish and cash a second diamond winner. However, she calls for dummy's queen, ruffs away South's king, and plays the ♠A and a spade to the queen to lead the ♡J, which von Arnim ruffs. Bessis overruffs and must play a diamond to get out for one down, but instead leads her penultimate trump to dummy's jack, drawing South's lurker as North carefully discards a diamond. The position is awful for Bessis now: she leaves the high heart in dummy and calls for the ◊K, which Auken takes to play a club through. Bessis ruffs the third club with her last trump, crosses to the ◊Q, and cashes the ♡9, her eighth and last trick: -500.

It might not be obvious why North must pitch a diamond and not a club on the third trump. If North releases an apparently idle club, declarer can cash the ♡9, pitching a club, and exit with a club. South wins and plays another club, but declarer ruffs, plays a diamond to the queen and exits with a heart, endplaying North, who must surrender a ninth trick in diamonds.

Closed Room

West	North	East	South
Rauscheid	Cronier	Nehmert	Willard
	pass	1♡	pass
2♠[1]	all pass		

1. 5-8 HCP, six-card suit.

When Cronier does not open the North hand, her opponents have the auction to themselves, and Rauscheid's response allows her side to stop at a safe level. North leads a club. South takes two club tricks and switches to the ♡K and another heart. Declarer ruffs, plays a diamond to the king and cashes the ♠Q. Best now is to come to hand with a spade to play a second diamond, but when instead declarer plays the ♡9, South discards a diamond. Declarer ruffs the heart and belatedly plays a diamond. North takes the ace and gives her partner a diamond ruff, but that is the last trick for the defense, +110. That is 12 IMPs for Germany, moving closer at 193-216. Although the French lead is still 23 IMPs, the team's camp followers have turned conspicuously silent.

To underscore the excellence of East-West's +110, consider that North-South can take at least ten tricks in their nine-card club fit. Indeed they might bid and make 5♣ with inspired play despite the bad heart break and location of the ◊KQ (declarer ruffs three spades in the North hand and concedes a timely heart to East, discarding South's last spade, eventually negotiating an endplay in diamonds). However, the truth may be that this deal is just too tough unless North can name both suits early without overstating strength. In the event, as we've seen, neither North-South pair mentions clubs.

Board 90. Both Vul.

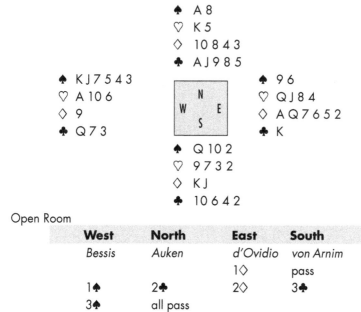

West	North	East	South
Bessis	Auken	d'Ovidio	von Arnim
		1◇	pass
1♠	2♣	2◇	3♣
3♠	all pass		

There can be no doubt that Auken knows her aggressive 2♣ overcall is a dangerous action, but here she catches a fit and succeeds in pushing her opponents to 3♠; mission accomplished. She leads the ♣A and switches to the ◇3. Bessis wins with dummy's ace and leads a heart to the ten and king. She wins the heart return with the ace, ruffs a club, and plays a spade to the jack and ace, essential to make the contract. She loses a trump trick to South, but that is all, +140.

Closed Room

West	North	East	South
Rauscheid	Cronier	Nehmert	Willard
		1◇	pass
1♠	pass	2◇	pass
2♠	all pass		

With no lead attractive on the auction, North goes for the gusto by leading the ♡K. Rauscheid misguesses on the first round of trumps, but North does not play on clubs, leading a second trump, so declarer loses only two trump tricks for +170; 1 overtrick IMP for Germany, 22 behind with six deals left.

I find it interesting that by overcalling, Auken gained enough information to avoid the unfortunate, otherwise reasonable lead of the ♡K, but at the same time gave Bessis enough information to play trumps to best effect.

Board 91. Neither Vul.

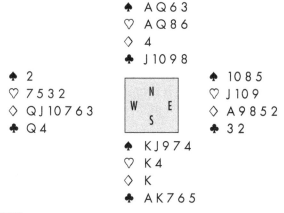

```
              ♠ A Q 6 3
              ♡ A Q 8 6
              ◇ 4
              ♣ J 10 9 8

  ♠ 2                        ♠ 10 8 5
  ♡ 7 5 3 2        N         ♡ J 10 9
  ◇ Q J 10 7 6 3  W   E      ◇ A 9 8 5 2
  ♣ Q 4              S        ♣ 3 2

              ♠ K J 9 7 4
              ♡ K 4
              ◇ K
              ♣ A K 7 6 5
```

Open Room

West	North	East	South
Bessis	Auken	d'Ovidio	von Arnim
			1♣¹
pass	1♡²	pass	1♠
pass	2♠³	pass	3♣⁴
pass	3♡⁵	pass	3NT⁶
pass	4♡⁷	pass	4♡⁸
pass	4NT⁹	pass	5♡¹⁰
pass	6♠	all pass	

1. Strong.
2. 8+ HCP, 4+ hearts.
3. 11+ HCP, 3+ spades.
4. Club ace or king.
5. Heart ace or king.
6. Serious slam-try, denies extra spade length.
7. Shortness in diamonds.
8. Last Train slam-try.
9. RKCB for spades.
10. 2 keycards without the trump queen.

It's unusual not to get into the mix over a strong club with a hand like West's but Bessis reveals later why she passes: '1◇ would show both majors, 2◇ would be a normal-strength 1◇ overcall, not weak, and 3◇ would promise a seven-card suit. Sad, but true!'

Against 6♠, West leads the ◇Q, and East wins with the ace and switches to an honest ♣3. Declarer wins, draws trumps, and, having seen West's singleton spade, is not going to credit her with another one after her silence in the bidding. East's ♣2 on the second round doesn't have to mean much, but does nothing to dissuade von Arnim from taking the winning line; she drops the ♣Q for +980.

The French have reason to be concerned about this deal, as they can see how vigorous defensive bidding could create problems for their North-South pair. And, assuming a slam is bid, hardly a certainty, might declarer not play the hand with the long diamonds for shortness in clubs? While everyone knows it's best not to dwell on such things and concentrate 100% on the next deal, doing so without exception in the heat of battle can be a challenge.

Closed Room

West	North	East	South
Rauscheid	Cronier	Nehmert	Willard
			1♣
2◇	dbl[1]	4◇	4♠
pass	4NT[2]	pass	5♡[3]
pass	6♣	all pass	

1. Negative double.
2. RKCB for spades.
3. 2 keycards without the queen.

It is standard French practice at this time to open 1♣ with 5-5 in the black suits. That agreement leaves room for Rauscheid to get her long suit into the mix at the two-level, which makes it attractive for Nehmert to bounce to the four-level. Willard has quite a bit in reserve for 4♠, but Cronier feels she has enough to bid again, driving to 6♣ after checking on keycards for spades. (Cronier: 'Sylvie responded keycards for spades, but I don't believe we have the agreement that 4NT confirmed spades; I chose clubs unilaterally because I was sure we'd have nine or ten trumps in clubs but quite possibly only eight in spades.)

Andrea Rauschied

Against 6♣, Rauscheid resists the temptation to lead her singleton spade. Instead she starts with the ◇Q to the ace and Nehmert switches to the ♡J.

Declarer does not have the luxury of testing spades and hearts before broaching the crucial club suit, something she could do if spades were trumps. Would she rely on the inference that an opponent who makes a preemptive bid (and is therefore likely to have some short suit) and then leads her own suit rather than one of the off-suits, is a favorite to have a singleton trump? To the VuGraph commentators, it seems there are good reasons for Willard to do the wrong thing in trumps after Rauscheid has done so well *not* to lead her singleton spade. That would have given Willard a clear line of play: two high trumps, intending to play on hearts to discard her diamond loser safely as long as the hand with the guarded ♣Q had at least two hearts, leading to an easy +940. But Willard wins the heart lead with the king, cashes the ♣A, crosses without incident in hearts, leads the ♣J, and plays... the king: +920. Whew!

2 IMPs to Germany; the deficit was now only 20 IMPs, 196-216.

Sylvie Willard

Board 92. N-S Vul.

```
                     ♠ A 5
                     ♡ K 9 8 7
                     ◇ A 10 9
                     ♣ K Q J 10
  ♠ 6 4 2                              ♠ K Q 9 3
  ♡ Q 10 6 4          N                ♡ A 3 2
  ◇ Q J 5 3      W          E          ◇ 8 6 4
  ♣ 9 4               S                ♣ 7 5 2
                     ♠ J 10 8 7
                     ♡ J 5
                     ◇ K 7 2
                     ♣ A 8 6 3
```

Open Room

West	North	East	South
Bessis	*Auken*	*d'Ovidio*	*von Arnim*
pass	1♣[1]	pass	1♠[2]
pass	1NT[3]	pass	3NT[4]
all pass			

1. Strong.
2. 8+, at least four spades.
3. Relay.
4. 8-10 with only four cards in spades.

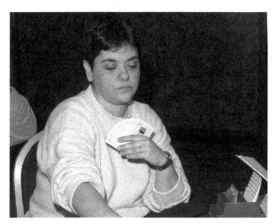

Catherine D'Ovidio

The camera work for the live VuGraph show is excellent, focusing on d'Ovidio's hand as she contemplates her difficult opening lead. Although dummy is known to hold four spades, the closed hand need not be balanced, and East seemed to be leaning towards a spade lead, her fingers alternating between the ♠3 and the ♠Q. The French supporters are quite vocal: shouts of 'Non, Cat, non,' alternate with chants of 'Carreaux, carreaux' (diamonds), but their united effort is to no avail as d'Ovidio finally decides on the ♠3.

Auken has a problem of her own at Trick 1, but has no losing option this time. She calls for the seven, which wins the trick, and leads dummy's ♡J, which West covers. East takes the king with the ace and, as her partner has given count at Trick 1 with the ♠2, continues with the ♠9 to knock out the ace. Auken drives out the ♡10, and the defense has two spades to cash, but that is all: +600.

Closed Room

West	North	East	South
Rauscheid	Cronier	Nehmert	Willard
pass	1NT	pass	2♣*
pass	2♡	pass	3NT
all pass			

Nehmert has more evidence than d'Ovidio, as she also knows about declarer's four-card heart suit in a balanced hand, so decides to lead a minor suit. She chooses the 'stronger', which turns out to be absolutely the best she can do. The ◇6, second- or fourth-best, goes to the jack and ace. Cronier leads the ♣J to dummy's ace (nine from West), to lead the ♡J, covered all around. Rauscheid hoped her ♣9 could be read as an encouraging Smith signal for diamonds, but this time Nehmert is going to play another diamond regardless. She continues with the ◇4, the honest card from that original three-card holding.

At this point, declarer can make sure of her contract by rising with dummy's king and playing on hearts. As the ◇J appeared on her right at Trick 1, the lead of the ◇6 could not be fourth-best from a five-card suit, and from six-four doubleton, Nehmert would have led the four. Similarly, East could not effectively disguise her holding by continuing with the eight rather than the four because if the lead were from eight-six doubleton or jack-eight-six, it could not hurt to win the second diamond. There is no danger of losing three diamond tricks by going up with the king unless Nehmert has done something unusual, but it soon becomes apparent that playing low from dummy is not completely safe.

Rauscheid wins with the ◇Q, and knows she can set up another diamond trick to cash when she gets in with the ♡10, but that would give the defenders only four tricks. Could partner's spade holding be strong enough to give the defense *two* extra tricks to go with two hearts and one diamond? Rauscheid switches accurately to the ♠4, middle from three, and Cronier has no good answer. When she ducks to the queen, Nehmert can either continue with a low spade or revert to diamonds, and chooses the latter. That is one down, -100, which gives Germany 12 IMPs, and the margin is down to 8 IMPs, 208-216. Someone calls for a knife to cut the tension.

Board 93. Both Vul.

```
              ♠ A K 5
              ♡ 9 4 2
              ◇ A Q J 9 4
              ♣ Q 7
♠ J 10 8 2                      ♠ Q 3
♡ K 7 5 3          N            ♡ A Q 8 6
◇ 3 2          W       E        ◇ K 10
♣ K J 10           S            ♣ 9 8 6 4 2
              ♠ 9 7 6 4
              ♡ J 10
              ◇ 8 7 6 5
              ♣ A 5 3
```

Open Room

West	North	East	South
Bessis	Auken	d'Ovidio	von Arnim
	1♣[1]	pass	1◇[2]
pass	1NT	all pass	

1. Strong.
2. Negative, 0-7.

Closed Room

West	North	East	South
Rauscheid	Cronier	Nehmert	Willard
	1NT	all pass	

Both Easts lead a club, d'Ovidio the four (count), Nehmert the six (attitude), ducked to the king. Both declarers take the ♣J continuation with the queen and play ◇A, ◇J, West giving count as East wins with the king. A heart switch would hold declarer to seven tricks, but it seems natural to continue clubs, and both declarers chalk up +120. Still 216-208, France.

Board 94. Neither Vul.

```
              ♠ A 10
              ♡ K 9 7 2
              ◇ A K 8
              ♣ J 10 6 3
   ♠ K J 3              ♠ 7 4 2
   ♡ 10 8 3      N       ♡ Q J 5 4
   ◇ J 10 5 3  W   E     ◇ 7 6 2
   ♣ A 8 5        S      ♣ K Q 4
              ♠ Q 9 8 6 5
              ♡ A 6
              ◇ Q 9 4
              ♣ 9 7 2
```

Open Room

West	North	East	South
Bessis	Auken	d'Ovidio	von Arnim
		pass	pass
pass	1NT	pass	2◇[1]
pass	2♠[2]	all pass	

1. Either: (a) transfer to hearts with at least invitational values; or (b) a signoff in spades; or (c) any three-suiter forcing to game.
2. If you have hearts, I want to be in game.

Closed Room

West	North	East	South
Rauscheid	Cronier	Nehmert	Willard
		pass	pass
pass	1NT	pass	2♡[1]
pass	2♠	all pass	

1. Transfer.

Both Easts lead the ♡Q, and declarer wins with the king to play the ♠A followed by the ♠10, losing two spades and three clubs, +110; no swing. Two to play.

Board 95. N-S Vul.

```
              ♠ K
              ♡ A Q 10 5
              ◇ A Q 10 8
              ♣ 9 8 4 3
♠ A J 8 7 6 5                    ♠ 10 3
♡ 8              N               ♡ J 7 6 3 2
◇ J 9 7      W       E           ◇ 6 2
♣ J 10 7         S               ♣ A K Q 2
              ♠ Q 9 4 2
              ♡ K 9 4
              ◇ K 5 4 3
              ♣ 6 5
```

Open Room

West	North	East	South
Bessis	*Auken*	*d'Ovidio*	*von Arnim*
			pass
2♠	dbl	pass	3◇
pass	3♠	pass	3NT
all pass			

South has a 'little something' when she could have nothing, but does she have enough to make a positive noise facing a takeout double of 2♠? A common strategy for dealing with enemy preempts is for intervenor to assume partner has roughly 6-7 useful points. Adherents to that approach could sensibly go either way with this South hand, but to a degree, the alternative responses can affect that decision. Perhaps the most popular treatment on the market is a variation of Lebensohl that defines three-level responses as constructive while weaker hands start with 2NT, requesting a 3♣ reply from doubler (after which pass, 3◇ and 3♡ would be weak) unless substantial extra strength is held.

Sabine Auken

These are the methods employed by North-South, but due to her assessment of the state of the match and protected by her first-round pass, which denied as many as 11 HCP, von Arnim makes the more aggressive choice. Although Auken can expect any game contract to be marginal at best, she is in sync with her partner about needing a swing; she probes with 3♣, which leads inevitably to 3NT.

If Bessis leads the ♣J, the rafters in the VuGraph theater will be in jeopardy of being raised by the French supporters, who so far have had little to cheer about in this session, but eventually she decides to go with her long suit and leads the ♠7, giving declarer a chance when the king holds (ten from East). Von Arnim cashes the top honors in diamonds ending in dummy, as East discards the ♡2, only because neither a club nor her remaining spade seem safe. Unfortunately for d'Ovidio, the 'not-so-idle' fifth heart discard strongly suggests that she is likely to hold significant length in the suit. At this point, declarer should cash one of dummy's heart honors to guard against a singleton jack in the West hand, while retaining a diamond entry to dummy after taking a successful second-round finesse of the nine.

Von Arnim, however, cashes the ◇10, East releasing the ♣2, West the ♠5. West is known to hold six spades and three diamonds, and therefore has only four unknown cards. Factor in East's heart discard and the absence of any club bid by East, and the odds certainly favor playing a heart to the nine. Declarer sees it this way too, and Germany has +600 in the bank.

For a moment there is a joint gasp of despair from the French fans, a bit more noticeable than the joyous 'Yes!' from the much smaller German cheering section, but then comes polite applause, recognition for a job well done. It is one of the more poignant moments in the exciting history of VuGraph presentations.

Closed Room

West	North	East	South
Rauscheid	Cronier	Nehmert	Willard
			pass
2♠	dbl	pass	3◇
all pass			

In the classic French style, bidding a suit directly at the three-level over the takeout double of 2♠ is the weakest move possible. In contrast, bidding 2NT would be a constructive move, in effect the direct opposite of Lebensohl. When Willard elects to go low, Cronier can't consider further action. Against 3◇, West leads the eight of hearts, and declarer soon claims ten tricks for +130, the best result legitimately available to North-South, but 10 IMPs worse than the result achieved by them in the Open Room.

The match has a new leader: it is Germany by 2, 218-216! The final deal is revealed:

Board 96. E-W Vul.

```
              ♠ 6 4 2
              ♡ 9 5 4 3
              ◊ 10 8 7
              ♣ 6 3 2
♠ A 7 3                      ♠ Q 10 5
♡ K Q J 2          N         ♡ 10 8
◊ J 5 4        W     E       ◊ A Q 9 6 3
♣ K J 8            S         ♣ 10 5 4
              ♠ K J 9 8
              ♡ A 7 6
              ◊ K 2
              ♣ A Q 9 7
```

Open Room

West	North	East	South
Bessis	Auken	d'Ovidio	von Arnim
1NT[1]	pass	3NT	all pass

1. 15-17.

Closed Room

West	North	East	South
Rauscheid	Cronier	Nehmert	Willard
1NT[1]	pass	2♠[2]	pass
3♣[3]	pass	3NT	all pass

1. 14-16 HCP.
2. Either weak with a long minor, or a balanced game invitation, or any 4-4-4-1 game-forcing.
3. Accepting the balanced invitation.

D'Ovido raises Bessis' 15-17 notrump to game, the normal decision with the East hand, which is worth significantly much more than its raw point count.

Rauscheid's notrump is a bit weaker (14-16) than Bessis', however, and Nehmert must decide whether to try for a game that would at best be a 24-point venture. In doing so, she might get the partnership to 2NT on a combined 22 points, jeopardizing the likely plus in 1NT. Although her side has played extremely well in this set, there hasn't seemed to be that much in the cards, and from her point of view it makes sense to stick to a policy of controlled aggression, so she moves forward with an artificial 2♠, most often a raise to 2NT

But even though Nehmert takes the aggressive course, it is still not clear for Rauscheid to treat her 4-3-3-3 'medium' hand with no nines or tens as sufficiently strong to accept a game invitation (via an artificial 3♣; 2NT would show a hand that would pass an invitational raise in notrump). But Rauscheid, following the same strategy as Nehmert, gets her side to game, and now the fate of the Venice Cup turns on North's opening lead.

At both tables all North knows is that dummy will not often deliver a four-card major, and that if South has a powerful major she has the option in the Open Room of doubling 3NT, and in the Closed Room of doubling 2♠ or 3NT. Although East's bidding points towards a major-suit lead, there isn't that much in it. Between the majors, the odds favor South being longer in North's shorter suit, but if South holds only four hearts there could still be an advantage in starting the defenders' eight-card fit, perhaps developing a long trick in the suit, with a late entry for North to take South off an endplay.

Cronier leads the ♡3 and Willard, still mildly hopeful, takes the ace and switches to ace and another club, although the main hope — king-jack doubleton in the closed hand — does not materialize. Rauscheid puts in the jack, and leads a diamond to the queen and king for a comfortable +630.

As the Closed Room finishes first, it is apparent to everyone watching that Auken's lead against 3NT is not going to affect the outcome, but she can't know that at the table, and will soon be relieved to learn that her choice, the same ♡3 selected by Cronier that leads to the same +630, has not cost Germany the match.

The only lead to beat 3NT is a spade, which gives the defense the timing to develop two spade tricks to go with South's two aces and the ◇K. Perhaps it is not surprising that there is some post-mortem discussion on the merits of doubling the artificial 2♠ with the South hand. Although it seems very risky, perhaps it's worth the effort because if South doesn't double, North will take that into account and probably prefer a red-suit lead. If 2♠ delivers an invitational hand, North will have nothing, so a spade lead will usually be best, and if 2♠ is based on a weak hand with a long minor, it may not be awful if North competes to 3♠. Of course, if someone were to redouble 2♠, this discussion might have a different flavor.

The match is over. The French race off first, eager to compare scores and find out whether they have held on to their lead. There is an almost eerie silence, and the hallway outside the playing rooms is almost deserted. There is a lone figure standing outside the door, Italy's Lorenzo Lauria, his face very grave. As Auken and von Arnim walk by behind the French, he tilts his right thumb up. That can only mean one thing.

Daniela von Arnim (Lorenzo Lauria in background)

A huge crowd is waiting for the players in the VuGraph auditorium, cheering and congratulating both the victors and the defeated home side. Germany outscored their opponents 51-2 in the last set, winning the match by 2 IMPs, 218-216 (really 215.5)!

It is a heartbreaking loss for the French, who had dominated during the round robin and performed at a high level throughout the knockout phase, only to lose the lead just two deals from the end in front of their home crowd. But moments after the comparison, they are there with their families, all of them congratulating, embracing and kissing their opponents.

To underscore the arbitrariness of intangibles in close matches, had North-South not been vulnerable on Board 95, France would have held on to win by half an IMP. Had North-South not held the ♡9 on either Board 84 or 95, the outcome would have been different too.

Better instead to reflect on the high quality of the bridge on many deals in a match played in an ambience of sportsmanship, friendship and respect.

Also Available

Close Encounters — Bridge's Greatest Matches Book 2: 2003-2017

978-1-77140-045-9

Eric Kokish and Mark Horton

The next installment in the two-book series that describes some of the most memorable bridge matches of the last fifty years. Book 2 begins with Italy's losing a world title in bizarre fashion on the final board, and ends with the USA's nail-biting 2-IMP victory over France in Lyon in 2017.

Contact Us

Master Point Press
214 Merton St. Suite 205
Toronto, ON M4S 1A6
(647) 956-4933

Master Point Press on the Internet

www.masterpointpress.com

Our main site, with information about our books and software, reviews and more.

www.teachbridge.com

Our site for bridge teachers and students — free downloadable support material for our books, helpful articles and more.

www.bridgeblogging.com

Read and comment on regular articles from MPP authors and other bridge notables.

www.ebooksbridge.com

Purchase downloadable electronic versions of MPP books and software.